MUSIC
IN THE LIFE
OF MAN

Detail from the amphora by the Berlin Painter: *A Young Citharoedus, singing to his own accompaniment*. Attic, early fifth century B.C. The Metropolitan Museum of Art, Fletcher Fund, 1956.

MUSIC
IN THE LIFE
OF MAN

JULIUS PORTNOY
Brooklyn College

GREENWOOD PRESS, PUBLISHERS
WESTPORT, CONNECTICUT

Library of Congress Cataloging in Publication Data

Portnoy, Julius, 1910–
   Music in the life of man.

   Reprint of the ed. published by Holt, Rinehart
and Winston, New York.
   Includes bibliographical references.
   1. Music—Philosophy and aesthetics.
2. Music, Influence of. 3. Music in art.
I. Title.
ₜML3845.P695 1973ⱼ   780'.1   73-9265
ISBN 0-8371-7000-1

Copyright © 1963 by Holt, Rinehart and Winston, Inc.

Originally published in 1963 by Holt, Rinehart and
Winston, New York

Reprinted with the permission of Holt, Rinehart &
Winston, Inc.

Reprinted in 1973 by Greenwood Press, Inc.
51 Riverside Avenue, Westport, CT 06880

Library of Congress catalog card number 73-9265
ISBN 0-8371-7000-1

Printed in the United States of America

10 9 8 7 6 5 4 3 2

To Alfhild

PREFACE

When white light is diffused through a prism all the colors of the rainbow appear—colors which man had sought out long before the scientific age to decorate and brighten his world. Man has also fashioned music out of natural sounds and beckoned her to be his handmaid. There are few activities in the life of man in which she does not participate. This book is a musical spectrum, a panorama of her many activities.

Music's role as a fine art is a recent one. She accompanied man in practical exploits long before coming to the concert hall. Music began her formal career joined to dance and words in the ceremony of the magic circle—perhaps the oldest form of religious rites. She helped man to hunt and fish, and to treat the sick in body and mind. In time, music became separated from dance and gave up her complete alliance with words. Now music is primarily a fine art, autonomous and exalted as the most evocative in the hierarchy of the arts. Modern man has changed her from a handmaid into a goddess of sorts.

The roles that music has played in our lives have undergone many changes. Our sacred music, for example, is quite different from that of ancient man. We have substituted verbal prayer for his rambling intonations, and whereas primitive man danced and waved his arms as he implored the gods for help, we now have dignified gestures in the ceremony of worship and stereotyped musical forms. Although a separation between sacred and secular music existed in the Western world, the distinction that we now make between classical and popular music did not actually emerge until the Renaissance, an era of wealth and learning that changed the values of the Western world. Our electronic age has enabled engineers to produce machines which emit sounds that are more exciting and varied than Pythagoras ever imagined existed in the harmony of the spheres.

Chapter I of this book presents theories about the creation of music, from earliest times up to the present day. A perusal of these theories shows that loquacious theorists are not at a loss to define this phenomenon. It is all quite plain to them. Creative artists, in comparison to these theorists, are mute about their creative powers. They bear out Socrates' observation that musicians cannot account for the origin of their art, or explain what it means after they have produced it. Creativity is still inexplicable; our efforts to fathom its nature, even in this psychological age, are only partially successful.

Chapter II deals with the making of music. Rhythm and melody, two of the basic elements of a musical work, are constructs of the human mind. With rhythm, man gave music the breath of life, and with melody, he enabled her to sing. He empowered music with his own voice to cry out against tyranny, and to sing in praise of love. Music has helped him to compensate for those necessities he has been deprived of in actual life.

Chapter III is devoted to values. What criteria do we employ to formulate a value judgment about a musical composition? What value does music have for enriching human existence? Although the first question is an esthetic one and the second is a practical one, they are not exclusive of each other in a musical experience. Of what value is a musical work if we are sound judges of its structural merit but it leaves us emotionally cold? Only music that has the power to communicate and enhance experience can broaden our perspective of life—the prime prerequisite of art's function in the world.

Chapter IV is concerned with the relationship of music to the other arts. Do musical terms mean the same thing when they are applied to visual arts; or, for example, does musical rhythm mean something else in comparison to the rhythm of sculptured figures on the façade of a Gothic cathedral? Is it possible for the poet and novelist to borrow musical forms, such as the sonata, and techniques, such as counterpoint, from the musician? Can we discern any similarity between an atonal style of composing and the creation of an abstract painting? Musical terms can only be used metaphorically when applied to her sister arts. Each art has its own vocabulary and, if artistic terms are used interchangeably without discrimination, a babble of tongues arises. The psychological process of creation is the same for all the arts but, however interrelated the arts may be, they cannot faithfully imitate each other.

In Chapter V philosophical theories about the metaphysical origins of music are examined; mathematical theories about music's structure are investigated; and a summation is given of what electronic music has thus far achieved. Philosophers of an idealistic strain have been prone to believe that music emanates from a source that transcends the physical world. They have stubbornly held to this notion for almost two thousand years after Plato's death, although there is no evidence to warrant it. Mathematicians divided the octave, worked out the ratios between intervals and helped temper them. In the modern world they have helped the musical scientist to expand the function of electronic devices to produce new sounds and musical compositions. Mathematical efforts, however, to reduce music to a set of formulas have proved to be as impracticable as attempting to explain beauty by a magic ratio.

Chapter VI deals with the therapeutic value of music in medical science, its use as a stimulant in mechanized industry, and as a form of relief to offset the boredom of tedious office work. The role of music in education and the function of music as entertainment make up the second half of this chapter. Ancient philosophers believed that music could steel the mind and discipline emotions; therefore, they thought, music should be an important part of a child's education. Music does train the mind but in a different way than logic does; it regulates the emotions, but not in the same manner as moral training attempts to do. Music does help a child, in his educational development, to become a social being and to exercise his emotions. But in the modern world music's primary function in the life of man has become essentially entertainment. Throughout the ages folk tunes and street songs filtered into the sacred liturgy, and were also brought into the home. In our time, jazz, born in tawdry surroundings, has influenced our serious musical entertainment, and is slowly finding its way into the religious service.

In Chapter VII musical traditions are described as part of an interminable struggle between the composer and the church, and the state. The latter two have very often taken the dogmatic view that they alone must decide what is right and wrong both in the construction and the appreciation of music; anyone who disagrees with their edicts and mandates, as humanists are apt to do, are, according to their judgment, in error. Musical myths, mysticism, and prophecies conclude the chapter. Poets created myths about the harmony of the spheres, and they, even more than philosophers, had perpetuated this myth up until the eighteenth century. Music without mysticism is the equivalent of a child's storybook that fails to evoke wonder and awe of distant and imaginary places. In the next thousand years electronic music will be prominent; it will exist side by side with the type of traditional music that we now have. The human voice, of all the musical instruments during the coming millenium, will be the most important. In a mechanized age, the singing voice will rise above the din of the machine, enabling man to assert himself.

This book is particularly suitable for courses in the humanities and the esthetics of music. It brings into focus, for the general public, most of the functions that music performs in our lives. Problems pertaining to music that vex, and not infrequently rob us of enjoyment, are examined with a fresh viewpoint. Out of this examination new musical insights emerge, the Muse of song appears in her original purity with a voice that is strong and clear. Her song fulfills the needs of all mankind and the needs of each of us.

J.P.

New York
January 1963

ACKNOWLEDGMENTS

I wish to express my thanks to Professor Milton Babbit of Princeton University for reading the section on electronic music, and to Professor Rudolf Arnheim of Sarah Lawrence College for his suggestions on pictorial illustrations. Professor Carl B. Boyer of the Mathematics Department and Professor John Hospers of the Philosophy Department of Brooklyn College read the manuscript with painstaking care, and helped me with their incisive comments. I am also grateful to the members of the Music Department at Brooklyn College for the generous aid that they gave me in preparing the manuscript for publication, and to Mr. James Bayley for his aid with the glossaries. To my wife, I owe the fullest measure of gratitude for helping me to bring to fruition *Music in the Life of Man.*

CONTENTS

xv

MUSIC
IN THE LIFE
OF MAN

CHAPTER I

CREATIVE PROCESS
in the ARTS and SCIENCES

THEOLOGIAN

Theologians once believed that music was divinely created when God first endowed man with speech. With the power of speech the great Diviner separated man from all other animals and with the gift of song raised him to a level one rung lower than the angels. The human soul was modeled and attuned to the spiritual *harmony** of a perfectly ordered world so that man alone, of all the creatures on the earth, possesses the capacity to imitate celestial harmonies in musical sounds.

⌐

Homer wrote in the *Odyssey* that the Greek minstrel was the favored mortal of the gods "whom the Muse loved above all other men, and gave him both good and evil; of his sight she deprived him, but gave him the gift of sweet song." [1] The theologian, Hesiod, related that the Muses appeared to him while he fed his father's flock and commissioned him to be their prophet and minstrel, and then adorned him with "the rhapsode's staff to betoken his mission as a singer." Plato gave full homage to both Homer and Hesiod by develop-

* Terms which are defined in the second part of the Glossary are *italicized* the first time that they appear in the author's text.

1

ing their supernatural theme into an ethically ordained reason for the creation of music as an art: "...music...is granted to us for the sake of harmony; and harmony, which has motions akin to the revolutions of our souls, is...meant to correct any discord which may have arisen in the courses of the soul, and to be our ally in bringing her into harmony and agreement with herself; and rhythm too was given by them for the same reason." [2]

Plato's theory of musical creation as it is described in the *Timaeus* is more picturesque than the one in the *Laws*. In the latter he also attributed the origin of music to the benevolence of the gods but now it is for bodily needs rather than moral reasons: "...the Gods, pitying the toils which our race is born to undergo, have appointed holy festivals," and then endowed man with a sense of harmony and *rhythm* so that he could imitate them in song and dance. [3]

Music and religion were thought by the Greeks to be divinely intertwined. Plutarch in one of his commentaries related that the statue of Apollo was placed in the Temple at Delos and was surrounded by a number of Graces who were holding various musical instruments. The Greeks looked upon the god Apollo as the founder and giver of song. He "was the inventor of all the music both of the flute [aulos] and harp. This is manifest from the dances and sacrifices which were solemnized to Apollo, as Alcaeus and others in their hymns relate. . . . Venerable is therefore music altogether," concludes Plutarch, "as being the invention of the Gods." [4]

Apollo was replaced by the God of Judea in biblical literature. Although very few references to the divine origin of music exist in Hebrew scriptures, the Jews have always believed that music is a gift of God. Jubal is referred to as "the father of all such as handle the harp and organ." In Genesis 4:21 and in Job 38:7 there is a poetic allusion that "the morning stars sang together." The Hebraic legend that David created the Psalms and invented musical instruments is based on the passage in II Chron. 7:6: "instruments of musick of the Lord, which David the king had made to praise the Lord." [5] However terse these remarks may be, they sufficed for the future scribes of talmudic lore to declare that music is not without divine law.

The Church Fathers believed that music was divinely created so that man might praise his Maker with holy text and song. St. Chrysostom in his admonitions to the faithful preached that God created the psalms as well as the music to accompany them. God "blended melody with prophecy in order that, delighted by the modulation of the chant, all might with great eagerness give forth sacred hymns to Him." St. Chrysostom also taught that God in His infinite wisdom might decree in a manner we cannot always comprehend. There are other times when God's mandates are expressly clear, particularly with reference to the psalms: "... lest demons introducing lascivious songs should overthrow everything, God established the psalms." [6]

St. Basil held not only that the prophet created the psalms in such a manner that they would best lend themselves to the accompaniment of the psaltery, but that the sounds of this musical instrument emanated from above in contrast to other instruments. The Lord "blended the delight of melody with doctrines in order that through the pleasantness and softness of the sound we might unawares receive what was useful in the words." The Christians did not favor certain instruments which might disclose them in secret prayer. Furthermore, the more zealous among them associated brass instruments with pagan religions and lustful ceremonies and so forbade their use. It was with good reason that St. Basil therefore stated: "brass wires of the cithara and the lyre sound from below against the plectrum, but the psaltery has the origins of its harmonious rhythms above." [7]

During the trying years of the Reformation Luther wrote in his *Eulogy of Music* that "music is a beautiful, gracious gift of God." Next in importance to sacred theology, he regarded music as a divine form of inspiration to guide him in his sermons. "That God preaches the gospel through music," is evident to all who are willing to listen and understand, he reminisced, recalling the music of Josquin des Prés which he so admired during his stay in Rome. Only a short time later came other members of the faith who preached that what Luther spoke of as a "gift of God" was actually a weapon of the devil. First these zealous men demolished church organs, then they burnt a great deal of the printed music—all because they thought that if God wanted His holy words set to music He would have done so Himself.

Calvin had no intention of doing away with music altogether in the Protestant service. What rankled him was that Luther had remained too much of a Roman ecclesiast by exhibiting such a love for Catholic music that he retained part of it, somewhat altered, for the Reformed service. Calvin therefore insisted that sacred music be limited to the singing of the psalms and other scriptural passages. He believed with Augustine that the beauty of a musical melody would detract from a devotional mood. Composers who created music that distracted the mind from the biblical text were, therefore, considered by Calvin to be guilty of heresy. Creativity and originality in musical matters were as sinful as vanity itself. All things begin and end in God, claimed Calvin, and everything exists for a purpose. Music was given to the faithful to draw them closer to God: "... we must think that it is a gift of God" so that when singing the psalms "we may be certain that God puts the words in our mouths as if Himself sang in us to exalt His glory." [8]

A good deal of similarity has always existed between Jews and Christians on such nontheological matters as the origin, function, and value of sacred and secular music. Both religious groups believe that music emanates from a higher source and they cite the Bible as their authority. The God who created Adam also gave him the power of vocal expression in speech and song. The human voice, they firmly believed, is an attribute of man bestowed on him by his Maker so that by this one distinguishing feature he would differ from all other forms of life. Nothing, however, is said about musical instruments in the Garden of Eden. Any musical instrument that man therefore creates can only be inferior to God's, for the human voice is the natural instrument of God's own creation, man. Music is of divine origin, according to Christian and Jew, but musical instruments that accompany the voice or simulate natural sounds are the handiwork of man.

The similarity of musical concepts between Christians and Jews was readily shared by the ancient Greek theologians, except that the Greeks believed that the gods and not man created musical instruments. The comparison of music to the movement of celestial bodies and the analogy of the musician's unusual powers to the supernatural actions of the Greek gods or God of Judea illustrate the human penchant for contriving mystical similes. These similes existed in antiquity and are still perpetuated. Christian theologians, with the help of the ancient and medieval philosophers, fostered the divine theory of musical creation through the ages by insisting that music has ethical significance. The doctrine of ethos, that music possesses powers that can degrade or ennoble character, implies that music is a moral echo of God's perfect world.[9] The composer's creative experience may be likened to a revelation in which the order and harmony of a perfect universe become brilliantly clear. It is this revealing moment of precious insight which he then imparts to us by re-creating in actual music an artistic testament of the pervading laws of God.

The Greek musician, like the Greek god, was a faithful imitator, a craftsman, even though he was the intermediary between the gods and man. The God of Christianity sets aside natural law and creates miracles at will. Those who draw an analogy between the musician and the Christian God believe that the musician also *transcends* natural restrictions when he is divinely inspired.[10]

The Greek musician was bound by the same laws in the creation of music as was the Greek god in the creation of the world. Although the bard did not create by rule, but by inspiration, the gods controlled his mind as they did his acts, and would not bestow a freedom on him, a mortal, that they would deny to themselves. The Christian musician emulates God but not as the recipient of direct guidance from above. He is endowed with a freedom, in a theological sense, that his pagan counterpart did not have. The Christian musician is a member of two worlds, the spiritual and the material. The choice is his: to create sacred music that is pleasing to God because it ennobles character or to defile the miracle of creation and produce secular music which arouses lust and desire.

PHILOSOPHER

Philosophers, like Aristotle and Lucretius, held a theory that music grew out of man's desire to imitate sounds in nature, first with the voice itself and then with crudely-made instruments. Other philosophers, such as Pythagoras and Plato, were more fanciful and claimed that music emanated from a more ideal source than the commonplace sounds in nature, probably from the movement of the stars. Musicians re-create this heavenly music by divine inspiration, never by rule only, claimed Plato. They are of a melancholic temperament, wrote Aristotle, which is brought on by the black bile in their veins that warms and excites them until they must create, just as wine intoxicates ordinary men and releases them from torment.

We could no more separate the musical beliefs of the philosophers from those of the theologians in Greek antiquity than we can separate the musical beliefs of the philosophers from those of the Christian theologians in the Middle Ages. The classical belief that the musician is controlled by a supernatural being was just as much in vogue in the Grecian schools of philosophy as it was among the temple priests who performed the pagan rites under the watchful eye of Apollo. Even such atomistic philosophers as Heraclitus[11] and Democritus looked upon the musician as blessed with divine inspiration, although they showed no disposition to embrace the Pythagorean theory of the spheres which found such favor in Plato's *idealism*. Pythagoras attributed the origin of music to the movement of the stars which were so arranged that they produced a harmony of celestial tones as they circled through the heavens. A divine hand created the stars, placed each in its proper orbit, and then set them in motion so that in their movement they would reflect the perfect order and harmony that governs the universe. There is also a legend that Pythagoras became interested in the science of music in the act of passing a blacksmith's shop, and upon hearing the clangorous sounds of the hammer blows he was moved to carry on experiments that enabled him to work out theories of tonal *intervals* and acoustical differences between *consonant* and *dissonant* tones. There is nothing in Plato that even alludes to this bit of fiction, although both he and Aristotle ridiculed the Pythagoreans for being more absorbed in the acoustics of sound than in the *esthetic affects* of music. Nevertheless, it is probable that

Pythagoras did learn how to produce the octave, fifth and fourth. What interested Plato, however, were the esoteric teachings of the Pythagorean school: that music is a reproduction of the *harmony of the spheres* and therefore has ethical qualities because it reflects the ideal order in the universe.

The image of a God as a supreme geometer who created the world and sent it on its way is introduced into Western philosophy for the first time in the Platonic dialogue *Timaeus*. Plato's God is a cosmic artist who fashioned the world out of geometric forms and then introduced music by setting the heavens in motion. He is a God who has favored the musician above all other men, for he deprived him of his mind and imbued him with divine frenzy so that in such moments of rare ecstasy men would know that he is a prophet of God: ". . . not . . . by any rules of art: they are simply inspired to utter that to which the Muse impels them, and that only; . . . for not by art does the poet sing, but by power divine . . . and therefore God takes away the minds of poets, and uses them as his ministers, as he also uses diviners and holy prophets, in order that we who hear them may know them to be speaking not of themselves who utter these priceless words in a state of unconsciousness, but that God himself is the speaker, and that through them he is conversing with us." [12]

Plato's musician is a God-intoxicated mortal who creates by inspiration and not by rule. "But he who, having no touch of the Muses' madness in his soul, comes to the door and thinks that he will get into the temple by the help of art—he, I say, and his poetry are not admitted; the sane man disappears and is nowhere when he enters into rivalry with the madman." [13]

The musician, wrote Plato, is "carried out of himself" and becomes deranged when creating.

For all good poets, epic as well as lyric, compose their beautiful poems not by art, but because they are inspired and possessed . . . the lyric poets are not in their right mind when they are composing their beautiful strains: but when falling under the power of music and metre they are inspired and possessed; . . . For the poet is a light and winged and holy thing, and there is no invention in him until he has been inspired and is out of his senses, and the mind is no longer in him: when he is not attained to this state, he is powerless and is unable to utter his oracles.[14]

So overwhelming is the human effort to create that the musician must be restored to his senses to realize what he has done. Even then, he can no more give acceptable reasons for his detachment than he can explain the meaning of his song, Plato has Socrates conclude:

I went to the poets; . . . I took them some of the most elaborate passages in their own writings, and asked what was the meaning of them. . . . I must say that there is hardly a person present who would not have talked better about their poetry than they did themselves. Then I knew that not by wisdom do poets write poetry, but by a sort of genius and inspiration; they are like diviners or soothsayers who also say many fine things, but do not understand the meaning of them.[15]

Aristotle believed that the creation of music grew out of man's need for emotional expression and a rational desire for order and form. But why, asked Aristotle, is the composer of a melancholy temperament? [16] What makes him different from other men that he possesses the unique capacity to produce in his music "not the outward appearance of things, but their inward significance?" Wherein lies his ability to abstract the essence from the sounds emitted by the movement of the heavenly bodies and so depict reality by producing for us in tonal form the order in the universe? The composer performs these tasks because he is not like other men, Aristotle finally decided. There is something strange about his nature. Creation "implies either a happy gift of nature or a strain of madness." The musician is artistically mad for "he is lifted out of his proper self." [17] Aristotle echoed Plato in calling this madness divine.

No age is without its opposition, and Aristotle's was no exception. Theophrastus, his student and successor, represented a minority group who agreed that musical creation is a form of emotional expression but disagreed that it has anything to do with the divine. He believed that music is an outlet for oppressed man, an expression of fleeting joy; but, above all, music has its origin in love. It is a feeling which is overwhelming; reason subsides and feeling gives vent in song. Love, wrote Theophrastus, "contains all the causes of music . . . it should incline us more than any other passion to poetry and songs." [18]

Seneca shared Aristotle's views that those who create are a blend of genius and dementia.[19] Cicero used Plato as his authority to comment that "no man can be a good poet without the ardor of imagination and the excitement of something similar to frenzy." [20] Plutarch compared the mad musician to an oracle who utters prophecies while in a state of trance.[21] Longinus noted that music which elevates the soul can only come from a musician inspired by a sublime force.[22] Lucretius held a *naturalistic* belief: man first learned to sing by imitating the birds, and then invented crude instruments to accompany him in song and dance.

It would be a mistake to think that the musicians in the Middle Ages were simply perpetuating traditional musical styles rather than creating new ones. The history of music is replete with struggles between the musician and both the philosopher and the theologian—the introduction of the novel and the retention of the old. Ecclesiastical composers were as daring in their creations as the trouvères and the troubadours were in theirs. The Church trusted neither group whether they were her own or were wandering musicians who often spread anticlerical songs. The restless nature of the musician—which philosopher and theologian well knew—and his longing for something new made him a subject of suspect by both church and state.

With the age of *humanism* in the offing, *Renaissance* scholars began to believe that the musician was divinely inspired in a figurative sense only. Plato had called the musician a rebellious spirit, in a state of perpetual revolt. The members of the Florentine Academy were in agreement with their Greek idol that the musician is a restless creature, an example of poor stability. But the musician's personality was not really their concern or interest. What did disturb them in this period of intellectual awakening was whether their master, Plato, erred or only symbolically said that the musician's power comes from God. Cardinal Cusa spoke for his Church in denying divine powers to a mere mortal whether it be in matters of sacred theology or in the creation of fine arts. The philosopher Ficino, who spoke for the musician on the grounds that he was one himself, maintained that creation is a miracle, whether it be God creating the world or man, in His image, making a song. The Renaissance men of letters eventually combined these contrary views by calling the musician divinely inspired and mad, in a figurative sense.

During all this time, as in times before, the musician marveled at the ease and wisdom with which the scholars, who do not create fine art, could speak about such matters, since he himself could not. Musicians mock at academies, even at Plato's and the Florentine's. They know full well that if God were the source of their creative power the Church would be more responsive to their Call. They are not the favored few. If anything, their lot is more precarious and less certain than that of other men. That salvation will not come from above, but rather from within, is a credo for living they all too soon adopt. The musician is the source of his own power.[23] It is not he who analyzes the symptoms of creation as a mental malady in which God takes away the mind of the musician for His use. Frenzy is not the presence of Godliness generating the musician's power, but rather rejection of God's world for a more personally imaginative one.

Leibniz, the most colorful of the European *rationalists,* gave credence to the theological precept that all ideas originate and terminate in God. "It follows from the supreme perfection of God that in producing the universe He chose the best possible plan, containing the greatest variety together with the greatest order; . . . For as all possible things have a claim to existence in the understanding of God in proportion to their perfections, the result of all these claims must be the most perfect actual world which is possible."[24] Music, claimed Leibniz, comes into being by imitating this worldly order. In his estimation, there is nothing more pleasant than the wonderful harmony of nature, of which music is only a foretaste and small evidence. However music may exalt us, "its beauty only consists in the harmony of numbers."[25] Music is a copy of God's perfect world.

The musician's "fire is not kindled from heaven." If anything, argued Hume, the *empirical* evidence is that "it only runs along the earth." [26] The artist is the source of his own power, a creator in his own right. "Creative power of the mind amounts to no more than the faculty of compounding, transposing, augmenting, or diminishing the materials afforded us by the senses and experience. When we think of a golden mountain, we only join two consistent ideas, 'gold' and 'mountain,' with which we were formerly acquainted." [27] To Hume, musical ideas come from sensory impressions just as all ideas do. There is nothing about the psychological process of the creation of music that differs, from that of a scientific idea. Both are born out of experience.

In the philosophy of Immanuel Kant the musician is compared to a genius who has "a *talent* for producing that for which no definite rule can be given; it is not a mere aptitude for what can be learned by rule. Hence *originality* must be its first property." Music must possess novelty and yet be created according to "a standard or rule of judgement for others." The creator of music "does not himself know how he has come by his Ideas." [28] The musician, according to Kant, is a highly imaginative mortal who cannot communicate to others the nature of his art so that they might reproduce it for themselves;[29] otherwise, music could be written by rule and measure and would become a kind of science instead of being an inspired form of art. The composer must be endowed with originality and have the technical means to give shape and coherence to his musical ideas. Music is born of imagination, and reason imposes its rules so that the vagaries of our sentiments and feelings find a rational expression in meaningful musical sounds. The musician must first be gifted, Kant believed, and secondly have the technical ability to create an imaginative bridge which helps us to span two worlds—one of sense and one of reason—so that we can reconcile the natural course of the starry heavens above and the rationality of the moral order within.

Hegel had the notion that music could be deciphered, as mathematics could, according to a man-made law. But however rational the phenomenon of musical creation may be, the composer's "true originality does not consist in merely conforming to the paramount conditions of style, but in a kind of inspired state." [30] According to Hegel, the composer by virtue of his own resources raises his art closer to the "Ideal" by clothing the subject matter of music with a sensuous medium of sounds. Thus, music is a synthesis of reason and feeling, namely the composer's own. The creation of music begins and ends with *dialectical* inevitability. The composer, in conflict with a world composed of contradictory forces, resolves opposing issues in imaginative musical forms. He uses these imaginative forms to transform things as they are into something more ideal. He creates in order to resolve conflict and, since conflict never ends, one creation begets another in an endless chain. The irrational becomes rational in the medium of song when a rational form embodies irrational emotions. To Hegel, the creation of something new is born out of conflict and reaction, be it the strife of men or the struggle of the state.

Music is not like mathematics. The arts, particularly music, cannot be rationally perused, for music is the *"copy of the will itself,"* objected Schopenhauer in giving voice to the *romantic* ideal. "The composer reveals the inner nature of the world, and expresses the deepest wisdom in a language which his reason does not understand; as a person under the influence of mesmerism telling things of which he has no conception when he awakes." [31] Life's cycle of desire and frustration drives the musician to near madness and contemplated suicide—he must escape from the will if he is to survive. In the process of creating music he denies the will, and in music itself he finds solace and ceases to know desire. Through music he is released from physical existence to escape in a make-believe world. The composer, like the genius, has "an abnormal predominance of sensibility over irritability," [32] the two prerequisites required in order to create, in the philosophy of Schopenhauer.

What do we mean by inspiration, asked Nietzsche? Have we forgotten in the late nineteenth century that artistic inspiration and theological revelation have their origin in a common source? The musician's inspiration is like the mystic's union with the infinite. Inspiration is an experience in which "something profoundly convulsive and disturbing suddenly becomes visible and audible with indescribable definiteness and exactness. One hears—one does not seek; one takes—one does not ask who gives: a thought flashes out like lightning." It were as though I were possessed, as though I were compelled to do what I must, continued Nietzsche. "There is an ecstasy whose terrific tension is sometimes released by a flood of tears, during which one's progress varies from involuntary impetuosity to involuntary slowness. There is the feeling that one is utterly out of hand, with the most distinct consciousness of an infinitude of shuddering thrills that pass through one from head to foot. . . . Everything occurs quite without volition, as if in an eruption of freedom, independence, power and divinity." [33] Here we have the most romantic version yet of artistic creation by the archenemy of romanticism himself. The musician forsakes the actual world for a fanciful one. His music is like a dream, a medium to help man reconcile the *Apollonian and Dionysian* elements in his being.

Nietzsche echoed Plato: the musician is different, he is rebellious, he is a coward. But Nietzsche went further: the musician escapes from reality into unreality and transfigures the world he left behind into something of his own choosing. It is a world which enables him to muse in Apollonian calm and soar to ecstatic heights in Dionysian frenzy and then, satiated, to return to the world he forsook, refreshed and calmed.

For Schopenhauer and Nietzsche the creation of music is an irrational process. It is an experience which transcends reason; it is a phenomenon which language cannot describe. Music is a nondiscursive language, and to try to explain how it comes into being by discursive language, added Bergson, would be just as futile as trying to explain *intuition* with reason or feeling with ordinary language. Musical creation is a mystery. The composer can hold the transient world of change at bay to catch a fleeting glimpse of "reality." He can no more tell us what it was like to achieve a union with the infinite than he can describe his powers of making music.

Santayana, however, voiced a different view: it is primarily reason which enables man to create music. Reason creates music to ennoble the emotions. Reason creates music as a means of organiz-

ing our chaotic and primitive drives and directs them toward something better than that which exists. It is our reason that imposes
order on our lives, legislates our behavior. Music is born of raw
emotion, the primitive and unbridled flux which will not be impeded
long in following its natural course. Reason gives form to this fury,
whether it be within us or at large. Music as a product of reason
gives order and direction to our emotions and echoes our most primitive thoughts. "Whatever writhes in matter, art strives to give form
to." [34]

Croce brought an idealism to the essence of creation which
makes the musician a divinity in his own right. Music has its beginning and end in the imaginative mind of the composer and there
alone. Music is not the printed score, not the sounds produced by
instruments. It is intuition, expression; they are one and the same
phenomenon for Croce. Expression does not mean externalization
for him as it does for other philosophers. Music is created by an
imaginative mind, not by labor as though it were a craft. Music is
music only while lodged in the composer's head. As the composer
gives physical expression to his musical image he ceases to be a
creator and becomes a craftsman instead. The creation of music begins in feeling, and not as a product of reason. Creation is a spiritual
phenomenon, a revelation in a highly personal way. The composer
has his musical visions and in him alone they live and die. This novel
view, that the mind brings music into existence by experiencing it
as intuition, makes the technical aspect of composition subordinate
to the musical idea. That creation is a spiritual phenomenon, not a
technical feat, is the core of Croce's esthetic theory.

Music comes from intuition, but this intuition is not antirational
for Maritain. The composer is a spiritual being and a laborer in the
Lord's vineyard. Music is the expression of the "spiritual unconscious
as well as the unconscious of blood and flesh." Music is only poten-
tially music when it exists as an idea. Not until the composer has
given it physical existence with the aid of technical skill has he
brought his art to fruition. However intuitive musical creation may
be, it cannot be isolated from reason. The intellect acts as the moral
censor in guiding the musician's craft to beget the sort of music
which will be pleasing to God.

The belief that the composer is divinely inspired is rarely accepted now. If there is a controlling force guiding the composer it resides in his own mind and body, and not outside in some transcendental realm. The composer is controlled by forces which reside in his very being and which are not voluntary or conscious but are unrestrained at the source. This is the realm of the *unconscious*, the storehouse of our repressed desires, the sanctuary of what is really man. For the Greeks the musician was a maker even if his art was divinely inspired. That the musician creates his music out of pure fancy, as the Hebraic and Christian God created the world ex nihilo, is only a picturesque analogy in which we must separate the supernatural from the natural and then cease to attribute to the musician what we have come to believe about God. Music arises out of our turbulent emotions to compensate for our daily needs. Creativity begins in feeling, and there is no certainty as to how it will be expressed. With few exceptions, the composer himself is unaware of what he is going to write before he actually does so. If he knew what he wanted to write, then there would be little if anything new to be said in a creative sense. He would be like a craftsman following a well laid plan and not a creator carried away by the pen. The craftsman is an imitator copying someone else's ideas. The creator is an originator of concepts and ideas. Ideas without craft, or vice versa, produce sheer sentimentality or exacting regularity. The creative composer feels his music so strongly that he says what he must, if not in a traditional form, then in whatever form he can. It is the novelty with which he bares his emotional life that enables his music to evoke from us what otherwise, long repressed, might never rise to consciousness.

SCIENTIST

Ancient magicians cured the sick and explained an eclipse with equal facility and assurance. They were known to have passed judgment on primitive crafts, created the tribal music, and led in ceremonial dances. After their power waned, the role that they performed was divided between the modern versions of artist and scientist. With the passing of time each went his own way; now they have grown so far apart that it is difficult to imagine that they both evolved from the magician.

⌣

Creating a work of art and inventing a new path to the stars are essentially alike in the psychological manner in which they are done. Artists and scientists differ very little in how they gather material for their projects, wait for it to germinate on an unconscious level, and live through the agonies and bliss of the creative act itself. Deep thought and good intentions alone will not create great art or scientific inventions. Creators are rare biological specimens, not trained technicians. A cultural environment that is overly oppressive may thwart as well as be their finest challenge. A cultural atmosphere that is overly abundant in freedom and luxury may be more conducive to lassitude than to creativity. Creative people do not think of themselves as benefactors of the human race.[35] They have a compelling urge to create, and do not take into account whether what they produce will be good or bad in its effect on mankind.

Scientists are driven by a desire for recognition and security as strongly as artists are. They are alike in the degrees of excessive vanity that they display and the contemptuous attitude that they take towards the public. Scientists and artists both view nature with the fresh and unmarred wonder of a child and, like children, they are eager to describe their visions and experiences, but in a lasting and organized way. "To carry on the feelings of childhood into the powers of manhood"; wrote Coleridge, "to combine the child's sense of wonder and novelty with the appearances, which every day for perhaps forty years had rendered familiar, . . . this is the character and privilege of genius, and one of the marks which distinguish genius from talents." [36]

Artists and scientists do not choose their professions to accumulate wealth. Biology and an insatiable curiosity decide the course they take, even if they themselves do not always know why. They are quite aware that the nature of their work requires dedication and uncompromising fidelity and that it may, in the end, bring poverty. The physical scientists have left us testimonies of their creative process in their own field. They have not seriously concerned themselves with creation in other fields. When Newton was asked how he made his discoveries he replied: "By always thinking into them." Edison attributed his inventions to "one percent inspiration and ninety-nine percent perspiration." William James gave academic approval to these observations by stating that creativity is associated with people who possess high powers of sustained attention. It is doubtful whether the discovery of the laws that describe nature is accomplished with mathematics and assiduous effort only or the creation of a musical masterpiece can be accomplished with theoretical studies and diligence alone. Creative people are not necessarily more conscientious and better informed than their colleagues; they possess biological and psychological characteristics that other men do not have. If hard work and erudition were the secret to creativity, then creators could be schooled as mechanics are. What clinical and literary evidence there is to account for the psychological process and the individual methods by which scientists create is not vastly different from that which artists have left us. The description given by Poincaré and Helmholtz of the creative process sounds very much like the explanations that artists give us in the following sections of this chapter on how they produce their work. According to Poincaré:

The part played by unconscious work in mathematical discovery seems to me indisputable. . . . Often when a man is working at a difficult question, he accomplishes nothing the first time he sets to work. Then he takes more or less of a rest, and sits down again at his table. During the first half-hour he still finds nothing, and then all at once the decisive idea presents itself to his mind. We might say that the conscious work proved more fruitful because it was interrupted and the rest restored force and freshness to the mind. But it is more probable that the rest was occupied with unconscious work. . . . There is another remark to be made regarding the conditions of this unconscious work, which is, that it is not possible, or in any case not fruitful, unless it is first preceded and then followed by a period of conscious work. These sudden inspirations are never produced . . . except after some days of voluntary efforts which appeared absolutely fruitless. . . . The necessity for the second period of conscious work can be even more readily understood. It is necessary to work out the results of the inspiration ... but, above all, it is necessary to verify them.[37]

Helmholtz gave this version of the creative process:

I must say that those fields of work have become ever more agreeable to me in which one need not depend on lucky accidents and "happy thoughts." But as I have found myself pretty often in the uncomfortable position of having to wait for happy thoughts, the experience I have gained on the question, when and where they came to me, may perhaps be useful to others. Often enough they crept quietly into my thinking without my suspecting their importance at first; and then it was often impossible later on to recall under what circumstances they had come; they were simply there and that was all I could say. But in other cases they arrived suddenly, without any effort on my part, like an inspiration. So far as my experience goes, they never came to a fatigued brain and never at the writing desk. It was always necessary, first of all, that I should have turned my problem over on all sides to such an extent that I had all its angles and complexities "in my head" and could run through them freely without writing. To bring the matter to that point is usually impossible without long preliminary labor. Then, after the fatigue resulting from this labor had passed away, there must come an hour of complete physical freshness and quiet well-being, before the good ideas arrived. Often they were there in the morning when I awoke, just according to Goethe's oft-cited verses, and as Gauss also once noted. But they liked specially to make their appearance while I was taking an easy walk over wooded hills in sunny weather. The smallest amount of alcohol seemed to frighten them away.[38]

One group of scientists maintains that their thoughts are clearly formulated in their minds before they express a creative idea: they know exactly what they wish to say or produce before they actually do it. Another group of scientists holds a contrary view: they maintain that scientific creativity is primarily a feeling, an intuition, and not a clearly formulated idea. It is only after the feeling is expressed that logic and analysis can be applied to determine its validity. Artists are divided, as the scientists are, on the nature of creativity. Some artists insist that their ideas are fully worked out and mentally complete before they express themselves overtly. Others hold that if an artist knew what he intended to say before he did so, he would be expressing something that already exists in thought and therefore it could not be considered a creative act.

A work of art or a scientific invention will not come about by itself without effort and direction. Giving birth to a scientific or artistic work is analogous to giving birth to a child. There are several stages of development and degrees of pain that must be endured before parturition arrives. Composers and scientists cannot tell in advance how their "offspring" will turn out, but once they sense the direction these ideas are taking, then they must shape and guide their development with all the critical faculties that they have at their command.

PSYCHOLOGIST

Sigmund Freud did not originate the theory that the creation of a musical work has its origin in the unconscious life of a composer. This view was expressed before him but he gave it credence with clinical evidence based on *psychoanalytic* techniques. Emotion, tension, and *anxiety,* which the composer can no longer endure, impel him to create. The cause of his anxiety may be more deeply rooted than he is able to discern.

The creation of a musical composition may take place in one of several ways. A composer who has received a commission, which he can ill afford to neglect, will start working on the score to complete it at a certain time whether he feels like doing it or not. If he were to sit around and wait for the Muse to stir him, he might never get it done. The same composer, on another occasion, may leisurely sit at his piano and improvise until he is smitten with a pleasing idea which he then goes on to develop into a definite musical pattern. This same composer might also feel impelled, at another time, to write because a gnawing sensation has taken hold of him that can only be alleviated by composing. Thus a composer may create out of economic necessity, or he may attempt to cull suggestive ideas from the unconscious, or a creative mood may come over him and force him to express himself. Some composers claim to use one method—usually the last of the three, the most romantic one. It is more likely that composers use all three.

Music may originate as a mental conception or music may arise from a feeling, but in either case the music has its source in the unconscious. Our mental processes and our emotional acts are governed by unconscious forces. Any composer who assumes that he creates in a purely conscious way is unaware that his musical ideas are embedded in layers of past experience, namely the unconscious. Composition is a confession of life's experiences, most of which have been consciously forgotten.

The composer lives with greater intensity than ordinary men do. He is by nature a more receptive person than most of us are. He is as rational as all men when he is not creating, and he is certainly not pathologically detached when he is creating. There is a difference between a deranged and hallucinated *psychotic,* and a composer in the throes of creation. The delusions of the madman lead only to eventual deterioration. The *phantasies* of the composer are converted into meaningful musical forms.

When the ancients spoke of the musician's madness they did not mean that he was actually deranged, but rather that he was "possessed" by what he was doing. Preoccupation and absorption are healthy forms of detachment and not necessarily symptoms of disease. The composer differs from the madman since he has the ability to vacillate between reality and unreality. He is in control of his medium when creating, else chaos instead of a musical form would evolve. The madman is no longer master of his thoughts but is incoherent; he is swayed by irrational impulses and no longer has the resources to separate what is real from what is not.

There is no such thing as a composer who is continuously "possessed," while the psychotic unfortunately is. The composer is a rational man. Perhaps not when he is composing; nevertheless, he has the ability to clothe his fancy imaginatively and bring forth a work of art. The whole life of the madman is one of delusion; what exists for him does not for anyone else. He is unable to share his private world or communicate with others.

The ancients quite rightly maintained that the composer has no understanding of whence he comes by his music or how to explain it to others. Only in this respect are musician and madman alike. The latter has no insight into his sickness and the composer cannot account for his art.

The psychologist has not been much more successful in unraveling the enigma of artistic creation than the ancient philosopher had been. Freud spent many years analyzing the works, diaries, and habits of several classical figures in the arts only to come to the realization that "whence comes the artist's ability to create, is not the question of psychology." Again, and with even more finality, he stated in an essay on Dostoyevsky: "Unfortunately, psychoanalysis must lay down its arms before the problem of the poet."

Freud would not agree with the unorthodox analytic methods of his estranged disciples who became more speculative than clinical in investigating the musician's motivating forces. He could not agree with Rank, who attributed the creative urge to an unconscious striving for immortality.[39] Neither could he accept Adler's thesis that the creation of music is a compensation for human deficiencies. Nor could he agree altogether with his archrival Jung who resigned himself to believing that the creative act "will for ever elude the human understanding."[40] The word "forever" is distasteful to a scholar who is naturalistically oriented like Freud. Psychoanalysis may not be able to fill this task, Freud maintained, but the study of biology may.

Freud originally thought that it would be possible to resolve the dilemma of artistic creation by comparing the creative process to the emergence of a dream. Sleep is sometimes characterized as a refuge from reality, in his writings, and art in a similar manner is called a form of escape. Thus, in sleep, we are freed from the moral censor—the conscience of our waking life—so that we might dream of fulfilling our desires and satisfying our needs. Dreams are nature's way of compensating in fancy what has been denied us in fact. Art, too, is wishful fancy; but at this point the analogy ends. Dreams remain amorphous and private, whereas art is formally structured and communicative.

The artist "understands how to elaborate his day-dreams," wrote Freud in his *Introductory Lectures on Psychoanalysis:*

...so that they lose that personal note which grates upon strange ears and become enjoyable to others; he knows too how to modify them sufficiently so that their origin in prohibited sources is not easily detected. Further, he possesses the mysterious ability to mold his particular material until it expresses the ideas of his phantasy faithfully; and then he knows how to attach to this reflection of his phantasy-life so strong a stream of pleasure that, for a time at least, the repressions are outbalanced and dispelled by it. When he can do all this, he opens out to others the way back to the comfort and consolation of their own unconscious sources of pleasure, and so reaps their gratitude and admiration; then he has won—through his phantasy—what before he could only win in phantasy.[41]

But Freud raised two fundamental questions in this passage and only answered one, and that much too briefly. First, what cardinal distinction sets the artist off from ordinary men? Secondly, what are these mysterious qualities which enable the artist to mold his phantasy into a work of art? To the first of these questions Freud answered that for "those who are not artists the gratification that can be drawn from the springs of phantasy is very limited; their inexorable repressions prevent the enjoyment of all but the meager day-dreams."[42] In answer to the second, Freud set forth his much debated theory that the artist is endowed with a powerful capacity for *sublimation.* Some years later Freud went on to add in his *Three Contributions to the Theory of Sex* that sublimation "through which the excessive excitations from individual sexual sources are discharged and utilized in other spheres.... forms one of the sources of artistic creativity, and, depending on whether such sublimation is complete or incomplete, the analysis of the character of highly gifted, especially of artistically disposed persons, will show every kind of proportionate blending between productive ability, perversion and reurosis."[43] Sublimation is then only one means of artistic creation and is not all-inclusive as a method of explaining the peculiar gifts of the artist. Psychoanalysis, Freud lamented, is not adequate to account fully for artistic creation. He was well aware of this fact in his earlier writings, even if some of his disciples were not, when he wrote in the closing pages of his *Leonardo da Vinci* that "the nature of artistic attainment is psychoanalytically inaccessible to us," and again, "It can do nothing towards elucidating the nature of the artistic gift, nor can it explain the means by which the artist works." [44]

The substance of the Freudian belief is that works of art are analogous in their modes of creation to dreams. Just as dreams afford us the experience of realizing our repressed desires in a world of phantasy, so the musician achieves *wish-fulfillment* through his creation. The dreamer does not share his phantasy with others; the composer does.

A dream cannot be considered a work of art even though it is created by the same laws which govern the creation of a musical score. Both the dream and music have their origin in a number of causes. Freud never insisted that sublimation of itself accounted for creation. He considered it the psychological process by which the composer converted inhibited primordial drives into what Santayana later called something better than had existed before. Whether the experimental psychologist can develop an operationally sound hypothesis which would lend itself to a rejection or verification of the sublimation theory is yet to be seen. It is quite evident that even though Freud developed his theories on artistic creation independently, the function of will, desire, and escape in Schopenhauer and the comparison of the dream to music in Nietzsche, found their way into his thinking. What was theoretical in these romantic philosophers was given clinical corroboration in Freud's empirical methods of mental therapy.

The basic similarity between Freud and Jung is their common belief that artistic creation has its source in the unconscious, even if the rational way in which the composer goes about his work would seem to deny it. The difference in belief between Freud and Jung is as wide as the gulf which separates the philosophical *materialist* from the theological idealist in accounting for their respective theories of knowledge. Freud believed that man is the sum total of his experience. Jung disagreed. He believed that man is more than his life experience. He is also a repository of the past. The unconscious is the subterranean chamber of symbols, myths, cultural and religious traditions. Man stands as a symbol of the collective unconscious, a recipient of a legacy, the heritage of the past. His life cannot be dissociated from the repressed vicissitudes of his race even though they may be consciously forgotten.

Man bears a burden of guilt, reasoned Jung, a feeling of revenge, and a sense of revelation too—the musician more so than other men. Salvation for him can be achieved through creation. He finds himself compelled to create in order to survive. In the process of saving himself, he saves humanity too. Jung expressed it in this way: "Art is a kind of innate drive that seizes a human being and makes him its instrument. The artist is not a person endowed with free will who seeks his own ends, but one who allows art to realize its purposes through him. As a human being he may have moods and a will and personal aims, but as an artist he is 'man' in a higher sense—he is 'collective man'—one who carries and shapes the unconscious, psychic life of mankind." [45]

Jung's theory that music, as a form of art, arises from psychic residua of ancestral experiences is summed up in the statement that the creative process "consists of an activation of the timeless symbols of humanity resting in the unconscious and in the development and refinement of them into the complete work of art." These primordial images, psychic residua of experience and ancestral beliefs, are the archetypes which the musician is unconsciously bound to and guided by in his mood of creativity. Those who speak of music as a timeless art may not be far wrong after all.

SOCIOLOGIST

Sociologists lay great stress on the role that environment performs in grooming creative personalities. They have statistics to show that creativity is found largely in middle and upper middle socio-economic groups. Their claim is that financial assurance and a scholarly home are more conducive to the development of creative personalities than a home in which there is poverty with no art and books. Environment is undoubtedly important in nurturing creativity, but not for the reasons that we so often think and that sociologists tend to favor. Creativity is a biological phenomenon primarily, and only secondarily a social one. A person who by nature is disposed to be curious, easily angered because of an over degree of sensitivity, and psychologically compelled to explode in order to maintain his emotional equlibrium, will create no matter what social system he lives under or home he happens to come from.

〜

One of the earliest references to the social origin of music is in Plato's *Laws*. It is the passage on human needs and the generosity of the gods and, quite properly, was referred to in the section on theology. Plato explained that music grew out of the festival dances which were held periodically in honor of the gods. The gods themselves created the festivals so that by honoring them men in turn would develop a sense of rhythm and harmony and thus be enabled to "alternate rest with labour" as well as "improve their education."

Quintilian expressed a similar belief, but he replaced the gods with nature. "Indeed nature of itself seems to have given music as a boon to men to lighten the strain of labour." [46] But even when a Roman referred to music as having a social origin it was usually done on the assumption that the gods could provide men with music directly or they could supply it indirectly through natural sounds such as Lucretius described in *Book V, On the Nature of Things*.

The Greeks and Romans were inclined to think of the origin of music in a *teleological* frame of reference. It mattered little whether music came from imitating nature, as Lucretius pointed out. Nature expresses the will of the gods; it has no will of its own. Music can, therefore, only emanate from the gods, even though man acquires it from copying natural sounds. A song that wells up from the throat of a bird and in time is shaped by man into a structured musical work still has its origin in the gods.

Theories about the social origin of music received their greatest impetus in the nineteenth century from scholars who tried to apply Darwin's findings to the beginnings and development of music. Spencer believed that vocal music originated in impassioned speech,[47] in the instinctive needs of man to express himself. The growth of music from a simple vocal utterance to a complex art paralleled the evolution of man and his institutions. As man's needs multiplied and his institutions prospered, music reflected these personal and social changes.

Kant alluded to the origin of art as man's need to spend his excess energy in play. The poet Schiller was so enchanted with Kant's remark, "Art compared with Labor may be considered as a Play," that he worked out a theory of his own concerning art and play. The art historian Konrad Lange elaborated Schiller's theory by maintaining that a composer creates music as a child creates a make-believe world. Both create in order to give free reign to their imaginative faculties to offset the curbs and restrictions that society and religion impose on us. The composer's creation and the child's phantasies are conscious forms of self-illusion, a necessary indulgence to grant them the means to equalize the balance between what society has deprived them of and what they require by nature. Both child and composer improvise, consciously deceiving themselves by pretending that the unreal is the real, a game of willful make-believe.

Social theories on the origin of music are closely allied with human behavior. Man is by nature a gregarious animal. He cannot exist for long, let alone thrive, in isolation. His gregarious instincts compel him to search out other men and establish some kind of union based on common interests. Hunting, magic rites, and religious ceremonies were early opportunities for primitive people to congregate and express themselves. It is quite probable that at such gatherings emotions ran high and expressions of sentiment, fear, and expiation eventually developed a structural semblance of song.

All our efforts to trace the beginning of music are speculative;

still, some theories are more tenable than others. As eminent a psychologist as Carl Stumpf seriously believed that music originated in the sending of signal calls from hilltop to hilltop. This feat was accomplished by a man lingering on one tone so that his voice would be heard at a distance. This in turn produced a tightening of his vocal cords. The tautness of the cords produced a higher pitch. Sustaining the higher pitch developed a vibrato, creating a high pitched vibrato tone—the beginnings of music as compared to articulate language. This theory may be more sophisticated than the one that music developed out of the wild cries of the savage, but it is as unconvincing as the latter is inconclusive. Music is a very ancient phenomenon whose origin is so uncertain that we do not know whether it preceded, paralleled, or followed language.

Darwin took a dim view of both the play theory and the notion that music has its origin in impassioned speech. He felt that Spencer and his followers had used the theory of evolution rather superficially and to poor advantage in tracing the origin of music to a stage in existence when man had conceptually developed language to an advanced degree. The play theory is again too advanced. Neither theory regresses back far enough into the history of life on this earth to be fully convincing. Darwin's own theory on the origin of music is essentially biological. In the sequence of natural events, speech came after song, not the other way around.

As we have every reason to suppose that articulate speech is one of the latest, as it certainly is the highest, of the arts acquired by man, and as the instinctive power of producing musical notes and rhythms is developed low down in the animal series, it would be altogether opposed to the principle of Evolution, if we were to admit that man's musical capacity has been developed from the tones used in impassioned speech. We must suppose that the rhythms and cadences of oratory are derived from previously developed musical powers....[48]

I conclude that musical notes and rhythms were first acquired by the male or female progenitors of mankind for the sake of charming the opposite sex.[49]

Jung's cultural emphasis in his psychology of behavior led

him to side with Darwin in assuming that "we discover the first instincts of art in animals used in the service of the impulse of creation, and limited to the breeding season." [50] Those scholars who believe that life began with *Genesis,* and that music probably evolved out of the offering of a hymn of thanksgiving to his Maker by Adam, would not be likely to accept Darwin's theory. If there is any evidence as to which belief to favor, it would appear that the proof lies with Darwin; but then, the man of faith invariably asks—how can we know whether the evidence is conclusive?

NOVELIST

The stories that novelists tell are products of their own experience or those of others. But their ability to relate these stories well requires insight and sensitivity. Not all storytellers have these qualities. The novelist differs from raconteurs in temperament and imagination and in the ability to be impersonal about his own experience. Some novelists write because they are emotionally burdened. They hide behind their characters while complaining to the world. Some write autobiographies so that they will not be forgotten. More novels of great merit have been born out of maladjustment than out of love and devotion.

So far we have dealt only with what men of faith and reason have had to say about the creative process. We have yet to allow the creator of fine art to speak for himself. But unlike the scholar, he becomes mute and retiring when it comes to discussing his artistic prowess. The average scholar somehow is never at a loss for an explanation; ask and ye shall be answered, even if it is about something so inexplicable as the glowing and stilling of artistic fire. Such scholars are not noted for their novel creations and yet many of them have no qualms about speaking out on matters which are outside their experience and ken, such as the creative phenomenon.

It takes a Shavian sense of humor to believe that the artist divines by inspiration all the great truths that the academician "grubs up" in musty libraries and the scientist discovers in his laboratory. The scientist and scholar are just as creative as the artist when their work has what the philosopher Whitehead called "the principle of novelty." The begetting of a new idea is what counts in this world whether it is by artist, scientist, or imaginative scholar. Ideas are what capture the imagination and change man and the world.

Most scholars are cautious men who are not likely to "let down buckets into the unconscious," compare their work with dreams, or dare to admit that they do not understand what they said after they have said it. E. M. Forster's pithy remark, "Think before you speak is criticism's motto; speak before you think is the creator's," if carried to a logical conclusion ends in an insoluble dilemma. How is a scholarly critic to go about evaluating, with intellectual criteria, a work of art born of impulse and emotion? The history of criticism is replete with men of reason who tried to evaluate something new and fresh, but with such reverence for the past that they were impervious to many works of great novelty.

Stephen Spender's observation that criticism justly deserves to be defined "as the substitute muse of the universities" illustrates the predicament that the creative person finds himself in when pitted against the complacent intellectual in established institutions. "In our form of society," wrote Gide in his *Journals,* "a great writer or great artist is essentially nonconformist. He swims against the current." It is hard to imagine such a creature rising to authority in church, state, or school. Yet everything great in this world has come from the erratic artist, wrote Proust. "They alone have founded our religions and composed our masterpieces." The world will never know how great a debt it owes artists, or fully understand how "they have suffered to enrich us."

The process of creation is the same for novelist and musician:

only the materials with which they express their art differ. One art is more definitive than the other. It may appeal more to reason than emotion, but the creation of a novel or a musical score follows the same psychological laws. The plot of a book and the theme of a score come from the same residua of experience and not from any other place. Stendhal's description of his creative process is similar to that of the composer working in a state of feverish excitement. Turgenev's frank admission that he "never attempted to create a type without having, not an idea, but a living person, in whom the various elements are harmonized together" is further assurance that art can only come from life. Dostoyevsky's description of his torments while creating seems to characterize the lot of all who create—they must suffer before their art is given. The artist amuses the public with his agonies, concluded Flaubert. Stephen Crane writing to an editor said:

The Red Badge of Courage... was an effort born of pain—despair, almost; and I believe that this made it a better piece of literature than it otherwise would have been. It seems a pity that art should be a child of pain, and yet I think it is. Of course we have fine writers who are prosperous and contented, but in my opinion their work would be greater if this were not so. It lacks the sting it would have if written under the spur of a great need.[51]

Not all novelists write, as Turgenev did, about their immediate friends and enemies, or create, as Stendhal did, in feverish heat. Chekhov "never wrote directly from life." He would not begin actual writing until a story was completely settled in his mind. When he felt ready to work, ideas flowed without respite, fully organized and complete "until the end." He once told his friend Bunin that "one should not write unless he is as cold as ice," otherwise he would lose control over his ability to express himself and nothing but rambling ideas might come out. Chekhov's method of creating would hardly fit in with that of Flaubert, although the psychological process is the same.

Novelists, as a group, do not use the same method of creation any more than musicians do. Richard Strauss[52] expressed views almost identical with those of Chekhov concerning the creative process. The creative method of Tschaikovsky was similar to that of Stendhal.

PAINTER

Do painters "see" what they paint on canvas, an image so complete that not one "jot" of it needs to be changed? Or do painters plan their work with the detailed care that architects use to prepare a blueprint for a house? Painters use both techniques. At one time painters copied master painters, hoping to find the secrets of their genius by faithfully imitating them. Most modern painters are introspective and highly personal in their work. They spend their lives looking for answers to the mysteries of life within themselves and not in the work of painters who have lived before or share the contemporary world with them.

The creation of a work of art is not necessarily a benevolent act on the part of the artist to transmit an emotional mood to others that would correspond to the mood that he was in when creating. He may wish to do so or he may not; there is no way of determining empirically, even if he wants to transmit such a mood to others, whether he was successful or not. The artist, generally, is a thoroughly selfish person whose interest is primarily in himself. He may create to satisfy his desires in phantasy, or he may create to cloak his aggressions and repressions and so use his art as a defense against a society which he fears and toward which he bears hostility. Whatever be the artist's reason for creating, it may seem like humility, but, more probably, is egocentricity. Even when an artist makes a specific effort to be clearly understood by the public, he does so on his own terms, without compromise to his ego; the sacrifice, if any, is with the public. An artist who is so full of solicitude for the masses that he uses commonplace and banal means of expression is by definition not an artist but an illustrator, an arranger, a jingle-maker, a dispenser in the market place.

Artists are not equally gifted. Some are originators, but most are imitators. Those who create, that is originate, are trying to resolve a conflict of which they may or may not be conscious. The lesser artists may have their share of inhibitions, but these do not add up to a combustible mixture that must find an outlet or explode. For the average person psychic tensions are ordinarily released through the more usual ways, such as play, work, and dreams. If these pressures are restrained to a point of being thwarted and cannot be expressed in a normal way, then they will find release in an abnormal way. When Freud said that the artist comes close to being a *neurotic,* he meant that the artist is still capable of resolving a conflict by formal art. But if the degree of inhibition becomes overly severe, then the powers of function are stifled by psychic paralysis inducing mental and physical incapacitation.

An artist cannot describe his feelings to us in his creations as he originally felt them, however he may try. Artist's diaries are not reliable in this respect. It is as if a painter, for example, were trying to describe in retrospect the agony of a feverish toothache and the painful associations that went with it. He could no more recapture the sickening sensations that the aching tooth produced than he could make us feel, through his painting, how he felt at that time. Memory and time color and distort original impressions. Painting, like poetry, is emotion recollected in tranquility. The painter does not give us a faithful reproduction of his impressions. He does not transmit his conscious and unconscious feelings directly. With the help of reason he is subtle, suggestive, evocative. Wittingly and unwittingly he scoffs, mocks, praises and condemns, but of course with esthetic symbolism. His appeal is on the basis of a common culture. It is reasonable to assume that the symbolic character of a quiet painting would not send us into convulsions. Its Apollonian qualities evoke a subdued, gentle response from our culturally conditioned faculties.

The field in which an artist expresses himself is more what Aristotle would call an accident rather than an attribute of his artistic nature. "My statues are poems of life," wrote Maillol. "Instead of using the medium of verse I explain myself in sculpture." [53] Painters strive for the same affects that poets do. "Why should we not exaggerate on canvas as poets do in metaphors?" [54] asked Gauguin. Painters follow the same psychological process of creation as poets and novelists do. A Millet landscape would belie the fact that his paintings are a transfiguration of anguished humanity. His letters spoke of suffering—his own and that of others. He converted the strife within him, "the one thing that gives an artist power to express himself" into "the calm, the silence," [55] of nature at eventide. Gauguin called his paintings "a human outcry" against a money-grubbing society, a colorless civilization in contrast to that of an aboriginal one. Van Gogh, distressed by the evil and misery in the world, painted with the fervor of a missionary to abolish the sin that vexed him. "I have tried to express the terrible passions of humanity by means of red and green," [56] he moralized. He found what Dostoyevsky's idiot, Myshkin, sorrowfully learned: that a moral man cannot survive in an immoral world, and in order to escape, must go mad. Tormented in adolescence, half-crazed in manhood, van Gogh was well-equipped by nature to follow his calling. Each painting that he created temporarily deterred his self-destruction, ironically pointing out that the creation of art apparently gives only transient respite from sin and sorrow; death alone is lasting. Matisse did not moralize but rather wished that his paintings should be judged *hedonistically,* on the basis of giving pleasure and relief. He decorated his canvases with bright, warm colors in the hope that "my paintings will give mankind a moment of repose." Picasso is more exacting of his painting: "I want nothing but emotion to be given off by it." [57] Art is born of emotion to appeal to emotion, for Picasso.

Painters, like their fellow artists, have left testimonies on the creative process. "When extreme sentiments blend in the depths of a person, when they burst out, and when the entire mind flows out like the lava from a volcano, is that not the enthusiasm of a suddenly created work,... The cold calculations of reason have not presided over this emission, but who knows when the work was started in the depths of a person? Perhaps subconsciously?" [58] was how Gauguin described the creative process. "How I paint I do not know myself," [59] wrote the more modest van Gogh. Do ideas come slowly, quickly? "Ideas for my work come to me in swarms...I am working like one actually possessed." [60] There are uncreative times too, when ideas come slowly and not at all, lamented van Gogh: "They are a kind of transformation period." [61]

Kandinsky described his creative process in the following way:

As far as I can look back, all and any forms I have ever used, came to me, as it were, by themselves. They either appeared before my eyes, complete and ready to be copied, or would form themselves gradually, during the hours of work. Sometimes they would prove obstinate, and then I would have to wait patiently, often with fear in my heart, until such times as they chose to reveal themselves to me. These inner revelations cannot be described. They are mysterious and are born of many hidden reasons. Their approach is heralded by, as it were, a ripple on the soul's surface, an increasing undefined turmoil, a tautening and intensifying of some deep-set force. They stay, sometimes for an instant, sometimes for days at a stretch.... After such exalted moments, during which one's analytical control disappears completely, there follows a period of deep emotional lassitude.... a painter must guide the talent that sweeps him along the road of creation. And even if he is capable of calling forth rare, fragmentary moments of self-willed exaltation, it is, nevertheless, given him to qualify its character, as also of those that arise in him independently of his will. [62]

Some painters work from nature and some from models since they need the presence of tangible objects to stimulate them; other painters create purely from imagination. Some painters are adept at using one method only, some use different methods at different times. The number of ways for calling on the Muse are as many as there are painters. But whatever the respective way of creating may be, the stuff of which the painting is made comes from the raw emotions buried deep in the vitals of the artist. Picasso said: "A picture is not thought out and settled beforehand. While it is being done it changes as one's thoughts change...." [63] "When I have found something to express, I have done it without thinking of the past or of the future....If the subjects I have wanted to express have suggested

different ways of expression I have never hesitated to adopt them....
Different motives inevitably require different methods of expression...." [64]

A painting is not simply an emotional outburst or purely a mathematical formula. Emotion of itself or reason alone is as incomplete a form of expression in life as it is in art. The painter is a member of two worlds, sense and reason, and his work is expressive of both. Creation is the outcry of the complete man as Gauguin said, the animal as well as the rational in him, raw emotion and refined form.

POET

All the works that have been published by me "are only fragments of one great confession" acknowledged Goethe on several occasions. Writing poetry is the equivalent of releasing "the lava of the imagination whose eruption prevents an earthquake," Byron pointed out in illustrating the therapeutic value of creating poetry. The creative act "is that pleasurable emotion, that peculiar state and degree of excitement, which arises in the poet himself in the act of composition"; it is purgation in its purest sense according to Coleridge. Creating a poem does the same thing that occupational therapy does, adds Robert Frost.

The Greek bard and musician were one. He created his poem and the music to accompany it. With *melody* and rhythm he rounded out the *meter* and *style* of the words. The Muse, the spiritual source of his music, inspired his poem too. Some Greeks considered the poem more important than the melody; but to the Muse they were inseparable arts, and if she had to choose it would be the melody rather than the poem she would prefer. Even though poet and musician went different ways, the Muse saw to it that they should always derive inspiration from the same source. Pope noted that although the poet and musician had separated and each had become autonomous, both these children of the Muse still created without rule, guided by inspiration with which she had originally endowed them when they were one.

The poet's preoccupation with inspiration is as old as poetry itself. The Muse is the poet's conception of whatever he wishes her to be. She may be personal or religious, a fetish or a ritual. Without her he would be lost. Whether the spectre of the divine Muse is real or not, Shaftesbury wisely observed, is not for the poet to decide. He must live and believe in order to create, for without any faith he could never exceed his bounds. There is a *pragmatic* strain in this credo which a visionary, like Blake, would deplore. "I do not pretend to be any other than the secretary"; he wrote, "the authors are in eternity." Here practicality is supplanted with faith, there is no doubt of the artist's source.

> *Hear the voice of the Bard,*
> *Who present, past, and future, sees;*
> *Whose ears have heard*
> *The Holy Word*
> *That walk'd among the ancient trees;*
>   William Blake

Some poets are stimulated to create by choosing words with an inner rhythm, a succession of words with similar sounds for purposes of alliteration; they may put their first draft away to work on it another day, years after, as Horace suggested, before the final poem is finished. The more romantic poets write in a frenzied state, as though they are carried out of themselves, completing their poem in one sitting. Another type of poet, however rare, will thumb through the dictionary searching for one word to kindle the imagination. The sight of a particular word may move the poet to associate it with something in his past, thus awakening a latent experience that can now be turned into art. Poe wrote that he created poetry with the precision of a mathematician. "The Raven" at "no one point in its composition is referable either to accident or intuition ... the work proceeded, step by step, to its completion with the precision and rigid consequence of a mathematical problem." [65]

Thumbing through a dictionary to induce a flow of ideas, and fretting and waiting for ideas to arrive, are reflective ways of conjuring up the Muse, in comparison to the creative method in which the Muse takes hold of the poet, making him "possessed." Some poets call for the Muse to inspire them; sometimes the Muse calls them. Either method bears out Wordsworth's belief that poetry is created from emotion recollected in tranquility. "The emotion is contemplated till by a species of reaction the tranquillity gradually disappears, and an emotion, similar to that which was before the subject of contemplation, is gradually produced, and does itself actually exist in the mind. In this mood successful composition generally begins, and in a mood similar to this it is carried on." [66] If it should seem that this does not apply to the frenzied poet, since he is not himself when creating, then indeed it would be true that the poem is not really his and does belong to the Muse. What is more actual than fancy is that his frenzy is brought on by the crystallization of certain feelings and ideas which he may consciously have thought about or unconsciously have harbored and could no longer repress. The poet's mind is a receptacle of life's experience.[67] After impressions are gathered they coalesce as they sink into the unconscious; in time they become compressed and eventually must be expressed, lest they erupt in some formless fashion. A poet is "possessed" only when his ideas are fully developed, after a period of waiting.

The poet, like the musician, is guided by feeling more than reason in the creative process. The affect always comes first, even when appearances would seem to deny it, concepts and forms only later. The poet cannot explain how he creates his poem or fully anticipate its outcome. To predict a poem, T. E. Hulme said, "would be to produce it before it was produced." The mind in creation is governed by some invisible influence buried deep in the life of the poet. Shelley wrote:

A man cannot say, "I will compose poetry." The greatest poet ever cannot say it; for the mind in creation is as a fading coal, which some invisible influence, like an inconstant wind, awakens to transitory brightness; this power arises from within, like the color of a flower which fades and changes as it is developed, and the

conscious portions of our natures are unprophetic either of its approach or its departure. Could this influence be durable in its original
purity and force, it is impossible to predict the greatness of the
results; but when composition begins, inspiration is already on the
decline, and the most glorious poetry that has ever been communicated to the world is probably a feeble shadow of the original conceptions of the poet.[68]

Poetry, like all art, is born of experience of a real or imaginary
kind. The poet creates because he must, to get relief from anxiety
that will not let him rest.[69] It is sometimes done in quiet indignation
and sometimes with a roaring blast. In whatever way it is accomplished, its source is from the life of man. At times it emerges
tormentingly slowly, on occasion even quickly and, sometimes, in a
brilliant glow. It is a vision, a feeling expressed, which the poet
cannot fully understand any more than we.

MUSICIAN

I compose for "the weary and the worn," wrote Haydn, so that they
"may enjoy a few moments of solace and refreshment." Haydn's
correspondence would show that this solicitude for the masses is a
projection of his own life. Composers cannot always tell what motives
guide them; at other times the reasons behind their creative urges
are crystal clear to them. Mahler wrote: "... so closely bound up is
the act of creation in me, with every experience, that when my mind
and spirit are at rest, I can compose nothing."

⌐

Musicians differ from ordinary men, but are they different from
other men who are also creators? The poet Browning thought they
were. He held that God endows the musician with near-omniscience.
While other creators question and wonder, the favored musician
knows. What is more, to Browning, God permits the musician to
create not in obedience to law, as all others who create must, but by
inspiration from above, free of governing law. The esteem in which

Statuette: *Seated Man with Harp.* Cycladic, about 2500 B.C. Marble. The Metropolitan Museum of Art, Rogers Fund, 1947.

the musician is held may be clearly seen, the sign is there. The finger of God is pointed at the musician, signaling him out from all the others.

Browning's appraisal of the musician, in *Abt Vogler,* outdoes the musician's evaluation of himself. His idolization of the musician is mere whimsy; it certainly is not based on facts. The finger of God is just as visible in the work of the poet and painter as it is in the score of the musician. Nature's inexorable law governs the musician in the same way that it does all who create. The musician is no better informed about the past or able to predict the future than any other creator. It is a myth that God favors the musician; at the risk of being iconoclasts, we must remember that it was Homer who invented, and the philosophers who perpetuated, the notion that the gods take away the minds of the musicians and make them their own. Those who create music are not controlled by external forces any more than those who create in the other arts. The spark that kindles the fires of creation comes from within the musician and not from without.

Philosophers in antiquity wrote erudite accounts of the musician's habits and symptoms associated with creativity. The little that we know about the Greek bard's music, for example, is based largely on philosophical writings rather than on the few fragments of music that are extant. The philosopher's description of a musician in antiquity composing an ode might well resemble a modern version of creativity. *Modes* and styles have changed in character through the ages, the musician's creative process has remained essentially the same.

Our knowledge of how the musician created in the Roman era also rests on what the philosophers have told us. There is a difference, however, between what the Greek and Roman scholar had to say. The Greeks described the musician's creative process as originating in divinity, followed by madness and frenzy. The Romans simply noted "the musician creates according to the Greek philosopher's description of him"—content to confirm what their predecessors had originally said, but adding nothing new of their own.

The early Christians were not awed by the musician's powers as those before them were. Only the Apostles were divine prophets, insisted the Church Fathers; musicians are like other men, there is nothing supernatural about them. Priests are more favored than musicians in Christendom. Priests are ordained, musicians are not. In Greece and Rome it was the musician who was the favorite of the gods, not the priests.

The Protestants scoffed at the idea that the musician was by temperament in a special category and should, therefore, be treated as an exception because of his inventive nature. Proper Christian discipline could easily induce conformity, ruled the Protestant clergy with reference to the musician. Then the Protestants learned, what the Catholics already knew, that any attempt to curb the composer made him sing more sublimely than before, in a manner that the religious hierarchy would abhor. The composer could not change his nature and conform to a rigid set of rules, even if he had so willed. If he tried to do what was contrary to his nature, he would be destroyed by his own deed.

Musicians are rebels and innovators by nature, but they are not inclined to indulge in self-analysis. They may fear to question the Muse, lest she disappear and never return. Some musicians believe, and this has been the case throughout history, that if the mystery veiling the creative personality were lifted, the composer might commit a sacrilege by learning the source of his art, and so lose his creativity. Other composers do not share this historical fear and speak freely about their creative process.

It seems likely that a church organist, such as Bach, who had to write a new score for each Sunday service, just as the minister had to prepare a weekly sermon, could not sit and wait for the Muse. He did tell us that he worked untiringly to produce his music whether he was in the mood or not. "Ceaseless work,... analysis, reflection, writing much, endless self-correction, that is my secret." Where did his ideas come from? In some few cases it is quite obvious. On one occasion he copied a toccata and *fugue* from Purcell. In a broader vein, his harpsichord *concertos* are transcriptions of violin concertos, many of which were not his own. Borrowing was not uncommon in Bach's time any more than it is now. But borrowing alone does not produce a great composer. He must possess certain biological and psychological qualities, in addition to being a craftsman, in order to be a composer of Bach's stature. Bach would get an idea for a musical setting and then not allow it to be marred by extraneous musical ideas which might detract from the cohesiveness of the work. A composer of smaller stature might unwittingly bring irrelevant musical ideas into his score which would subvert his original idea and in the end leave him with a composition full of esthetic incongruities instead of a logically consistent piece of writing.

Handel wrote with ease but lacked the discipline to express

himself with the same cogency as Bach. Although both composers have made lasting contributions, still the music of Bach is more durable than that of Handel. Creative ideas and originality cannot always be equated with the quantity of a composer's output. Some composers with a paucity of ideas write endlessly and abundantly. Others produce slowly, deliberately, and in small amount, and each work is a masterpiece.

Haydn's music hardly gives the impression that it is the work of a tormented soul. Aristotle's observation that creative men are of a melancholy temperament would in that respect at least place Haydn in the class of creators. "The unstrung state of my nerves so completely crush me to the earth that I fall into the most melancholy condition so much so that for days afterwards I am incapable of finding one new idea." But Providence has its ways. "When my work does not advance I retire into the oratory with my rosary and say an Ave, immediately ideas come to me." Haydn retiring to the oratory with his rosary to say an Ave poignantly illustrates his efforts to invoke the Muse. The power of prayer has an overwhelming affect on one who is a supplicant. It is a time for introspection and confession which brings to the surface the guilt of yesterday's sin, remorse for something that could have been. But however sacred such a ritual may be, its psychological value is not unlike the age-old practice of the artist who sketches and waits, the poet who broods until distraught, and the composer looking at a blank sheet of paper or improvising at the piano, hoping for one theme on which to build all the rest.

If musical creation has its source in a life burdened with anxiety, then how do we account for the productivity of a youthful Mozart? A *Singspiel* written in early adolescence is a technical feat, not a demonstration of original ideas. Mozart showed himself to be an accomplished interpreter and performing virtuoso of other peoples' scores, but he did not display his creative powers until he left his youth behind. Youthful prodigies are technicians and interpreters, not creators. One must first have endured life's experiences before he has something to write about. A musician is not like God who can create ex nihilo.

Mozart's method of creating could just as well fit Beethoven or most other composers in its initial stages. Both composers made a practice of jotting down ideas that came to them in whatever place, at whatever time. These impressions underwent a period of germination or unconscious elaboration and then rose to the conscious level in response to some inward need or external stimulus. Mozart usually began a score by putting down his themes and then working around them. Ideas for portions of his *operas* flowed with a grace and ease that is foreign in experience to the average human being. His later quartets, that were written in dedication to Haydn, only came as the fruit of long and painful labor. Beethoven's sketchbooks lend themselves to the belief that he started with a tonal conception of a movement and then wove his melody into the structure of the work. "I carry my ideas about with me for a long time—often a very long time—before I write them down ... then begins in my head the working-out in the broad, in the narrow, in the height, in the depth; ... the fundamental idea never leaves me; it mounts, it grows, I see before my mind the picture in its whole extent, as it were in a single projection (in einem Gusse)." [70]

Whereas Beethoven worked tirelessly to satisfy his thematic demands, Schubert was known to produce a *Lied,* on occasion, as fast as he could write it down. Schubert wrote easily and without any overt evidence of pain. This itself is not beyond comprehension. It certainly is not a unique phenomenon which distinguishes Schubert from all the other composers in his time. This could just as appropriately be said of Handel, Gluck, and Mozart. Psychologically, such dexterity may come from the crystallization of musical ideas in the unconscious which come to the conscious level fully developed and are then transcribed unhaltingly on paper. Beethoven, it seems, was of a different nature. He worked out his ideas in sketchbooks; and in the process of revising an idea, over and over again, he achieved in a conscious and laborious fashion what more fortunate composers accomplished less painfully on the level of the unconscious.

Chopin's musical ideas came to him with a certain spontaneity, but then followed a period of writing and rewriting, fretting and weeping, bordering on maniacal frenzy. He would spend days on a single passage and then leave it as he had noted it down originally. Liszt's music was a direct reflection of his life. He created as he lived—vivaciously, flamboyantly, ingratiatingly.

Brahms's ideas came "in a flash," then followed the customary work and more work. Unlike Mozart and Schubert, he could not create with chatting friends around him. He needed isolation, privacy, and quiet surroundings to become absorbed in his work. Like Mozart and Beethoven, he jotted down whatever thematic ideas came to mind. "I let them germinate, sometimes for years." Turning out a score "is an intellectual process as far as the mechanics of composition are concerned"; but inspiration, the birth of an idea, "is a spiritual process."

Musical ideas have their origin in any number of sources and are expressed for a variety of reasons but the stimulus which brings them to the surface is confined to a two-fold need. Tschaikovsky wrote his benefactress that he created in response to a personal impulse, at which time ideas all but swarmed around him; or he composed to fill a commission by trying to evoke a mood conducive to creation which only came with much effort, if at all. The intrinsic merit of a work had little to do with one method or the other, Tschaikovsky was frank enough to say, whether it evolved out of his own initiative or was written in response to an external circumstance.

Tschaikovsky also insisted that during the actual period "of creative activity complete quiet is absolutely necessary to the artist." He then went on to make a pertinent statement that gives additional weight to Wordsworth's remark about creation.

Those who imagine that a creative artist can—through the medium of his art—express his feelings at the moment when he is *moved,* make the greatest mistake. Emotions—sad or joyful—can only be expressed *retrospectively,* so to speak. Without any special reason for rejoicing, I may be moved by the most cheerful creative mood, and, *vice versá,* a work composed under the happiest surroundings may be touched with dark and gloomy colours.[71]

The composer leads a dual life. He is practically schizoid when creating, and just as normal as anyone else when he is not. "In a word, an artist lives a double life; an everyday human life, and an artistic life, and the two do not always go hand in hand."[72]

The length of time that ensues between a mental impression and its germination into a musical idea depends on the nature of the composer and a number of circumstances. It is possible for a composer to become so excited by an event that he may express his feelings directly. There are also times when a composer is so affected by an experience that he must retire from the scene or remain inexpressive. Debussy found that the mighty ocean so overwhelmed his creative faculties that he had to go back to a quiet studio inland to express the surging dynamism of the sea in music.

Wagner found that his early efforts to give vent to his immediate feelings in music proved that the inexorable laws of nature do not permit the creative process to be circumvented in time and experience. His ideas for the stupendous music dramas came only after long brooding, sketching—spinning the threads of his own life into a mythical fabric of lore. Creation itself he called a limitless dream, an escape to another world. The actual writing part he repeatedly referred to as drudgery—drudgery, and nothing more.

What seemed so unbearable for Wagner appears rather pleasurable for Stravinsky. "The very act of putting my work on paper, of, as we say, kneading the dough, is for me inseparable from the pleasure of creation. So far as I am concerned," continues Stravinsky, "I cannot separate the spiritual effort from the psychological and physical effort; they confront me on the same level and do not present a hierarchy." [73]

Stravinsky does not sit around waiting to be inspired when there is something to do. He begins his task as a craftsman would, whether he feels like it or not. His method often consists of writing down the "first chord" in anticipation of the total score. This primary *chord* is the nucleus, sometimes called the "spiritual tonic," around which the tonal and rhythmic character of the composition is structured.

The creation of music, according to Stravinsky, is a God-given ability to give expression to vague intuitions, whose origins are unknown and whose meanings are unclear, through a "vigilant technique" that will add material substance to the spiritual idea. The composer is a mixture of thinker and doer, not one or the other alone. Creation is making, but the mystery of whence comes the composer by his ideas eludes understanding. Man is a spiritual as well as a material being, a duality which enables him to beget ideas and enjoy the power of making. "All creation presupposes at its origin a sort of appetite that is brought on by the foretaste of discovery. This foretaste of the creative act," writes Stravinsky in the vein of a *metaphysician,* "accompanies the intuitive grasp of an unknown entity already possessed but not yet intelligible, an entity that will not take definite shape except by the action of a constantly vigilant technique." [74]

Stravinsky would be at odds with the philosopher Croce. The latter held that music is intuition, not a physical phenomenon. It is a spiritual experience which ceases to be when given physical embodiment. Stravinsky maintains that actually there is no music until the intuitions are expressed. Croce would agree with this, but to him the expression of intuitions is personal, it need not be shared with another person in the world. Technique, in one sense, is not important for Croce in the creative process since music is a mental experience and not a printed page or tonal sounds produced by human voices and instruments. Technique is of the utmost importance to Stravinsky. Without it, the composer would be unable to develop his potential ideas into actual musical *form.*

Paul Hindemith's description of his process of creating music is reminiscent of Athena emerging from the head of the great god Zeus. "If we cannot, in the flash of a single moment, see a composition in its absolute entirety, with every pertinent detail in its proper place, we are not genuine creators." [75] On first thought this statement sounds like sheer rhetoric, but reflection soon bears out that what Hindemith says is essentially what does happen to some who create, only there are reservations which should be taken into account. It is doubtful whether a composer can visualize a composition complete in every respect, no matter how small or large the form. Mozart may have been the rare exception, but how many Mozarts are there in the world? Nevertheless, there are scientists and artists who insist that a phenomenon similar to the description which Hindemith gives of creation does take place; ideas fully realized, each part in its place, nothing extraneous, come into consciousness as a relevant whole.

There is nothing mysterious about this spontaneous form of creation in which the total plan of a musical structure is laid wholly bare, complete in its entirety. A scientist will carry latent ideas around with him for years, and then in the least expected place, at the most unusual time—voilà! A composer's ideas which have lain dormant for years suddenly burst out in glowing splendor—ideas fully crystallized, condensed, in meaningful symbolic expressions of rhythm and melody. It is like a dream in which our waking lives appear to us in fleeting symbols, making known to the mind in the night what it had been unaware of during the day. Perhaps Hindemith presents his case rather strongly, but then musicians are not known for their temperance.

SUMMARY

No one theory fully explains the creative process, although one theory, more than any other, stands out in analyzing it. Freud and Jung held the common belief that the unconscious is the "primary and creative factor in man, the never failing source of all art and of all human productivity." [76] Our dreams as well as art emerge from unconscious sources. Those few who are endowed by nature with sublimating powers and imagination are able to convert their dreams into art, concluded Freud, while the less fortunate are limited to satisfying their wishes in fancy alone.

Fancy of itself makes for pleasant dreams. Art is a product of imagination, and imagination is the creator's means of converting his fancy into art, [77] a feat the dreamer cannot do, for by nature he is not imaginative, but only a prosaic individual. The dreamer diffuses the unresolved conflicts of his daily life into personal fancy. The creator imaginatively resolves the problems which confront him into impersonal fancy and then communicates them to others. The dreamer can quite often communicate his dream, but even then, it sounds like any other. Through imagination, the creator so embodies his dreams that the result is unlike any other. We find in his "objectified" dream, as Emerson put it, "our own rejected thoughts; they come back to us with a certain alienated majesty."

The whole life of the creator comes to expression in his art and though it is inevitably molded by his environment and technique, it basically springs from emotion. He is not a faithful recorder of his age or a transmitting instrument for what is most current in his time. In order to create, some degree of isolation from his fellowmen is necessary, so that he will be part of the worldly scene and yet be sufficiently detached to keep a proper perspective.

The artist's eccentric character forces him into isolation and compels him to work out his salvation in creation. Even if society accepts his contribution and invites him to join the brotherhood of man, his perverse nature would make adjusting to a mundane existence so intolerable that he would revert to his former behavior in short time. Like a true neurotic, he is not able to live with himself or share existence with others. Even if it were possible for others to arrange their behavior to fit in with his, he would revolt against the conformity.

A creative musician is something of a paradox. He is caught betwixt society and isolation, without a place of his own. On the one hand, he must avoid isolating himself from society for too long a time; and on the other hand, he must guard against being absorbed into society. One extreme would stifle creativity and the other extreme would moderate his originality. Composers who mentally isolate themselves from the changing world for too long a period become warped and distrustful, as, in time, any human being who rejects the world would be. Such composers inevitably find that what they create is emotionally void, is highly refined, and full of technical stratagems. It is as though the composer were saying, "I wish to be as far removed from the public musically as I am in worldly matters."

The composer will create just so long as he is inwardly "afire." Creation is not continuous; there are periods of artistic sterility. If a composer were free of anxiety, would he not use all his energy for creation instead of expending so much of it wastefully? But this is an impossibility. There is no such thing as artistic creation without anxiety. Anxiety is the catalyst of human emotions which in response to the delicate stirring of the composer's exquisitely pitched sensibilities boils over into the conscious life and is imaginatively converted into music. We cannot actually prove that anxiety is the source of all great music, but if we look back on the history of this art we find that our monumental scores primarily come from men burdened with great distress.

Social scientists lean toward the view that the more ideal a society is the greater are its chances to produce creative personalities. Mozart, Haydn, Beethoven, and Schubert were products of "gay" Vienna and were composing almost as contemporaries. What kind of cultural environment made such genius possible? It was the same kind of social order that produced the giants of the Renaissance, benevolent despots ruling with an iron hand hidden in a velvet glove. These societies were less humane than ours is but we have not produced artists more outstanding than they did. The more humane a society is the more apt it is to ease the irritants and lessen the deprivations which produce anxiety, the storehouse of creative energy. Under ideal conditions instinctive drives are dulled, mental and physical needs, as well as biological and spiritual, are channeled into courses of commonplace activity. Creativity thrives when the artist is thwarted and angered, not when he is being coddled and assured of security.

The social climate in which we live has not affected the creatitve scientist as seriously as it has the artist. The scientist is faced with the challenge of conquering outer space and discovering a cure for cancer at home. But artists enjoy such an over abundance of good things that they have little to complain about. Artists thrive on poverty, misery, and discontent, more than they do on happiness and good times. Now that these three social evils have been partially erased society has moderated the extremes of the artistic temperament with other evils—comfort and luxury. What our artists consequently produce are not complaints against the world but art born out of boredom and monotony, which is usually frivolous and amusing, not educational and *entertaining*. In a society that is completely ideal, if that were possible, the artist would be an anachronism, there would be no place or need for him.

NOTES

[1] Homer *Odyssey*, Bk. VIII. 63.

[2] Plato *Timaeus*. 47.

[3] Plato *Laws*, Bk. II. 653-654.

[4] Plutarch *Concerning Music*. 14. [Aulos is a more proper translation than flute. The instrument resembles an oboe more than a flute.]

[5] I Chron. 23:5. ". . . and four thousand praised the LORD with the instruments I made, *said David,* to praise *therewith."* II Chron. 9:11. "And the king made . . . harps and psalteries for singers; and there were none such seen before in the land of Judah."

[6] Oliver Strunk, *Source Readings in Music History* (New York: W. W. Norton & Company, Inc., 1950), p. 67.

[7] *Ibid.*, p. 65.

[8] *Ibid.*, pp. 347, 348.

[9] In the *Sophist* Plato describes God as a divine artist who created the universe and in the *Timaeus* God is called a master craftsman (29a) who is the author of law and order in the cosmos (30a). St. Augustine maintained that the world was created not from any pre-existing archetype but from nothing. God created substance itself and then law and order. The view that nothing can be created out of nothing, even by divine fiat, is denied in the writings of Parmenides, Aristotle, and Lucretius. St. Thomas, as every orthodox Christian, repeated Augustine's view that God created the world not as an artist fashions an object out of existing material, but by divine command, out of nothing.

[10] Milton C. Nahm, *The Artist as Creator* (Baltimore: The Johns Hopkins Press, 1956), p. 68. "The presumption that the artist is capable of transcending natural law is but a specification of the theory that God has power to perform miracles. The two general issues are among the principal points of differentiation between the Hebraic-Christian theory of God's creativity and the classical view of 'Making' put forward by Plato." p. 43. ". . . the artist is receptive rather than productive, an unfree mime rather than a free creator, one who merely appears to produce novelty. . . . Craft or making does not produce novelty."

[11] Heraclitus *Fragments*. 12. "And the Sibyl, with raving lips uttering things mirthless, . . reaches over a thousand years with her voice, thanks to the god in her."

[12] Plato *Ion*. 534.

[13] Plato *Phaedrus*. 245.

[14] Plato *Ion*. 533-534.

[15] Plato *Apology*. 22.

[16] Aristotle *Problems*, Bk. XXX. 1.

[17] Aristotle *Poetics*, Bk. XVII. 1455a.

[18] *Plutarch's Symposiacs*, Bk. I. Quest. V, 2.

[19] Frederick Clarke Prescott, *The Poetic Mind* (New York: The Macmillan Company, 1922), p. 265.

[20] *Ibid.*

[21] *Plutarch's Symposiacs, loc. cit.*

[22] Longinus *On the Sublime.* XXXIX.

[23] Girolamo Fracastoro, *Naugerius, sive de Poetica Dialogus,* trans. Ruth Kelso (University of Illinois Studies, IX, No. 3, Aug. 1924), p. 65. "God is not the cause, but music itself, full of a sort of great, exalting wonder which makes the pulse beat with the rhythm as if stirred by some violent frenzy, and takes away self-possession, and rouses one to ecstacy. . . . Rightly indeed do the poets deserve to be called divine, since they alone have invented that divine speech by which the gods have condescended to speak in oracles to men."

[24] Gottfried Wilhelm Leibniz, *Philosophical Writings,* "Principles, 10," trans. Mary Morris (London: J. M. Dent & Sons, Ltd., 1934), p. 27.

[25] *Ibid.,* "Principles, 17," p. 30.

[26] David Hume, *Essays,* "The Rise and Progress of the Arts and Sciences" (New York: The Liberal Arts Press, 1953), p. 111.

[27] David Hume, *An Inquiry Concerning Human Understanding* (New York: The Liberal Arts Press, 1955), p. 27.

[28] Immanuel Kant, *Critique of Judgement,* 46, "Beautiful Art is the art of genius," trans. J. H. Bernard (London: Collier-Macmillan, Ltd., 1914).

[29] *Ibid.,* 47, "Elucidation and Conformation of the above explanation of Genius," ". . . artistic skill cannot be communicated; it is imparted to every artist immediately by the hand of nature; and so it dies with him, until nature endows another in the same way, so that he only needs an example in order to put in operation in a similar fashion the talent of which he is conscious."

[30] Georg Wilhelm Friedrich Hegel, *The Philosophy of Fine Art,* I, trans. F. P. B. Osmaston (London: G. Bell & Sons, Ltd., 1920), p. 400.

[31] Arthur Schopenhauer, *The World as Will and Idea,* I, trans. R. B. Haldane and J. Kemp (London: Routledge and Kegan Paul Ltd., 1909), p. 336.

[32] *Ibid.,* III, (1948), p. 159.

[33] Friedrich Nietzsche, *Ecce Homo, 3,* trans. Clifton P. Fadiman (New York: The Modern Library, Inc., 1937), pp. 99-100. From *The Philosophy of Nietzsche.* Copyright 1927, 1954 by The Modern Library, Inc. Reprinted by permission of Random House, Inc.

[34] George Santayana, *Reason in Art* (New York: Charles Scribner's Sons, 1931), p. 66.

[35] Arnold Schönberg, "The Musician" in *The Works of the Mind,* ed. Mortimer J. Adler (Copyright 1947 by The University of Chicago), pp. 69-70. "I believe that a real composer writes music for no other reason than that it pleases. Those who compose because they want to please others, and have the audience in mind, are not real artists. They are not the kind of men who are pressed to say something whether or not there exists one person who likes it, even if they themselves dislike it. They are not creators who must open the valves in

order to relieve the interior pressure of a creation ready to be born. They are merely more or less skillful entertainers who would renounce composing if they could not find listeners."

[36] Samuel T. Coleridge, *Biographia Literaria*, I, ed. J. Shawcross (London: Oxford University Press, 1954), p. 59.

[37] Quoted in Robert S. Woodworth, *Experimental Psychology* (New York: Holt, Rinehart and Winston, Inc., 1938), pp. 818-819. For a fuller description of the creative process in mathematics see H. Poincaré, *The Foundations of Science* (Section: Science and Method), trans. George Bruce Halsted (New York: The Science Press, 1929), Chap. III (Mathematical Creation), pp. 383-395.

[38] *Ibid.*, p. 818.

[39] The association of the creation of art and immortality is quite ancient: Sappho, Bergk, 10.

> To me the Muses truly gave
> An envied and a happy lot
> E'en when I lie within the grave,
> I cannot, shall not be forgot.

Plato *Symposium*. 208.

. . . all men do all things, and the better they are the more they do them, in hope of the glorious fame of immortal virtue; for they desire the immortal.

Shelley, *Prometheus Unbound*, Act I, lines 743-749.

> He will watch from dawn till gloom
> The lake-reflected sun illume
> The yellow bees in the ivy-bloom
> Nor heed nor see, what things they be;
> But from these create he can
> Forms more real than living man,
> Nurslings of immortality!

Horace, Bk. 3. Ode xxx.

> A monument I've achieved more strong than brass,
> Soaring kings' pyramids to overpass;
> Which not corroding raindrip shall devour,
> Or winds that from the north sweep down in power,
> Or years unnumbered as the ages flee!
> I shall not wholly die!

Shakespeare's Sonnet LV.

> Not marble, nor the gilded monuments
> of princes, shall outlive this powerful rime.

[40] Carl G. Jung, *Modern Man in Search of a Soul* (New York: Harcourt, Brace and World, Inc., 1934), p. 177. "Any reaction to stimulus may be causally explained; but the creative act, which is the absolute antithesis of mere reaction, will for ever elude the human understanding. It can only be described in its manifestations; it can be obscurely sensed, but never wholly grasped."

[41] Sigmund Freud, *Introductory Lectures on Psychoanalysis*, trans. Joan Riviere (New York: Liveright Publishing Corporation, 1935), pp. 327-328.

[42] *Ibid.*

[43] Freud, *Three Contributions to the Theory of Sex*, trans. A. A. Brill (New York: The Modern Library, Inc., 1938), p. 625.

[44] Freud, *Leonardo da Vinci* (New York: Moffatt Yard & Co., 1916), p. 128.

[45] Jung, *op. cit.*, p. 195. *Also:* Jung, *Contributions to Analytical Psychology*, trans. H. G. and Cary F. Baynes (London: Routledge and Kegan Paul Ltd., 1928), p. 248. "The creative process, . . . consists in an unconscious animation of the archetype, and in a development and shaping of this image till the work is completed. The shaping of the primordial image is, as it were, a translation into the language of the present which makes it possible for every man to find again the deepest springs of life which would otherwise be closed to him."

[46] *Quintilian*, Bk. I. X. 16.

[47] The theory that music grew out of impassioned speech is actually Greek and not of nineteenth century origin. Plutarch summarized Theophrastus' discourse on music in the following way: "Theophrastus lays down three causes of music,—grief, pleasure, and enthusiasm; for each of these changes the usual tone, and makes the voice slide into a cadence; for deep sorrow has something tunable in its groans, and therefore we perceive our orators in their conclusions, and actors in their complaints, are somewhat melodius, and insensibly fall into a tune."—*Plutarch's Symposiacs, loc. cit.*

[48] Charles Darwin, *The Descent of Man* (New York: D. Appleton and Company, 1899), pp. 584-585.

[49] *Ibid.*, footnote 39, p. 585.

[50] Jung, *Psychology of the Unconscious* (New York: Dodd Mead & Company, Inc., 1937), p. 145.

[51] *Stephen Crane* ed. Robert Wooster Stallman (New York: Alfred A. Knopf, Inc., 1957), p. 628.

[52] "I work very coldly, without agitation, without emotion even. One must be completely master of oneself to organize that changing, moving, flowing chessboard; orchestration. The mind which composed *Tristan* must have been as cool as marble."—Harold Osborne, *Aesthetics and Criticism* (London: Routledge and Kegan Paul Ltd., 1955), p. 162.

[53] John Rewald, *Maillol* (Paris: Editions Hyperion, 1939), p. 23.

[54] Joseph Pijoan, *An Outline History of Art*, III (Chicago: University of Knowledge, Inc., 1938), p. 358.

[55] Julia Cartwright, *Jean François Millet, His Life and Letters* (New York: The Macmillan Company, 1902), pp. 79, 106.

[56] *Further Letters of Vincent van Gogh to His Brother, 1886-1889.* (London: Constable and Co., Ltd., 1929), p. 17.

[57] From Christian Zervos: *Conversation avec Picasso* in "Cahiers d'Art," 1935, volume 10, number 10, pp. 173-178. Translation, based on one by Myfawny Evans, appears on p. 15 of *Picasso: Forty Years of His Art* (1939) by Alfred H. Barr, Jr., New York: The Museum of Modern Art.

[58] John Rewald, *Gauguin* (Paris: Editions Hyperion, 1938), p. 29.

[59] *The Letters of Vincent van Gogh to His Brother, 1872-1886*, I, (London: Constable and Co., Ltd., 1927), p. 510.

[60] *Further Letters of Vincent van Gogh . . . 1886-1889, op. cit.*, pp. 176, 373.

[61] Vincent van Gogh, *Letters to an Artist, From Vincent van Gogh to Anton Ridder Van Rappard, 1881-1885* (New York: The Viking Press, Inc., 1936), p. 9.

[62] *Wassily Kandinsky Memorial*, ed. Hilla Rebay (Museum of Non-Objective Paintings. The Solomon R. Guggenheim Foundation, 1945), p. 61.

[63] From Christian Zervos: *Conversation avec Picasso* in "Cahiers d'Art," 1935, volume 10, number 10, pp. 173-178. Translation, based on one by Myfawny Evans, appears on pp. 272-3 of *Picasso: Fifty Years of His Art* (1946) by Alfred H. Barr, Jr., New York: The Museum of Modern Art.

[64] From Marius de Zayas: *Picasso Speaks*, translated into English and first published in "The Arts," New York, May 1923, appears on pp. 270-271 of *Picasso: Fifty Years of His Art* (1946) by Alfred H. Barr, Jr., New York: The Museum of Modern Art.

[65] *The Works of Edgar Allen Poe*, IV, (New York: The Colonial Co., Ltd., 1903), p. 33.

[66] William Wordsworth, *Preface to Lyrical Ballads, 1800* (London: Oxford University Press, 1957), p. 246.

[67] Goethe wrote: "And thus began that habit from which I could not break away my whole life through—the habit of turning into an image, into a poem, whatever delighted or troubled, or otherwise occupied me, and thus of coming to some definite conclusion with regard to it. . . . Whatever, therefore, of mine has become public, are but fragments of a great confession."—Johann Wolfgang Goethe, *Poetry and Truth*, I, trans. Minna Steele Smith (London: G. Bell & Sons, Ltd., 1930), p. 252. *Also:* "I have never affected anything in my poetry. I have never uttered anything I have not experienced, which has not urged me to production. I have only composed love-songs when I have loved. How could I write songs of hatred without hating!"—*Conversations of Goethe with Eckermann*, trans. John Oxenford (London: J. M. Dent & Sons, Ltd., 1935), p. 361.

[68] Percy Bysshe Shelley, *A Defence of Poetry* (New York: The Modern Library, Inc., 1951), p. 517.

[69] William Butler Yeats wrote: "We make out of the quarrel with others, rhetoric, but of the quarrel with ourselves, poetry. Unlike the rhetoricians, who get a confident voice from remembering the crowd they have won or may win, we sing amid our uncertainty. . . . He only can create the greatest imaginable beauty who has endured all imaginable pangs, for only when we have seen and foreseen what we dread shall we be rewarded by that dazzling unforeseen wing-footed wanderer."—*Anima Hominis, Writers on Writing*, ed. Walter Allen (London: Phoenix House, 1958), p. 45.

[70] Ernest Newman, *The Unconscious Beethoven* (New York: Alfred A. Knopf, Inc., 1930), pp. 145-146.

[71] Modeste Tchaikovsky, *The Life and Letters of Peter Ilich Tchaikovsky*, trans. Rosa Newmarch (New York: John Lane Co., 1914), p. 306.

[72] *Ibid.*, p. 307.

[73] Reprinted by permission of the publishers from I. Stravinsky, *Poetics of Music in the Form of Six Lessons*, trans. Arthur Knodel and Ingolf Dahl (Cambridge, Mass.: Harvard University Press), p. 51. Copyright 1947 by The President and Fellows of Harvard College.

[74] *Ibid.*

[75] Reprinted by permission of the publishers from Paul Hindemith, *A Composer's World* (Cambridge, Mass.: Harvard University Press), p. 61. Copyright 1952 by The President and Fellows of Harvard College. *See also:* Schopenhauer, *The World As Will and Idea*, I, trans. R. B. Haldane and J. Kemp (London: Routledge & Kegan Paul Ltd., 1906), p. 321. "... genius holds up to us the magic glass, in which all that is essential and significant appears before us collected and placed in the clearest light, and what is accidental and foreign is left out."

[76] Jung, *Contributions to Analytical Psychology, op. cit.*, p. 365.

[77] S. T. Coleridge, *op. cit.*, II, p. 14.

CHAPTER II

The ELEMENTS of MUSIC

RHYTHM

What is music? It may be described as an aural image of our emotional experiences. Of all the elements contained in music, none is more important than rhythm, which is similar to the breath of life in a living being. Melody is to music what the power of speech is to man; harmony is comparable to skeletal structure. Rhythm, melody, and harmony are the sources of motion and life to a musical work. From these elements emerge shape and character—form and style.

⌣

What is rhythm? No one definition of it would be universally acceptable. Music without rhythm, however, is an impossibility.[1] Music is a temporal art. A musical composition may be described as a structure in time, a "movement." Time in music is manifested by movement between two points. This movement, the flow of sound, is called rhythm. Rhythm is what gives music a semblance of organic unity, a feeling of momentum, an illusion of time.

Unfortunately, a confusion in terminology often exists because the word "rhythm" has a two-fold meaning. The *Harvard Dictionary of Music* states: "Rhythm is everything pertaining to the temporal quality (duration) of the musical sound." This means that rhythm concerns general time flow, the measurement of time, and the actual length of specific notes. Under this broad view of rhythm are three categories: *tempo,* meter, and, for lack of a better term, rhythm.

Tempo is the rate at which sounds proceed in a composition. This rate refers to the speed of the underlying pulses which are in all movement. The relative durations of musical sounds (and of silence) are indicated by note values (whole-note, half-note, etc.). Duration is relative to tempo: a note value determines the number of pulses or the fraction of a pulse given to a symbol written on the staff, the tempo determines the amount of time allotted to each pulse.

Tempo is most precisely indicated by markings of the metronome, a mechanical device which ticks even pulses at any desired speed. The marking $\quart = 96$ means that a minute is divided into 96 quarter-note pulses. The use of exact metronome indications is not always the ideal way to show tempo. Physiological and psychological factors enter the picture. What may be the correct tempo in a small, "dead" rehearsal studio may not be suitable in a large, resonant concert hall. The technical facility of the performer may influence the speed at which he performs a fast passage. The tempo of a march or a waltz may be partially determined by the spirit of the group participants.

Often, composers use more general markings which allow for some freedom of interpretation by the performer. That tempo is closely related to psychological factors is shown by descriptive words and phrases frequently used. The mood of a composition and the emotional response of the listener may be drastically changed by an alteration of the tempo.

TABLE OF MAJOR TEMPOS

1. Steady Rate of Speed

Speed	Term	Meaning
Slow	Largo	broad, large, stately
	Grave	heavy, solemn
	Adagio	slow, tranquil
	Andante	moving at a walking pace
Moderate	Moderato	at a moderate pace
Fast	Allegro	cheerful, brisk
	Vivace	lively, vivacious
	Presto	rapid, very quick

2. Changes in Rate of Speed

Speed	Term	Meaning
Faster	Accelerando	accelerating, gradually increasing in speed
	Stringendo	swiftly accelerating
	Più mosso	more movement, faster than preceding tempo
Slower	Rallentando	becoming gradually slower
	Ritardando	becoming gradually slower
	Allargando	becoming broader
Flexible	Tempo rubato	"robbed," fluctuation due to prolongation of important notes and acceleration of lesser notes.

Examples of Metrical Patterns

Simple duple meter

Compound duple meter

Simple triple meter

Compound triple meter

Meter is the grouping of strong and weak pulses, accented and unaccented notes, into repetitive patterns which provide the underlying skeleton for rhythm. The ear tends to organize pulses of equal duration into groups of two or three. These groups are perceived by natural accent, the stress which falls on the first pulse of each pattern. The two basic forms of meter are duple and triple which give rise to a variety of other patterns. These patterns are made known visually in conventional notation by the time signature and the bar line. Occasionally, even frequently, changes of meter may occur within a single composition. This is accomplished by changing the time signature or by shifting the metrical accent for a period of time by stress marks (— ∧ >, etc.).

Meter is also described as being simple or compound. In simple meter, each basic pulse is subdivided into groups of two, four, eight,

Examples of Metrical Patterns *(continued)*

Combination of duple and triple (irregular meter)

Change of meter

The above pattern may be notated without change of meter as below:

etc. The triplet subdivision is the foundation of compound meter: the basic pulse is subdivided into groups of 3, 6, 12, etc.

Rhythm in its more specific meaning is everything about musical time which is not in the realm of tempo or meter. It was noted that meter is the grouping of repetitive patterns of notes with equal duration and regular accent. Rhythm embraces flexible patterns of notes with varied duration and sometimes irregular accent. Meter is the underlying skeleton for a superimposed rhythmic pattern.

Music would be uninteresting if all its sounds paralleled strict metrical patterns. Rhythmic patterns enable a composition to have variety and interest, and coherence as well; they disguise the obvious metrical patterns. Just as one pattern approaches monotony, a composer will introduce a new pattern of fresh, interesting activity; when the music seems to stray too much from the main material, he may bring back a pattern heard before, thereby helping the listener to feel at home again.

What does a composer do to create rhythm, and how does rhythm relate to meter? The answer to both these questions is contained in the following statement: "Rhythmic pattern may act upon metrical pattern in four ways: (1) it may divide the metrical unit into notes of shorter duration; (2) it may combine metrical units into notes of longer duration; (3) it may shift or displace the metrical accent [commonly called "syncopation"]; (4) it may coincide exactly with the metrical pattern." [2] Thus [3] if the basic metrical pattern is

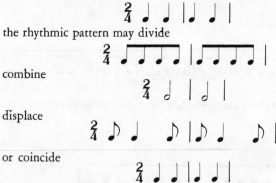

the rhythmic pattern may divide

combine

displace

or coincide

What musical devices does a composer employ to make rhythm

meaningful in a composition? A flowing melody, a harmonic progression, a resolution of a dissonant passage, a *syncopated* note that enters before it is expected, these are all ingredients that go into the making of rhythm. A reversal or delay in the continuity of what we have been conditioned to suppose would happen in a musical work, a pause or short "run" that disrupts our equilibrium, the desire which these create to restore our sense of balance and order are additional characteristics of rhythm. Two qualities produce rhythm perhaps more than any other: tension and relief.

How does rhythm affect us? Rhythm induces a feeling of anticipation and preparation for what is to follow in the music and then leaves us surprised, pleased, or frustrated at what has come to pass. Rhythm thus creates tensions in us and resolves tensions carried over from previous musical episodes. Rhythm gives us a sense of motion, a line of direction, a feeling of beginning and end.

In Greek music the song and poem were wedded and a bard rendered his ode in declamatory style. The rhythm of his delivery was dependent on the text: one note set to each syllable, each syllable treated as either long or short, the long syllable ordinarily equal to two short ones. A poem was sung according to its nature and mood—usually, in a traditional meter, memorized and passed on from one generation to another. The medieval *plain song* was also rhythmically set to the text. Choirs sang these sacred chants, just as they do to this day, with the rhythm and melody closely wedded to the word. Medieval *polyphony* in its early stage consisted of "a double plain-song." With the further development of polyphony it became necessary to use more definite rhythmic practices than had existed previously in order to ensure uniformity among the voices. Medieval composers used rhythmic modes which were similar to the rhythmic feet of classical poetry; the rhythmic modes of the various voices were usually not identical. Around 1600, rhythms with characteristics that are associated with the dance—strong accents recurring regularly—became prominent, and this prominence was retained for about three succeeding centuries. In our own century rhythms suggested by techniques of early jazz made exciting inroads on serious composition.

Rhythm cannot be explained as tension and relief only. The

steady beat of a drum, the simple flow of a nursery song, have a rhythm of their own. Rhythm in its most elemental form is, after all, the dynamism we experience in nature, the thunderous roar that follows lightning, the timid wave that breaks into surf and recedes to be washed in once more. Musical rhythm came into being when man learned how to gather the sounds he heard and then arranged them as he wished, sometimes rearranging rhythmic patterns which exist in nature. Musical rhythm is actually a creation of man, a mental phenomenon,[4] by which man creates an order of his own to express his needs and wants in musical form.

MELODY

"Melody is the most essential of . . . [the] elements, not because it is more immediately perceptible, but because it is the dominant voice of the symphony—not only in the specific sense, but also figuratively speaking."[5]

What is melody? Most of us are inclined to identify it as that which is "singable." We assume that we should be able to hum parts of a composition after hearing it; or, if this is beyond our technical ability, that we ought, at least, to be able to retain the shape or character of various parts of the work in our memory. We frequently judge the effectiveness of a whole composition on our own receptiveness to the melodic content, reacting to music on the basis of what we most readily grasp.

Upon closer examination, a description of melody concerns much more than a simple test of "singability." Few of us come away from a performance of a Josquin des Prés mass humming a tune. Yet, a chorus member is likely to say that this music ranks among the most effective works composed for voice. Even trained musicians are not ordinarily able to sing Bach's *Magnificat* or Stravinsky's *Symphony of Psalms* without diligent rehearsal, although these compositions are recognized masterpieces of choral literature. A melody which is easy to sing is not always good esthetically. When a "rock 'n' roll" tune, certainly easy to sing, is heard without the customary strong rhythmic accompaniment, a musically literate person is aware of its esthetic weakness which is caused by the monotonous repetition of the small variety of notes contained in the melody.

Melody is extremely difficult to describe. Since the sensation of movement and the organization of tones are fundamental qualities of melody, it is impossible to separate this element from either rhythm or form. Melody is also closely related to harmony.

Nature does not supply us with a system of melody. Melody is a creation of man, a mental achievement in bringing together certain sounds in nature and arranging them according to his desire. Man cannot imitate nature faithfully. He alters her varied sounds and tonal patterns with rule and imagination to create a world of his own.

A song that wells up from the throat of a bird has a melody of its own, and yet it is not a melody in a musical sense until man gives it balance and form. Natural sounds alone are not a melody even though melody is made up of sounds. "Consider it well: each tone of our scale in itself is nought," the poet said, and the same thought fits the concept of melody. A melody must have a relationship between tone and tone, possess continuity and expectancy, and instill, in the listener, a feeling of beginning and end.

A melody consists of a series of tones of varying pitch and duration. The tones must have a cultural relevancy one to the other, and the sequence of tonal sounds must also have continuity and a suggestion of forward motion. The unity and mobility of a melody is not in the melody itself, but actually in the listener's mind. We often come to regard a series of musical tones as being a melody only through hearing it repeatedly; we become accustomed in our expectations to what a melody should be. We are like lesser gods in our own right—creating and arranging, not according to eternal archetypes, but from the need for symmetry and order in our lives.

A melody does not move in the same sense as an object that is pushed through space, or as a brook flows through marshy land; it proceeds from note to note when activated by rhythm. Melody is a series of musical tones that can instill varied tensions in us; it can suggest a change in mood, a feeling of hurrying or being at rest, moving up or coming down, or going forward.

A melodic line does not really flow or sing, it merely initiates a mental state. What is to follow? How will it end? We develop certain tensions in the process of mentally following a melody upward, become more relaxed as it moves downward. It is an example of *empathy;* reacting to a melody as though it really ascended or descended, when we know very well that only fluctuations of frequency produce a sensation of rising and falling. A melody gives the illusion of going forward, up or down. The movement is in us; the musical line is only suggestive. A melodic line of itself has no magical status, it has no existence of its own as a melody; only what we confer upon it, from our culture and experience, makes it a melody for us.

Should a composer mar the flow of a melodic line with boring repetition, he would destroy the basic element in melody, the sense of moving and reaching for some end. The continuity of a melody is sustained only so long as we are inclined to follow it to a logical end, with a feeling of finality in the near offing.

Melodies differ with each culture and generation; no two conceptions of melody are alike. Music that had been considered unmelodic in the past is considered melodic today and wonder is expressed that it could have been otherwise. We also do what our predecessors did by failing to recognize new melodic ideas when they appear. But then only a small minority of us are receptive to new ideas, in music or in life.

How can we explain why melodies which are so warmly regarded now were not considered melodies in the past, except by a very few? Perhaps melodies have objective qualities that are peculiar to various cultures which can be detected by a well-trained elite or a select few of unusual sensitivity. The evidence is that there is nothing by nature in a series of tones that gives it an autonomous status as a melody, even in a certain culture or at a particular time. Brahms's followers said that Wagner's music was unmelodic. Wagner's adherents said the same thing about Brahms. Each group was right about its own idol, wrong about the new ideas in the music of the other. A child's response to a new musical idea is fresh and uninhibited; he does not have our prejudices. The ears of a child are not yet conditioned to anything old, so he reacts like the little animal he is, instead of as a rational being who compares, by antiquated rules, newly heard music with music he has heard before. Sometimes our reaction is like a child's in this respect; but on the whole, we respond to what we hear for the first time with outmoded criteria as our guide. If we find eventually that our criteria are unwarranted, we modify our judgment, and what we considered unmelodious by archaic rules becomes a melody; or what we considered a melody again becomes only a series of tones without unity and coherence, just as it was before we attributed melodic properties to it.

HARMONY AND POLYPHONY

Pythagoras heard the harmony of the spheres, and Moses listened to the moon sing in concert with all the other stars in the sky. Musical harmony is a gift from God, wrote the Christian theologians in the late Middle Ages, but polyphony is of the Devil's making—it disrupts and tears apart a musical work in the same way that Satan tries to destroy God's well-ordered world.

Both harmony and polyphony consist of a combination of two or more tones sounding simultaneously. Harmonic tones are chordal (vertical) in structure; the strength of harmony depends on the relationship of the chords to each other. Polyphonic music is melodic (horizontal) in structure and, although it may visually appear chordal, it is linear in the sense that its individual voices are relatively independent of each other in the separate courses that they follow. In harmonic music the lower voices in a chord support the upper voice or voices carrying the melodic line. Polyphonic music is actually a type of harmonic writing but harmonic music is not necessarily polyphonic music.

Harmony and polyphony are older than we think. Their origin, however crude, may be found in antiquity.[6] The bard who sang his ode so that voice and instrument each went its own way, instead of being sung in unison, was in a primitive sense producing polyphony. Greek music was essentially *monophonic*; a single tune accompanied the poem; word and tone were one. Part-singing did not actually appear until the medieval Christian learned how to improvise an unpretentious tune that he could sing as a countermelody to a Gregorian chant.

Medieval *organum* is the earliest form of polyphony, if we are to be exact. It went through several stages of development, from a lowly two-part composition to a complex several-voiced one, from the ninth to the thirteenth centuries. The medieval composer was fascinated by its imaginative possibilities. No other musical form had thus far allowed him to express himself so fully in rhythm and melody. His ingenuity, alas, was so daring that the Church finally had to object. He thought of polyphony as such a wonderful "game" of *counterpoint* (note against note) that he would devise a motet for the religious service in which three different melodies, with varying texts, were sung simultaneously, in independent rhythms, against a Gregorian tune. The clergy thought that such music would well pass as a technical exercise but was not suitable for worship.

Composers in the *baroque* era thought of music not primarily as horizontal lines of successive voices but as a progression of related perpendicular chords. This chordal progression was a new concept, the beginning of a revolution in musical thought. The type of music in which a predominant melody is supported by chordal accompaniment is called homophony. The baroque composer had learned how to hear music not as isolated voices or separate parts, as his ancestors did, but as a cluster of tones arranged in chords which were harmonically related and continuous.

After about 1600, composers boldly began to alter chords, employ *chromatic* progressions, and finally to *modulate* freely. During the romantic period harmony, in the traditional sense, almost disintegrated as a system. Chromatic effects, unresolved chordal progressions, and modulation from one key to another without preparation were characteristic. In the dawn of the twentieth century, composers such as

Debussy and Scriabin virtually abandoned traditional harmony in their compositions.

Schönberg defended his system of *atonality* as a substitute for traditional harmony on the thesis that Wagner and Debussy had already "dethroned tonality in practice." Simultaneously with the breakdown of tonality, the public became accustomed to the startling dissonances of late romantic music and, in Schönberg's estimation, a "radical change in compositional technique" was required. Strict atonality, however, proved itself to be an inadequate musical system.

Stravinsky began to employ unusual dissonances within a harmonic context which retained some vestiges of traditional practice. His style was called *neoclassicism*. For a while twentieth century music appeared hopelessly divided into two camps—neoclassicism and atonality. Stravinsky, searching for new areas to explore, turned to some of the techniques of Schönberg and aptly showed that the two musical languages are not as far apart as they were once thought to be.

The melodic line was uppermost in the musical considerations of the ancients; even when supported by some accompaniment, nothing would detract from its nature. In time, the composer learned how to enrich his music by writing melodies that could be sung together and produce a pleasant duet. Then he boldly wove his melodies in and out, learned how to invert and reverse his melodic figures, and contrast them with each other. In time he carried his ideas to extremes and introduced such rare novelties that he all but pushed traditional harmony to the brink of an esthetic catastrophe. A reaction to these extremes followed, and a search for new esthetic criteria was undertaken. Then a new problem arose on the musical horizon to vex those whose ears had been accustomed to traditional harmonic tonalities: *electronic music*. The composer of electronic music is no respecter of the past; sonority in the conventional sense is all but foreign to him.

INTERVALS

The interval of an octave was called "diapason" in medieval theory because it is the interval which includes "all the tones" of the octave. In "A Song for St. Cecilia's Day," John Dryden wrote:

> *Through all the compass of the notes it ran,*
> *The diapason closing full in Man.*

Not all the intervals within the octave have fared as well as the octave itself at the hands of poets and theorists. An interval of a seventh was called "Satan's seventh" because it excited the flesh; as a discordant note it could only be resolved if a tone true to nature followed.

⌣

    Intervals are the differences in pitch between one musical tone and another, and the relationship between these tones. Musical intervals are natural like the colors that fall on a canvas when a ray of white light breaks through a prism. Of musical intervals, *scales,* and keys, intervals alone are autonomous; scales and keys are man-made.

    Paul Hindemith [7] states that the interval "is the basic unit of musical construction." Intervals sounded in succession have a melodic function; intervals sounded in combination have a harmonic function.

    The Greeks believed that the octave, fifth, and fourth were consonant intervals and that the third and sixth were less so. The Pythagoreans originally thought that they had discovered the explanation for the acoustical difference between a consonant and dissonant tone. The octave, fifth, and fourth, in their estimation, reflected the mathematical order in the universe and were therefore considered consonant. Dissonant intervals, reasoned the Pythagoreans, consisted of ratios which are incongruous with natural order. Some few philosophers, of whom Aristoxenus was one, differed with the Pythagoreans. Aristoxenus wrote that consonance and dissonance were relative distinctions which can only be discerned by "the two faculties of hearing and intellect." But the Pythagorean theory appealed more to the Greek mentality than that of Aristoxenus. What caught the imagination was more readily accepted than anything so commonplace as the position Aristoxenus had taken.

    At the time of organum, vocal parts were arranged a fourth or a fifth above and moved parallel with the theme. Medieval man had remained faithful to Pythagoras throughout these centuries until he learned that adding intervals of thirds and sixths for contrast and variety, and then hearing them over and over again, became pleasing after all. Since the late Renaissance and early baroque eras, composers have employed musical intervals in their compositions in more complicated and novel ways. The invention of new instruments and the

Basic Types of Intervals Within the Octave

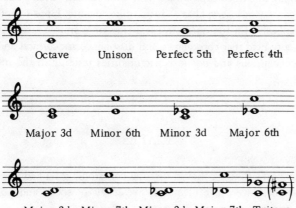

Octave   Unison   Perfect 5th   Perfect 4th

Major 3d   Minor 6th   Minor 3d   Major 6th

Major 2d   Minor 7th   Minor 2d   Major 7th   Tritone

Note that an octave inverted becomes a unison; a third becomes a sixth; a second becomes a seventh. A tritone (three whole-tones) divides the octave in half; its inversion is a tritone.

development of instrumental techniques have encouraged composers in these activities.

Musical intervals by themselves are not music; they become music only in some organized formal arrangement—a *symphony*, a sonata, a *Lied*. They change in quality and suggestiveness in the context of different musical works and forms. They are disturbing or restful, anticipatory or final in their relationship to other intervals. Our response to any musical combination of sounds is personal and culturally conditioned. What sounds consonant to one listener may sound dissonant to another. The same interval appearing in one context may affect us altogether differently in another context, and the same interval may affect us still differently when heard alone.

Composers are interested in what esthetic relevance an interval has in producing a desired psychological affect. The psychologists have offered different explanations on what consonance and dissonance are. Helmholtz identified consonance with "smoothness." Stumpf believed that a consonant interval has a "fusion-like" quality. Lipps maintained that the basis of a consonant interval rests on a simple ratio.[8] Ogden and Moore held that consonance and dissonance are cultural and personal conceptions and not intrinsic qualities residing in the interval itself.

SCALES

The classical Chinese believed that the pentatonic scale had five notes because there were five elements, five levels of social and political life.

Musical scales are man-made in contrast to the interval of an octave which has a natural origin. Scales are traditional means of sustaining tonal order in music. Every musical system has its own set of scales which depend on the manner in which the interval of the octave has been divided. The Hindus and Chinese have a system of musical scales, and so did the classical Greeks.

Scales are written on arbitrary esthetic principles. They are what one musician and eminent psychologist has referred to as: "First, any scale is a construct of the social mind, a phenomenon of social agreement. Second, any scale establishes what the logicians call an order-system and what the musicians call a tonality system—a pattern of relationships that do not depend upon convention or habit, but are the unalterable and inevitable consequences of the scale-system itself." [9]

Some Frequently Used Scales

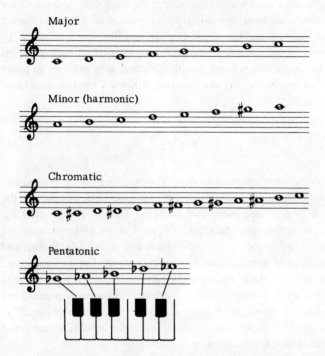

Note that the black keys of the piano form a pentatonic scale.

The human penchant for giving the elements order and a sense of purpose is well illustrated in the structure of the musical scale.

Our own system of scales (diatonic) has its source in Greek music. But not until the late baroque era did the Western scales become the well-tempered structure of intervals that we take so much for granted. It was then that our present chromatic scale—a sequence of twelve equal half-tones rising or falling in pitch—was developed, along with the pattern, or modes, of the major and minor scales.

Not all the music that our Western composers have produced is based on our major and minor scales. Debussy, for example, was so impressed with Oriental music that he used old modes and the whole-tone scale to achieve his ethereal musical affects. Then during the first half of the twentieth century tonality was challenged by atonality, and our musical values were turned upside-down. Composers created music which was not tonally oriented; they went ón to prove that music can be moving and affecting without a fixed tone and key.

KEYS

The Chinese were once taught that "The music of Cheng is lewd and corrupting, the music of Sung is soft and makes one effeminate, the music of Wei is repetitious and annoying, and the music of Ch'i is harsh and makes one haughty."[10] The Greeks believed that the Ionian and Lydian modes were effeminate and soft and the Dorian and Phrygian modes were military in tone and strong. Luther wrote: "we want to take the sixth mode for the Gospel: . . . we want to arrange the eighth mode for the Epistle." Much later, F major was called the pastoral key, F minor and F sharp minor the tragic musical keys. The notion that certain keys and modes symbolize moods, seasons, and character is probably as old as music itself.

A musical key consists of a family of tones which are held together by their relationship to a fundamental tone. It is from this fundamental tone, the tonic, that the key derives its name. The scales set the sequence of the tones; the key sets the starting point and is used to identify the scale.

Our musical keys are an outgrowth of the Greek modes, which

were based on the Pythagorean division of the octave. Since the cycle of fifths cannot lead to a perfect octave, a problem in musical tuning developed in the Pythagorean system which became more noticeable as music became more complex. Aristoxenus suggested that, in order to remedy this tuning problem, the intervals within the octave be tempered "to make each half-step equal in ratio to every other one." [11] His suggestion was eventually followed—more than two thousand years after his death.

Various methods of overcoming this tuning problem were tried —particularly by changing the structure of the scale—but none of them were acceptable to the musical world as a whole. In the eighteenth century, however, the equal temperament principle of tuning the interval by dividing the octave into twelve semitones equal in ratio but not acoustically perfect was universally accepted. According to this principle only the interval of the octave is acoustically correct.

Because of their differences in ratio, the original Greek modes could not be modulated directly. With the development of harmony in the music of the Western world, modulation with ease became a necessity. The principle of equal temperament esthetically satisfied this musical necessity by enabling the composer to modulate freely from one key to another. This in turn led—in the romantic and particularly in the post-romantic period—to an overabundant use of modulation. The composers of the *classical* era had used diatonic harmony and modulated discreetly from one key to another using *accidentals* for embellishment. Romantic composers used accidentals freely and modulated at every opportunity, as though they were trying to express the surging dynamism and churning emotionalism of their age. Their use of chromaticism and ceaseless modulation pointed the way to atonal music.

In the Greek period, each mode expressed a particular mood. Most philosophers in that era attributed ethical qualities to these modes, believing that their structure bore out acoustical laws that were inherent in nature. Views not too far removed from those of the Greek philosophers still persist. One notion is that modes have a fixed character; that major is "bright" and minor is "dark." It is also believed that certain keys are symbolic of moods and seasons; by their

Circle of Fifths

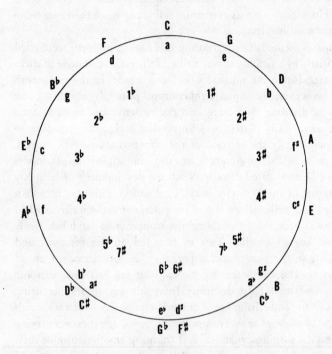

On the outer edge of the circle are major keys with the number of sharps or flats appropriate to their key signatures; minor keys are inside the circle. The major and minor keys opposite each other are called relative keys because they share a common key signature.

very nature they express our feelings and the time of year. Composers have been known to seek out specific keys to express certain moods. Composers have also relied on certain keys to give their music a particular kind of figurative colorization. Perhaps the two best examples that exist are found in the contrasting views that Rimsky-Korsakov and Scriabin made on key-color association.

FORM

A musical form in its original state is the configuration of a composer's ideas. Traditional musical forms rest on time-honored principles. Style, on the other hand, is the way a composer writes, what use he makes of his ideas, and how they are expressed. By analogy it is like character in ourselves.

Form is the most essential element in all beautiful art, wrote Immanuel Kant. It is a frame which contains the creator's ideas. Style is the way the composer's ideas are expressed within this frame.[12] Repetition and variation, contrast and balance are common to all art forms; the first two are particularly important in musical forms. Repetition gives emphasis to the motifs in a score, which are not immediately discernible as they are in the other arts. Variation is the diversification of the composer's primary musical ideas.

Musical forms are more like the forms of poetry, essays, and classical ballet than the forms of painting and sculpture. The latter two are visualized almost at once, in a Gestalt-like motion, while a period of time must follow before the former ones are discerned. Forms sometimes are used interchangeably in the arts, as when an essayist such as De Quincey, in *The English Mail-Coach,* employs the form of a musical fugue to express a literary thought; or, when a musician like Liszt composes a symphony as a poet would construct a poem.

Whether artistic forms can be successfully blended is an old controversy in esthetics. When the form of one art is applied to another art, two pure art forms turn into a hybrid one and a new form is developed. For a while it is looked on as a blend, but before too many decades pass it will be considered pure and chaste; and then, perhaps, it may even be merged with another art form to beget still another one. It is also worthy of note that the larger musical forms contain a number of smaller forms as part of their structural comple- ment, forms existing within an overall form without any loss of iden- tity to one or the other.

How do we distinguish one musical form from another? Through a learning process, there is no other way; forms are not disembodied ideas, something apart from our experience. Through a process of education we develop the capacity to recognize and associate the existence of certain principles which the composer has musically employed to express esthetic ideas. There is some music that is so vaguely ordered that it leaves us undecided on a first hearing as to exactly what form it has.

We must distinguish between the structural form within a musical work and the form, or design, of the work itself. A classical symphony or a sonata is a formal outline comprising musical sections divided and contrasted according to moods and tempos. What char- acterizes a classical symphony or a sonata as musical forms in com- mon is that each of these forms is only the configuration of a musical content. This content is made up of the musical techniques and devices which the composer employs to express his ideas. A serious musical form is a complex enterprise and, in the process of working out his ideas, a composer will use shorter single forms to produce the larger compound forms.

Those who hold, like the ancients, that a form must be "imposed" on musical elements before music can actually exist are not in dis- agreement with the view that if tones and rhythms are arranged in a certain way a desired form will emerge.[13] Forms, as scales and keys, are creations of the human mind. Although the basic traditional forms that man has made exist as a universal set of principles, they have no practical value until they are applied in the construction of a musical work. A musical form, like an architectural blueprint, is only an out- line for action.

An elementary set of principles by which a composer may work out his musical ideas is called a ternary, or ABA, form. The process is simple: a first section presents the initial ideas; a second section which contains contrasting material follows; and then a return to the first section rounds out the final portion of the work. The ternary form is the basis of a great many musical works; although, of course, there are other forms too, such as the basic binary, or AB, form. Others which are quite complex are really elaborations and modifications of either the basic binary or the basic ternary forms.

Musical forms are like rules which children abide by in play. When they play hide-and-seek they do so in the same way that children have done for centuries. If they decide to change the rules somewhat it does not affect the game too seriously just so long as not being "caught" remains the most important feature, and one child wins and another loses. Composers create their musical works according to established principles, just as children play their games. They alter traditional forms, as children vary the rules of their games, but retain the essential features of a form to separate it from other forms, as children differentiate between the rules for playing hide-and-seek and those for London Bridge. Musical forms, like rules for children's games, do not come ready made; they emerge, in their original state, out of the structure of the work from which they draw the breath of life. In time, these forms acquire a traditional status, are universally accepted, and, with some exceptions, are commonly used.

SUMMARY

Rhythm in music is what energy is to matter, what blood is to the body. Music is not possible without rhythm; it would be like inert matter, something altogether lifeless. We no longer think of rhythm as the Greeks originally did; we are well aware that it is a construction of the mind, culturally conditioned, varying throughout the world in style and expression.

A melody without rhythm is an impossibility. Melody expresses the will, the life of man. It is a form of phantasy akin to a dream in which we vicariously experience freedom from tension and guilt. What we do not achieve in our own dreams is more fully realized in the dreams of others, in the melodies they write, the songs they sing to lament or exult their lot in life. To achieve variety, a composer may pause in the continuity of a passage or replace one melodic progression with another. Perhaps one of the most effective ways of achieving his end is to introduce an element into the continuity of the melody that is different from what we expect.

Primitive music was monophonic. It remained essentially so until the late Middle Ages when organum emerged. Harmony and counterpoint are relatively late arrivals, as the history of music goes. At its inception, polyphony was called a babble of tongues which could only bode ill for man. This new music was confusing, not as satisfying as old unison singing which was easier to understand. Polyphony took man's mind away from the Holy Text; it hindered devotion rather than helped it, the Catholic hierarchy said.

Composers during the baroque era were pleased with themselves; they finally had learned how to think and write harmonically instead of in the old linear style. Now, composers have knowledge of a diversity of approaches. They freely use both chordal and contrapuntal techniques in one composition.

The interval of an octave is a natural phenomenon; the tempered intervals within the octave are man-made. Consonant and dissonant intervals have been explained on the basis of ratios, smoothness, "fusion-like" quality, and cultural and personal conceptions. A cadential process is resolved only because we have come to expect that it should be, and when this does not happen, we either feel thwarted or mentally resolve it for ourselves. We attribute psychic qualities to musical tones, and endow them with ascending and descending properties. The properties are not actually there, they are creations of the human mind.

Scales and keys are technical aids to give music a firm tonal structure and coherence. Every musical system in the world has its scales. Scales in our culture are figuratively like ladders in which the tonal rungs are arbitrarily arranged in rising pitches. Because of changes in tonal concepts new modes have emerged in different phases of our musical history.

Musical keys are peculiar to European music. They differ from scales by containing tones, such as accidentals, which are not included in our major and minor modes. Our system of keys emerged, as did our scales, from the Greek modes. A musical form is the design of a composition. Style is a manner of expression, very often characteristic of a historic period in a civilization. We usually associate the form of a musical work with a particular style, but this is not always true. A musical form is only a plan of the music we are to hear, a guide to what should follow and how it should traditionally end; style recalls the time in which the musical work was written or the epoch in which it belongs, and indicates how the composition should be rendered to fit in with the time in which it was composed.

NOTES

[1] W. Fleming and A. Veinus, *Understanding Music: Style, Structure, and History* (New York: Holt, Rinehart and Winston, Inc., 1958), p. 28. "Rhythm is at once the life's breath that animates the spirit of every musical organism, the life's blood that courses through the arteries and veins of its circulatory system, the heartbeat that pulses throughout the body of a musical composition, and the life cycle that covers the span between the birth of its initial upbeat and the death of its closing cadence."

[2] Allen Forte, *Tonal Harmony in Concept and Practice* (New York: Holt, Rinehart and Winston, Inc., 1962), p. 24.

[3] *Ibid.*, p. 27.

[4] James L. Mursell, *The Psychology of Music* (New York: W. W. Norton & Company, Inc., 1937), p. 162. "... *the ultimate foundation of rhythm is to be found in mental activity.*" Curt Sachs, *Rhythm and Tempo* (New York: W. W. Norton & Company, Inc., 1953), p. 38. "... rhythm comes from the mind and not from the body!"

[5] Reprinted by permission of the publishers from I. Stravinsky, *Poetics of Music in the Form of Six Lessons*, trans. Arthur Knodel and Ingolf Dahl (Cambridge, Mass.: Harvard University Press), p. 40. Copyright 1947 by The President and Fellows of Harvard College.

[6] Aristotle *De Mundo*, trans. E. S. Foster (Oxford: Clarendon Press, 1914), Chap. VI, 399a. "The single harmony produced by all the heavenly bodies singing and dancing together springs from one source and ends by achieving one purpose, and has rightly bestowed the name not of 'disordered' but of 'ordered universe' upon the whole. And just as in a chorus, when the leader

gives the signal to begin, the whole chorus of men, or it may be of women, joins in the song, mingling a single studied harmony among different voices, some high and some low; so too is it with God that rules the whole world."

[7] Hindemith, *The Craft of Musical Composition,* trans. Arthur Mendel (New York: Associated Music Publishers, Inc., 1942), Bk. I, p. 57.

[8] Lipps, *Psychological Studies,* II, trans. Herbert C. Sanborn (2d ed.; Baltimore: The Williams & Wilkins Company, 1926), pp. 138-265.

[9] J. L. Mursell, "Psychology and the Problem of the Scale," *Music Quarterly,* XXXII, No. 4 (1946), p. 564.

[10] *The Wisdom of Confucius,* trans. Lin Yutang (New York: The Modern Library, Inc., 1938), p. 264.

[11] Paul R. Farnsworth, *The Social Psychology of Music* (New York: Holt, Rinehart and Winston, Inc., 1958), p. 20.

[12] Eduard Hanslick, *The Beautiful in Music,* trans. Gustav Cohen (New York: The Liberal Arts Press, 1957), p. 75. "Style in music we should like to be understood in a purely musical sense: as the perfect grasp of the technical side of music, which in the expression of the creative thought assumes an appearance of uniformity. A composer shows his 'good style' by avoiding everything trivial, futile, and unsuitable as he carries out a clearly conceived idea, and by bringing every technical detail into artistic agreement with the whole . . . we . . . apply the word 'style' to a composer as we apply the word 'character' to a man." Stravinsky, *op. cit.,* p. 70. "Style is the particular way a composer organizes his conceptions and speaks the language of his craft."

[13] Dante *Divine Comedy,* Paradiso. Canto I. 104.

> *All things, what'er they be, an order have*
> *Among themselves; and from this order is.*

CHAPTER III

MUSICAL VALUES

SACRED VALUES

Jews   Jews once sang and danced in praise of God to the accompaniment of timbrel and psaltery.' In Solomon's Temple an organ and trumpets were used. The Second Temple had brass ensembles and an organ as part of the religious service, but not so grandiose as in Solomon's original house of worship. After the Romans destroyed the Second Temple and dispersed the Jews, worship became less elaborate and instruments were no longer used.

⌣

The Song of Songs is a biblical story which became a prophecy. It is a narrative of a lone woman, of unquiet love in ancient Judea. In it the scribes of Judea relate how this woman searched for inner contentment and did not find it in the land of her God and King. It was as if she was a stranger to her own people, destined to wander alone.

The great Temple fell and the second one arose, but the Jews found no peace in their souls. The educated and cultured people sang Greek songs and imitated Greek ways in order to overcome their inner discontent. The Rabbis complained that these Jews, influenced by the Greeks, were acting like strangers in their fathers' land. Soon the Second Temple was demolished and the Jews became wanderers throughout the lands of the earth. Wherever they went the psalmist

was heard: "How shall we sing the LORD'S song in a strange land?" [2]
The Jewish people had become, like the lone Jewess who sang for all
the Jews, strangers in foreign lands.

To Jews scattered throughout the world the voice of the prophetic
psalmist was heard: perpetuate the traditional songs of Judea or per-
ish from the earth. Wherever the Jews went they preserved their faith
and strength by singing the songs that their fathers sang when Israel
was great. But they remained dispersed so long that many Jews tired
of being strangers, sang the songs of their benefactors, and became
like them in their ways. Those who held fast to their faith throughout
two thousand years of wandering still sing the songs that were sung
at the sacred service before their Temples were demolished.

The sacred songs of Israel and the holy written works kept the
Jews united after the dispersion, however far away they went from
the promised land. Jews who eventually lost contact with other Jews
were swallowed up in the cultural life of the lands in which they
stayed. Their music became a polyglot adapted to foreign ways. They
sang and danced in the styles of their adopted countries until they
had little in common among themselves except the Old Testament.
Jews who preserved their songs found them a bulwark against alien
influences that challenged their way of life.

The sacred songs of Israel are the songs of the synagogue. The
Jews have always insisted that religion cannot be based on a code of
ethics alone but should have ritual, ceremony, and songs of praise.
Their music cannot be fully appreciated unless its significance is
understood in the ceremony of worship. After Richard Wagner visited
a synagogue to hear a sacred service, he came away grumbling about
the babble of sounds he had heard; the only meaning the sacred songs
had for him was unintelligible wailing and groans of remorse. But not
all Jewish sacred music is tragic in tone. Some of it is gay and light,
such as the songs of spring planting and autumn harvesting which are
sung in the synagogue on different holidays.

The sacred service of the Jewish faith has not remained the same
since the First Temple stood in Solomon's time, and neither has the
music. After the Second Temple was destroyed by the Romans, about
A.D. 70, organs and musicians disappeared from the religious service.

Jews, turned into nomads, could not cart grand organs and brass ensembles of instruments with them wherever they went. Their music became purely vocal, and so it has remained to this day in synagogues that are orthodox in faith.

The secular music of the Jews was often borrowed from the peoples who gave them shelter. When they were quartered in ghettos they created secular songs of their own. Thus they gave and they borrowed music from every country in which they lived. What they contributed they often brought with them; what they took, they carried to some other place. They remembered the songs of many lands in their travels and, like bees pollinating varied beds of flowers in a garden, they enriched each place that gave them refuge.

Catholics The early Christians were in agreement with Aristotle's dictum that musicians with corrupt souls compose music which reflects their being and that those who listen to this music will become like the musicians themselves. The Fathers of the Catholic faith also abided by Plato's admonition that since the souls of the young are malleable and tender they are more susceptible to moral corruption than those of their elders. The kind of music that is to be used in the education of youth is, therefore, of the utmost importance.

The original music of the Catholic Church came from the synagogue. St. Paul [3] is the source of our knowledge that the earliest Christian hymns were of Jewish origin. Musical instruments were forbidden at the first Christian meetings since instruments were symbolic of pagan religions. Early Christians were also fearful that, if they used instruments during their secret prayer meetings, they could be easily detected by the Romans.

Plato's writings had a strong influence on Catholic theologians. St. Augustine, more so than any other Patristic, helped to make Plato's philosophy of music the official view of the Church. He exhorted the clergy to rid their services of profane tunes that had associations with pagan worship. If that could not be done because the tune was too firmly entrenched, the next best thing would be to marry it to a holy text. In time the melody would come to be thought of in a sacred context and not as having come from a profane source. Music that excited undesirable emotions would ruin a man's character; sacred music could lift one's thoughts toward God.

In the sixth century Gregory the Great "cleansed" his diocese of pagan influences in his capacity as a bishop. When Gregory became Pope, he banned secular learning—science and art were ruled out as worthwhile studies. When complaints reached him that members of the clergy officiated at the altar like actors in a Roman theater who try to charm an audience with their singing, he reminded the offending priests of St. Augustine's saying: "I am moved not with the singing, but the thing sung." [4] Vocal gymnastics shorn of piety was a form of personal vanity as far as he was concerned, an evil all men must guard against, particularly Catholic priests.

A thousand years after Gregory died the Council of Trent was still carrying out his work with edicts and decrees to "cleanse" the Church of its musical improprieties. The *liturgical drama,* which began as a form of troping, an educational effort to teach illiterate parishioners about the content of the service, came to a bad end. The Council banned it on the grounds that it had defiled the sanctity of the service and must be cast out of the Church. The same Council ruled that polyphony drowned out the text, confused the ear, and was not suitable for worship.

Even today, in the Catholic Church, music is watched with infinite care. In the *Motu Proprio of Pope Pius X on Sacred Music,* the musical philosophy of the Church in the twentieth century is reaffirmed in the spirit of St. Augustine and Pope Gregory the Great. This document states that the principal office of sacred music "is to clothe with suitable melody the liturgical text . . ." Sacred music must possess "sanctity," "goodness of form," and "universality," the three qualities that predominate in the ancient Gregorian chant, the supreme model of sacred music. Modern music may be used in the religious service if its tone has a character of sanctity about it and if the form in which it is performed is modest. "Still, since modern music has risen mainly to serve profane uses, greater care must be taken with regard to it, in order that the musical compositions of modern style which are admitted in the Church may contain nothing profane, be free from reminiscences of motifs adopted in the theatres, and be not fashioned even in their external forms after the manner of profane pieces." [5] Singers must perform during the service with piety and devotion, and "noisy or frivolous instruments" are forbidden in the Church itself. Each bishop is to institute a commission in his diocese to watch over the music that is used in religious and social functions sponsored by the Church.

Protestants   Luther could see no reason why "the devil" should have "all the good tunes" and so he borrowed melodies wherever he could to make Satan envious of him. He borrowed from Gregorian chants and the songs that the minnesingers sang. Sacred words were added to the music of the popular ballads of the day.

Music and theology instill calm in the human soul; that is why the prophets preached "the truth" with songs and psalms, Martin Luther believed. This belief was not shared by all the Protestants. Those who dissented with this view were of the conviction that only the word of God could bring lasting peace to troubled souls. Music's value they believed to be primarily sensual, more conducive to idleness than worship. Luther conceded that the wrong kind of music could debase a Christian soul, but he was equally certain that the proper kind of music could just as well ennoble it.

Music is a "disciplinarian and moral trainer" in Luther's estimation. Every child should be given instruction in music; it will make him "more gentle and refined, more conscientious and sensible." The "heterodox" who teach theology but not music to children make a grievous error; both theology and music are blessed gifts from God.

Luther never outgrew his love for the music of the Mother Church. He borrowed freely from the Catholic repertoire. ". . . we have made some selections from the beautiful music and hymns used in the papacy. . . . However, we have changed the texts. . . . The songs and music are precious; it would be a pity indeed if they perished."

Calvin disagreed with Luther about music. He regarded it as an

Angel with Rebec. South German, about 1500. Wood, painted and gilded. Height 22 in. The Metropolitan Museum of Art, The Cloisters Collection, Gift of Mrs. John D. Rockefeller, Jr., 1947.

invention of the Devil, an instrument to prey on men's emotions. What little music he permitted to be used in the religious service must be simple and suited "to the spiritual import of the words." His views spread like an infection among his zealous followers. They imprisoned a composer for altering the tunes of several psalms. They closed theaters and barred secular singing on the Sabbath. Musical performances were associated with idleness; even singing in one's home had an element of guilt about it. Calvin's fanatical views finally extended beyond his expectations. Even today, in certain Protestant services not a single musical note is sounded; prayer and worship are carried on with words alone.

SECULAR VALUES

Origins and Influences   Much music in the world is of folk origin— something that we often forget. Music which grows out of work and play, as folk music does, has qualities that are universally infectious. Melodic themes in some ancient Gregorian chants have their source in work songs and play songs, and so do some of our cultivated art songs and elaborate symphonic scores and operas. Sometimes folk themes are retained in their purity when used in another work and at other times they are cleverly concealed against a backcloth of sensuous polyphony.

Folk music was sung in parts long before harmony and counterpoint were invented. Primitive people sang in unison, parallel fourths, and fifths. They used simple drum beats, cross rhythms, syncopation, and varied dynamics of mood and sound on percussion instruments. Some tribes sang in high pitched voices and others in throaty tones. Each group had its stylistic and cultural traditions that came out in the character of their performances through their songs and accompanying gestures.

Folk songs have their origin in work and play. They have been associated with each other from their first stages of existence.[6] Primi-

Lorenzo Costa (1459/60—1535), *A Concert*. Reproduced by courtesy of
the Trustees, The National Gallery, London.

tive people did not distinguish as sharply between music used for hunting or playing at games, and ceremonial music, used for worship, as we do between secular and sacred songs. In Greece and Rome there was a distinction made between folk songs and religious songs but this was not as sharp as it became in Judaism and Christianity after their religious service had been developed and matured; they had at the beginning accepted folk music and adapted it to their needs. This distinction between folk and religious songs is still made but is more evident in the Catholic faith than it is in the other faiths.

Musicians have borrowed folk songs freely for their own works. Traveling minstrels in antiquity sang the songs of the people in the hills or valleys more often than their own creations. Greek playwrights rounded out their plots with folk songs that were familiar to their audiences. Roman playwrights hired composers to create music that would be novel and infectious to accompany their plays. The first opera was written by an itinerant musician [7] in the Middle Ages and was composed of folk tunes. Opera composers have been using traditional folk tunes ever since. Composers of instrumental music appropriate folk music most liberally. Sometimes they have these tunes stand out clearly by themselves and at other times they are woven into the fabric of the work in an effort to minimize their status.

Industrial mechanization has affected folk singing. Where people once sang as they worked, now the machine is heard. In modern factories and office establishments music is piped in from a central source to relieve fatiguing nerves. This music is produced by machines and is "scientifically" controlled to fit the mood of the day and the nature of the work in every office and factory that it "services." Industrialization does many things for us that we once did ourselves. We listen to accomplished singers perform the songs of many lands, of work and play, satire and hate, love and death, without any desire to sing about our own lives as our forefathers did.

In play children sing, as they always have, but adults rarely do. Adults now associate singing at play with childish ways. They, in their maturity, use music as an accompaniment, a tranquilizing agent as it were, to keep them calm and relaxed and to help them be as precise in play as they are in work.

Traditional folk tunes lose their character and virility when they are sung away from home in stylized musical arrangements. When a song of the field, that a peasant woman with a raw and vibrant voice once sang, is sung by a person with a well-trained voice, the song is not the same; only the skeleton is preserved. When a folk song that was sung as a simple round is elaborately developed, it loses the infectious quality and simplicity that once bound peasants together. When a song that was modal in tone and sung by one person is arranged for several voices in a tonally centered work, it is an art song for cultivated voices and no longer a folk song. Our oldest folk songs were performed as purely vocal feats. Modern folk singers who add instrumental accompaniments to these ancient songs commit two grievous sins: they detract from the melody of the song, and they are compelled to fit the tune to the chords of their instrument, thereby marring the original character of a once unaccompanied folk song.

Greece and Rome   Although the Greeks and Romans had a system of musical notation, we cannot interpret what little music we have of theirs with the same accuracy as we can translate the words of their poets. What we know of Greek and Roman music is primarily what philosophers and theologians have told us.

Words from Greek folk songs have survived, but the tunes to which they were sung have disappeared. Greek musicians had a system of musical notation which was far enough advanced to record their music. However, they taught their music to each other mainly by rote and memory.

Those texts of Greek folk songs that have survived in poems and historical documents are about love and loneliness, pestilence and debts, but mostly about the hardships of work. Fishermen's songs and farmers' songs existed in abundance. Young girls had songs of their own when they gathered at a well to draw water and gossip; old women sang their songs about spinning and about the loneliness of old age. There were songs for harvesting and the treading of grapes and sailors had songs to accompany them in coiling rope and trimming sails.

We actually know very little about Roman music, but it is quite likely that their folk songs were similar to those of the Greeks. In all lands farmers and fishermen sing alike about their work, as do tradesmen and shepherds. The first Roman mimes were Greek bards and they set the styles and character of the early Roman songs in the same way that Greek painters, poets, and architects influenced their Roman successors.

Wherever the Roman army marched, minstrels shortly followed. Roman citizens serving their government in outlying posts of the Empire must have felt as modern servicemen do in far away places when traveling entertainers sing to them about life at home. Folk songs to Roman soldiers were nostalgic reminders of family and friends and of what awaited them after military service was over.

Three Faiths Protestants are so divided in the modern world that they have no one policy on sacred and secular music. If Ariadne were to unroll a thread through the labyrinth that the Protestants have traveled, she would be puzzled to see how different sects, founded on a single revolt against the Mother Church, can be from each other. Denominations with rich musical services encourage secular music among their parishioners, and those that use music sparingly in their religious service discourage secular music in social life.

Folk music in ancient Israel was as popular as it is in modern Israel but there is a difference between the songs of the old and new nation. ". . . in ancient Israel a 'secular' folk-song flourished—a folk-song of war and carnality and lust inspired by wine and women—a folk-song against which the prophets and the sages carried on a battle for centuries." [8] Many of these folk song melodies nevertheless became the sacred tunes that were used to accompany holy words in the Temple service [9] and which Jews still sing in their synagogues and on festive occasions. In modern Israel newly created folk songs are revolutionary and idealistic—about a new nation fighting for a place in the sun.

The first Christians brought their local customs to church, and they also brought their secular songs with them to sing during the religious service. After a period of time, these songs became the hymns and sacred melodies. Once the liturgy was unified throughout the entire Catholic world, the separation of sacred and secular music was made more pronounced, and so it has remained. Folk music is now associated with six days of toil and sacred music with the seventh day of rest.

The first Protestant services resembled the early Christian meetings in the type of music the worshippers sang. Luther encouraged his congregation to sing native folk songs during the religious service. Music that he borrowed from the Mother Church was translated from Latin into German so that it could be understood and sung in their homes and in the fields and not be reserved for Sundays only.

Calvin did not believe that German folk songs, or music borrowed from the Catholic Church, should be used in the Protestant service. Folk music had its place, but not in the house of worship. Less music at the service would allow more time for prayer; very soon after this declaration, singing at work, not too surprisingly, diminished. As Protestant life became more grim, less music was permitted in it. The Puritans who came to America sang psalms and hymns when they embarked; the folk songs of their ancestors they no longer sang even when they worked.

POLITICAL VALUES

Greece Music has been a handmaid of politics from very ancient times. Our first systematic exposition of its dangers to the state are found in Plato's *Republic*. His theory is that innovations in music eventually lead to innovations in the state. Innovation is an infection which spreads and destroys and, in the case of the state, leaves anarchy in its wake. Music which enervates and waters the emotions also undermines a country.

Complete freedom for a musician to express himself as he wishes is a relatively modern concept. It was a tradition in the ancient world that music should be controlled. Greek bards would not have thought of modifying metrical rules in a musical selection any more than they would have thought of compromising the law of the land. This tradition of strict musical control prevailed in Greece until after tne Periclean Age.

The statesman Solon, who lived almost two centuries before Pericles, declared that music's value is in promoting good citizenship, strengthening the state, and making men loyal to their government. Music must be disciplined, exacting in rhyme and meter, if it is to achieve this goal. Damon, the philosopher and teacher of Pericles, maintained that music "could not only arouse or allay different emotions, but also inculcate all the virtues—courage, self-restraint, and even justice." [10] Appropriate harmonies could create new character formations, draw latent characteristics of virtue out of young and old alike. But innovations in musical styles and rhythms, Damon warned, would inevitably lead to social changes and perhaps to a revolution in the state. Plato, through the voice of Socrates in the fourth book of the *Republic*,[11] strongly agreed with this view.

War between the Greeks and the Persians and the wars of the Greek city-states resulted in physical exhaustion and spiritual decay, and, eventually, to the dissolution of traditional musical forms in Greece. A new kind of music has driven out the old, Aristophanes wrote. This new music is a mixture of incongruous melodies without rhythm or any semblance of sanity. Musicians seek only popularity now, lamented Aristophanes. They try one novelty after another; each daring experiment is more presumptuous than the one that came before it. Soon the habit for innovation will infect the entire state.

Since Plato believed that music could mold character, he instructed statesmen and educators that it was their duty to condemn music that was, in their judgment, bad. The Guardians of the State must be well educated and discerning so that they will know what they are doing and not make indiscriminate judgments. Music with incongruous texts, music that provokes obscene gestures, music that attempts to make one instrument sound like another or imitate the human voice, should be strictly forbidden. Mixed styles are confusing. Using one instrument for another is deception. Both tendencies are detrimental and cannot be tolerated in a perfect state. Furthermore, the Elders of the State must remember that moderation and not extremes should be the guiding rule in instrumental education, and students should be informed that music without words may bring harm to their souls without their being aware of it. The average citizen cannot distinguish good music from bad. In an aristocracy of intellects, the *Republic* itself, the wise and learned must guide the less informed and decide what is best for them. The populace does not always know what is to its advantage in either politics or music.[12]

Plato's advice, to the State Guardians in the *Republic,* on the value of music in education and citizenship is the core of Aristotle's musical philosophy in the *Politics.* Aristotle wrote that students must be taught the various modes, rhythms, and melodies; their moral affinity to the revolutions of the soul should be carefully explained. Greek students ought to acquire technical skill in playing instruments, but they must not attempt to become so proficient in this task that they will rival professionals who vie with each other for the plaudits of the crowd. The paid performer practices his art not to improve his character, "but in order to give pleasure, and that of a vulgar sort, to his hearers... he makes them what they are, and fashions even their bodies by the movements which he expects them to exhibit." [13]

Discipline, a virtue which Plato so ardently admired in politics and art, reached such a low ebb among Greek musicians that a strange kind of license, mistaken for freedom, became the mode of the time. This condition began before Plato arrived on the scene and was getting progressively worse in Aristotle's estimation. The Cynics reflected this state of affairs by calling music a useless pastime, an utter waste. Musicians are people whose souls are out of tune; what good could possibly come from such a source? Plutarch related a story about Antisthenes the Cynic who said "when he heard that Ismenias was an excellent piper: 'But he's a worthless man,' said he, 'otherwise he wouldn't be so good a piper.'" [14] Plutarch continued this tale by describing how Alexander was berated by his father for playing a musical instrument too well. Such things are unfitting a king; musicians are idlers, contestants at carnivals, activities a monarch should abhor. A king should listen to others perform, and thus pay his deference to the Muse.

Rome   Both music and politics are arts. Aristotle called politics the noblest of the arts because it is concerned with governing and making wise decisions which affect our way of life. Politics is thus an art which requires wisdom and knowledge. Music is born of inspiration and nurtured by waves of emotion. One is a practical art, like medicine and teaching; the other is a fine art, such as poetry, painting, and sculpture.

⟶

Aristoxenus, the Greek musician and philosopher, commented that the subtleties of the Greek musical system were wasted in a civilization where the colosseum took the place of great tragedy, and military trumpets were more in evidence than shepherds' pipes. Aristoxenus was referring to his Roman neighbors in the north whose influence would soon spread throughout the Western world. The music of Rome must have taken on some bizarre aspects in the following centuries, judging from three famous contemporaries. Seneca complained that music was given a degree of importance that was out of proportion to its social contribution. Quintilian wrote that Roman music would sap the strength of every citizen in the land and eventually destroy the Empire.[15] Horace, in a satirical poem, described a visit to a musical contest and the degradation to which it sank.

When, on a day of revels, to begin
The feast from noontide was no more a sin,
A larger license and a scope less rude
Both to the music and the verse accrued.
For what should that mixed audience have of taste,
Clown grouped with cit, and boors by nobles placed?
Thus did the piper superadd erelong
The charms of gesture to the powers of song,
With pantomimic grace his sense expressed,
And trailed along the boards the floating vest.
Thus too, its tones increased, the lyre severe
Poured richer warblings on the ravished ear;
The muse in loftier numbers learned to soar,
Imped her bold plume for flights untried before,
And, fraught with fire prophetic, bade each line
Rival the raptures of the Delphian shrine.
        He that in tragic lay late strained his throat
To win the paltry prize—a shaggy goat,
Soon bared upon the stage a sylvan crew

And brought the wanton satyrs forth to view:
The solemn tone not wholly laid aside,
To humor and burlesque his hand applied;
And sought by grateful novelty of song
To rivet to their seats a boozy throng
From festive rites and revels just set free,
Ripe for loose pranks and full of tipsy glee.
Yet so to shift from grave to gay 'twere fit,
So temper the light satyrs' saucy wit,
That not each god, each hero, that of late
Stalked forth in purple robes and royal state,
Anon should all his pomp of speech let down
To the low slang and gabble of a clown,
Or, steering heavenwards his flight too fast,
Grasp empty clouds and soar into bombast.
The Tragic Muse, with bashfulness severe,
Disdaining the base gibe and trivial jeer,...[16]

Rome was not lost because of its enervating music, as its moral guardians had feared. But as the Empire was being dissolved, Boethius, adviser of state to King Theodoric, took on the task of fusing the musical precepts of Plato and Aristotle for the future guidance of the Western world. He noted that music is inherently ethical in its nature, a reflection of the mathematical order in the world. It surpasses any other discipline in the educational quadrivium in shaping the mind and body of the young. Music can therefore ennoble or degrade character, make men better or worse than they are. It is of the utmost importance to the state that music should not undergo frivolous innovations that will mar its natural order. Music that is not in harmony with nature will blemish the human soul and eventually lead to revolt against authority in the state. Boethius' musical precepts became the measuring rod with which to judge music for a thousand years after his death. His influence upon music in the Western world is equal to the hold which Aristotle kept on science and thought in the civilized world throughout the Middle Ages.

Nationalism   Musicians in one form of government do not produce better music than those in another form with a different political label.

Musicians in governments with Spartan tendencies toward militarism are capable of producing music of esthetic merit that equals or surpasses that of musicians in peaceful democracies. The creative nature of a composer is not stifled by government politics, unless the oppression is excessive. Perhaps the greatest music that has been produced in the Western world in the previous two centuries was composed under the auspices of benevolent despots.

Composers of a chauvinistic bent who wish to fire our political emotions have musical symbols at their disposal that can be understood without any loss of significance around the whole of the Western world. These symbols are the folk songs, the music of the people. Folk music is associated with specific social groups, countries, and historical events. Composers make full use of these symbolic references when they wish to introduce a nationalistic strain or cultural association into their musical work. They will either use indigenous folk music or create melodies that resemble those of their native land and display them as boldly as they can in the context of the work.

XNationalistic symbols in music are to a nation what hymns and chants are to a religion. Music of this kind is educational as well as entertaining. During the classical and romantic eras in music, composers used their scores to further nationalistic causes. *The Beggar's Opera* with simple songs of the countryside and pub was produced to liberate England from the musical esthetics of the Italians. Pergolesi struck back for the honor of Italy; he wrote *La Serva Padrona* and rivaled the musical triumph which *The Beggar's Opera* had received. The philosopher Rousseau decided to save France single-handedly from taking third place in the musical war of the time. He composed a folk opera of his own, *Le Devin du Village.*

⚑ Notes of political significance dart in and out of Mozart's operas and in Beethoven's songs of freedom. Liszt acted as the champion of the working class, and Wagner set out to rejuvenate the German State with his music drama. Verdi fired the Italians with the torch of insurrection by using tunes that eventually became associated with the struggle for Italian freedom, and Glinka set out to promote Russian

Winslow Homer (1836-1910), *Amateur Musicians*. Oil on canvas, 18 by 15 in. The Metropolitan Museum of Art, Samuel D. Lee Fund, 1939.

nationalism with native folk themes. Songs that were written and sung during the great War between the States in America are as accurate a chronicle of the mood which raged through the land at that time as any literary document that we have in our possession.

Although nationalism in music is very old it received a strong impetus artistically during the nineteenth century. The political upheavals that rocked the world in that century were as strongly presented in Glinka's *A Life for the Czar* and *Russlan and Ludmilla* as the overtones of the Communist revolution were in Prokofiev's *cantata Alexander Nevsky* and in the opera *War and Peace*. The same kind of patriotic pride that inspired Glinka and Prokofiev to write for their country also inspired Sibelius to write the *tone poem Finlandia* for his "oppressed" nation. Because of its incendiary political character the Russian government at one time forbade the performance of this work in Finland. Music that is written in a strongly nationalistic idiom, such as Smetana's *Bartered Bride,* can become a historical document of a way of life in a land that has since lost its political independence.

In the twentieth century music has become a weapon in the ideological struggle between two ways of life. The communist countries firmly hold that the value of music is not only to amuse and titillate the senses but to serve the state—to educate and enlighten the masses. In their political order music is expected to be composed on a level equal to the understanding of the people. Therefore, if the composer's music is too complex to listen to, it will be confusing and wasteful; if his music is alien to the needs of the masses, it will deter the cultural growth of both the individual and the s.ate. If composers place their personal feelings above political policies, they must be publicly reprimanded so that others will not emulate their actions. Folk melodies and patriotic texts ought to be encouraged—one engenders a spirit of brotherhood, and the other teaches the history of the Marxist revolution.

ESTHETIC VALUES

Composer The composer and poet were once one and the same person. Music and poetry were a unified art—not separated as they are today. Music has retained the powers of a language with a grammar and syntax of its own and has become a complex art which can express several different ideas simultaneously, but poetry, her "blessed sister" [17] can only express one idea at a time.

⌇

What are the composers' intentions? Composers are divided among themselves as to precisely what their intentions are. One group believes that music is a trustworthy image of their life experiences. A second group maintains that their scores express musical ideas only. Tschaikovsky is a representative of the first group: "I do not wish any symphonic work to emanate from me which has nothing to express, and consists merely of harmonies and a purposeless design of rhythms and modulations." [18] Shostakovich says the same thing: "I suddenly realized that music is not only a combination of sounds arranged in this melody or that, but an art which is capable of expressing the most varied ideas and feelings by means of its specific qualities." [19] Stravinsky takes a position opposite to that which the former two Russian composers hold. He insists that it is impossible to express specific feelings, "translate dramatic situations" into musical compositions or imitate nature with tones and rhythms. "For I consider that music is, by its very nature, essentially powerless to *express* anything at all," [20] he concludes in his autobiography.

How are a composer's ideas conveyed to us? Sometimes he performs his music for us himself, but generally others do it for him, even during his lifetime. Some composers do not agree with their interpreters; other composers hold that professional performers give fuller justice to their music than they can themselves. A composer may think that his intentions are clear and evident in the structure of his musical work, but when the work is performed it may not sound as he thought it would. The composer may have some qualms about whether he recorded his intentions accurately. He may be unable to reconcile, to himself, what he meant to convey with what came out in sound. If he is conducting his own work, it may be that the talent that he has for recording his ideas in written musical form he cannot equal in actual performance. Someone else may perform his work while he is present, and it may sound just as he intended it should. A member of the Bach family was frank enough to write that composers are not always the best spokesmen for what they have to say; Robert Schumann also believed this to be so and wrote a short commentary giving the reasons for his view. "Those opposed to this stand are often incapable of doing justice," wrote C. P. E. Bach, "despite their technique, to their own otherwise worthy compositions. Unable to bring out the content of their works, they remain ignorant of it. But let someone else play these, a person of delicate, sensitive insight who knows the meaning of good performance, and the composer will learn to his astonishment that there is more in his music than he had ever known or believed." [21] Schumann's reasons are summarized in this passage: "Experience has proven that the composer is usually not the finest and most interesting performer of his own works, especially his most recent ones, which he has not yet mastered from an objective point of view. Other people often know how to express our meanings better than we do ourselves. . . . We have seen instances when composers have wholly misinterpreted their own works." [22]

Richard Wagner was adamant that his intentions be carried out by conductors and singers performing his works. Everyone who worked with Wagner knew how tyrannical he was on this point. But as a conductor himself Wagner was less obedient to the wishes of other composers. He thought it quite proper to correct "errors" in Beethoven's *Ninth Symphony* by altering tempi and dynamics, rephrasing passages, and adding ideas of his own. This practice of altering a composer's work was more prevalent before the romantic age. Bach and Handel rearranged the music of their contemporaries, either directly or by incorporating it into a work of their own.

Conductors sometimes understand a score better than the composer who wrote it, but two modern composers would take very strong exception to this view. According to Igor Stravinsky, they are often prone to substitute their own intentions for those of the composer. He contemptuously compares conductors to army sergeants, and orchestra members to soldiers under their command. Military men obey orders handed down by their superiors, and in the musical world conductors and performers should obey the directives of the composers who are in a higher artistic echelon than they. Other artists are not plagued with this problem. "Composers may well envy the lot of painters, sculptors, and writers, who communicate directly with their public without having recourse to intermediaries." [23] Paul Hindemith agrees with Stravinsky that performers distort a composer's intentions to exalt their own vanity. "Those performers who, craving a modest share of the creator's glory, feel unable to compete with the glorious deeds of the arranger, find their satisfaction in adding fingerings, slurs, dynamics, and other symbols to other people's compositions. This means that they leave the mere notes of a piece as they are, but otherwise feel free to forge, interpolate, and adulterate as they please." [24]

What musical qualities should the composer's score possess? His ideas and sentiments must be expressed with logic and consistency. The entire work must be unified, and there must be as little as possible that is superfluous in it. Every part of the score must be related to every other part so that the complete work possesses coherence. A musical work is like an ideal state; it has its similarities and dissimilarities in personalities but these are subordinated for an ultimate ideal.

A musical work must have variety and contrast. The contrasts must not be so bland that they are ineffectual as emotional stimulants. Nor should the contrasts be so severe that we are emotionally incapable of bridging the differences between the moods that they present. A certain amount of time must elapse before we can become accustomed to incongruities that shock and stun; and this is as true of life as it is in listening to music.

Repetition is extremely important in a musical work. It enables a composer to expand his ideas and bind them together. Recurring themes are also a source of satisfaction; they remind us of old friends who disappear and then return again. Because we are familiar with their ways, we feel at ease with them. Recognizing musical themes that we previously heard has a stabilizing influence; we assume that they will end as we heard them do originally.

A musical work should not be of such length as to tax our endurance or be so short that it only whets our appetite. A score that is too long can become fatiguing, thus diminishing our pleasure in listening to it. Musical selections that are too brief, as primitive melodies so often are, lack repetition and contrast. Without recurring themes and contrasting elements there cannot be a serious amount of interest and tension in a musical work.

A musical score is in a sense like a human life. A person grows and develops, or becomes enmeshed in insolvable problems from which he cannot extricate himself. In the first case, a human life is fully realized through successful accomplishments. In the second case, a person will tend to become stunted and warped by not being able to rise above the problems that enter into his life. The composer, by analogy, must have the ability and character to surmount the musical problems that each step in creating a score presents. The value of his finished work will depend on how well he resolves these problems.

Listener Music surpasses all the other fine arts in its power to create suspense and relief, tension and repose. Its therapeutic values are balm to our souls. In music all the facets of our lives are symbolized, paraded before us to review in the same way that images of our waking life appear in dreams. But music has greater therapeutic value than dreams possess. Dreams confuse and mislead, they distort when they please, and send us back to the actual world beguiled and perplexed. Music is like an open book in comparison to dreams; it does not compromise with truth or delude us about ourselves. Music is a "playback" of our failures and successes, the hurts that we seemingly had forgotten, a renewed wonder about the world, and a feeling of thankfulness for being alive.

$\backsim$

Purists point out that a line must be drawn between the structure of a musical work and the emotion that it arouses in us. One is a matter for an objective value judgment, and the other is personal. The emotion that music rouses in us is a psychological phenomenon that concerns us and no one else. Only sentimental people, continue the purists, talk about letting their feelings run over into tones, rhythms, and of hearing echoes of their lives in musical elements. They confuse the intrinsic value of a musical composition with their private emotional experiences.

Very few listeners hear music as tones and rhythms without any reference to their experiences in the actual world. Most of us hear in music a composer's confession of faith, and echoes of our own complaints against the world. We use words such as "sad" or "gay" to describe how music sounds to us. We associate certain tonal combinations of tones and rhythms with life experiences.

... there do seem to be mysterious affinities between life-experiences and musical ones; for music does evoke in us experiences sufficiently like some experiences in life to make us use the same characterizing adjectives in describing them, inadequate as they are, and to do so with considerable regularity and insis ence. The sadness we feel in hearing the music is never the sadness of personal bereavement, and yet the word is used in describing the music because of some felt correspondence between it and the emotion of daily life. There is a recognizable similarity, yet when we want to describe our musical experience, the words used in doing it seem even more inept than they do for describing our experiences in life from which the words we apply to music were derived.[25]

Listening to music properly can be learned through training.[26] There is no royal road; it takes effort and diligence and a great deal of listening. But a listener must also possess sensitivity to derive the fullest benefits that music can offer. This quality can be developed through guidance and exercise. A listener who is ably trained develops the discipline necessary to follow a musical score of length and complexity without tiring or wandering mentally soon after the performance has begun. Learning how to listen to music is no different from learning how to participate in any other mature activity.

A listener must also be able to project, transfer his feelings, and endow tones and rhythms with his life's experience. A listener whose life is not burdened with tragedy and given to hope will find no joy or sadness in music. Without anxiety there could be no tension and suspense in music. One who is not receptive to surprise and who is not tired of waiting will miss the climaxes in music just as he misses the climaxes in every full day of his life. A knowledgeable music listener who is unable to effuse feeling and pathos is no better than a metronome as far as the Muse of song is concerned.

A listener who can analyze the mechanics of a musical composition while hearing it but does not experience the pleasure of phantasy, tension, and release is like an automobile mechanic who enjoys listening to the hum of motors if they are properly tuned but who rarely takes a ride. Listening to music is a form of escape much like motoring out into the countryside away from everyone else, picnicking in a natural paradise, and then returning home.

Listening to music gives us temporary release from moral restraint and envy. It is the equivalent of honey mixed in a *cathartic* potion of tones and rhythms which purge the emotions with sensations that are both pleasant and disturbing. Music helps us work off destructive impulses which we might otherwise turn inward upon ourselves or direct outward against our neighbors. Music is able to block and to dull but not entirely to erase our deep-seated hurts and hates—at least for a short while. Music can help us dispel in phantasy problems of a lesser kind in the same way that opiates blot out minor problems from our troubled minds; but, whereas music raises the level of our morale, it does not leave us depressed or enervated over an extended period of time as opiates do.

We listen to certain musical compositions over and over again, probably for two reasons more than any other: music of great intrinsic value excites us with its rich ideas every time we hear it; other types of music may have purely sentimental value for us even though they may be shallow. Repetitious listening does not diminish our appetite for music which nourishes our particular constitution. Through repetition we may even come to know some music so well that none of its intricate nuances slip by us, and yet our pleasure remains undiminished every time we hear it. But the joy that we get from hearing an old favorite, however it may affect us, is never quite equal to that when hearing a new musical work that draws ecstatic sensations from us. Still, as we mature musically and listen to our favorites, we find that they are very much like human friends. In some we discover certain qualities that we missed before because of our own limitations. In others, although we realize how shallow they are, we enjoy having them with us simply because they are so pleasant.

As a rule we listen to music not as a duty but to entertain ourselves. No one is adversely affected by our doing this or in competition with us for our experiences. It is purely a game of make-believe and, like play in general, music permits us to discharge pent up emotion, to drain the pus that might poison us from festering wounds. In music, as in games, we learn about ourselves—what our strengths and weaknesses are and how we act at the point of a climax. We listen to music for escape and strive for fulfillment by exerting ourselves in a make-believe way.

A listener's response to a musical work depends on his age and maturity, his beliefs and convictions, prejudices and sympathies, and the mood that he happens to be in at the moment. A child will not get the full measure of pleasure from a musical work that is beyond his grasp. Ordinarily an adult will find children's music pleasant, not challenging. But on the adult level there is music that does not warrant being reheard, so weak is its appeal to a person with disciplined musical habits. A mature listener will outgrow certain kinds of music, just as a child will give up infantile ways in the process of becoming an adult. Mature people do not stand still; they become more discriminating and esthetically demanding as they move along in life, providing they are sensitive and curious.

We make judgments about music by different standards, not all of which are of equal value. Some of us decide on the merit of a work on the basis of its structure and the logic and consistency with which the composer develops his material. Others equate the value of a musical composition with the amount of self-reference that they can associate with what they assume to be the composer's intentions. These are the two usual ways of making value judgments about music. Some listeners, however, make their value judgments about music primarily on the basis of personal prejudices. A temperate listener moderates between extremes. He tries not to confuse the structural merit of the work with his private life. He follows the structural development of a musical work as best he can, but he does not keep his imagination under wraps as to what the music may signify to him emotionally. He does not limit his musical diet to modern music alone or, the other extreme, old music. He avoids *dogmatism* in musical matters just as he shies away from fanaticism in life. His entire life is a search for understanding, and as he looks to a learned man for intellectual enlightenment, so too he follows the guidance of a competent authority in musical matters until he, himself, has developed sufficiently to be his own authority.

Performer A language has little value if it does not help us to communicate with one another. A language is meaningless to us if we do not understand it. Since most of us cannot read or understand a musical composition, we count on the performer to communicate the composer's intentions to us as he understands them. Sometimes the performer is the composer himself, but usually it is someone trained to interpret what he says. It would seem that the basic feeling of a musical work would be best brought out by its composer if he were alive; but this is not always so. Performers trained in the art of interpretation may get more out of a score than its composer was aware it contained.

Between the listener and the creator stands the performer as an intermediary. The role of performer is a relatively modern practice; it has not always been this way. In ancient times performers created their own music and played and sang it as well. Creative artists still perform their own work, on occasion, usually as conductors of symphonic orchestras. Somewhat oddly, certain performers appear more important than creators, judging by the position they hold in society. This shows a rather poor sense of values as far as the public is concerned. Even if the performer should be considered as a lesser creator in his own right, rather than an intermediary, his interpretation can generally not equal the contribution of the composer from whom the music stems.

It is a rare composer indeed who performs as well as he creates. Nature separates the performer from the creator by the amount of psychic discomfort she permits each to bear. The performer is not original because there is not as much psychic conflict in his being as there is in that of a creator. Performing requires technical skill which must be cultivated as diligently as composing itself. Without gifted performers we could not possibly have symphonies, operas, and the variety of solo work as beautifully performed as it now is.

Symphonic conductors are not ordinarily thought of as performers, although they do conduct and perform simultaneously at times. Nevertheless, the conductor will be treated as a performer because he is an intermediary between the creator and the listener. He is the director of other performers. A modern orchestra without a conductor would be a near impossibility. Composers have clearly indicated in their scores, since the romantic period, what dynamics and tempi should be followed. Orchestral works, and opera too, became so complex that such markings were necessary if the music was to be performed with a fair degree of uniformity wherever it was sung or played. The conductor acts as the composer's representative to see to it that his directions are obeyed. He takes on the task of a catalyst for all the talented musicians of varying temperaments in the orchestra. He gives their performance balance and direction on the basis of his understanding of the composer's intentions. Musical markings, like written words, convey different shades of meaning to each member of the orchestra. One member must lead if harmony is to prevail. This the conductor does.

Performers do not have the initiative and independence that composers display. Their position is that of a middle man in the entertainment field—a precarious one at best.[27] Their lack of self-assurance shows itself by adherence to traditions that a composer would never tolerate. They program concerts, for example, with historical continuity simply because it is the fashion, even though a single artist cannot do justice to all the musical styles that exist. Performers labor under the illusion that unless certain works are included in their program they will lose caste with their colleagues. They become half-crazed with work and fear trying to do what they are emotionally and technically not suited for but which is demanded of them, nevertheless, by a fickle public.

Most performers are too timid to chance unpopular or unknown music, and thus they deprive the public of hearing new and good music. The rare performers who befriend the moderns and try to enlarge our musical diet with works we will probably enjoy if we hear them often enough are deserving of more of our gratitude than they receive. Concert managers and board members are not any kinder to them than the public. Performers, therefore, spend their energies repeating standard works and only sparingly perform the moderns or little-known works that should not be forgotten. A small group of performers go to the other extreme; they will only perform old music or new music.

Performers not only differ from each other in their interpretation of musical works, but never perform a work in exactly the same way a second time. Each performance differs from the last one, and that is one reason why recordings, however well rendered, do not measure up to live presentations which are as varied as the facets of a musician's life. The mood of the audience, the nervousness and exhilaration which grips the performer, come through in his interpretation and technique. In a sense there is no one *Komm süsser Tod* that Bach wrote; but as many as there are performers to sing and play it.

A performer can bring out hidden nuances in a musical work that the composer himself was unaware of. A performer can also inject feelings into a musical work that are irrelevant to its character. Liszt altered the scores of practically every composer whose music he performed at concerts, as other performers did in his time, so that he could display his fiery technique and the breadth of his emotional range to his worshipful admirers. Mature women screamed and fainted at his concerts, just as immature girls become ecstatic and swoon with delirium when listening to our popular idols. A performer who renders musical works note for note with mechanical precision and leaves his audience unmoved is the very opposite of a composer such as Liszt. Both types of performers are undesirable extremes. But if a performer is incapable of feeling the fundamental tone of a musical work, he will often compensate with devices of his own, such as liberties in interpretation, that are hardly in character with the original composition.

A performer can never know with certainty what the composer's intentions were. Composers themselves are not always able or willing to tell us what they were trying to say. Performers must subordinate themselves to the work as best they can according to their feeling of what they think the composer meant to convey. Knowing the history of the period that the work was written in, its styles, and instruments, is a prerequisite for an intelligent and sensitive performance.

A performer must remain in control of his emotions and his instrument during a performance, or chaos will result. Performing with passion and forceful dynamics must never be so extreme that the basic character of the work is lost in pyrotechnics. Exaggerated gestures and bodily movements will encourage the audience to watch the antics of the performer instead of listening to the musical work. A performer who uses a composer's work for self-aggrandizement is unworthy of his craft.

Critic   The critic has a three-fold task: he acts as an appraiser of the composer's work; he watches over the performer to see that the composer's music is rendered with fidelity; and he teaches the public how to develop discriminating habits which will help it to formulate a musical judgment. This last task is perhaps his most important function.

⌣

Music criticism became a profession about one hundred and fifty years ago when men of letters and professional journalists assumed the task of informing the public about the merits and deficiencies of musical works. They used various standards to formulate judgments, and to this day they cannot agree among themselves on one standard. Posterity has reversed many of their judgments and pointed out, all too clearly, how inept they were at sensing new musical trends. Music critics have never claimed infallibility, but their contributions as appraisers are so few alongside the errors that they have committed, that many people believe we can well get on without them. They appear as prophets without honor in the modern musical world, not highly regarded by composers or an enlightened public, however seriously they may take themselves. Critics may not have oracular powers, but they cannot be dispensed with altogether. They are, as a rule, more discerning and disciplined listeners than the average person and, usually, are sufficiently well-equipped to be our teachers in musical matters.

What qualities should a music critic have to fulfill the obligations of his calling as an appraiser of the composer's creation and of the merits with which it is rendered by a performer? He must possess the indispensable quality of liking music. If he is indifferent to its charms, his criticisms will lack the effusive ingredient that is required to motivate and enlighten the public. A critic must be sensitive and learned. Musical subtleties are wasted on an insensitive person, whether he be a critic or a layman. Without a sound knowledge of music history, structure, form, and style his evaluations will be shallow indeed. A music critic must go beyond declaring what he likes or dislikes purely on personal considerations if he wishes to be an effective teacher. He should employ esthetic criteria in his criticism and explain the arguments that he used to arrive at his conclusions. These criteria are considerations of the musical ideas expressed in the work, of the merit with which they are developed, and of their originality. Judgment must be passed on the logical consistency of the actual structure of the work, and on the manner in which the composition is rendered by the performer. A music critic has to be emotionally mature and not allow sentimentality or individual idiosyncracies to interfere with his judgment. He should have wide musical experience so that he will be able to make comparisons and contrasts between different works and performances and suggest how they can be improved. He must be precise and articulate whenever possible, but he must also have the capacity to employ poetic metaphors and similes when ordinary words fall short of his descriptive needs. Prose is twice removed from music in emotional overtones; poetry, only once.

Vitriolic language and euphemisms must never be used to cover up a critic's ineptitude. A music critic must steel himself against making musical judgments based on impulse, whim, and arbitrary preferences. He must be capable of passing judgment on the work itself and of evaluating the excellence, or lack of it, with which it was performed without confusing the actual merits of the score and the performance. He must not decide whether a musical work is good or bad purely on the basis of how he thinks the public may respond to it. It is a critic's duty to go contrary to public clamor for a particular work if, in his estimation, the score is not worthy of the esteem in which it is held.

A music critic must be a Socratic gadfly, a zealous and challenging force. Should he cease being incisive and forthright in his criticisms, then he can only function as an apologist, and not as a challenger and examiner of musical ideas. He need not be the equal of the composer whom he challenges or be capable of creating a work of the dimensions that he is evaluating. A critic need only be able, intelligently and courageously, to pass judgment on the works of others in order to fulfill the requirements of his calling.

SUMMARY

Sacred music and secular music associated with politics have several features in common. The primary purpose of such music is to promulgate religious and social ideals. It is usually composed in a clear, simple fashion so that it will be easily remembered. It adheres strongly to traditional patterns and eschews innovations.

Folk music is the "original melody" of man, it is "the musical mirror of the world," wrote Friedrich Nietzsche in *The Birth of Tragedy*. Folk songs are historical documents of the human race, of the coming and passing of cultures, of the rise and fall of nations. They are sources of emotional outlets for those burdened with work, and rhythmic accompaniments for children at play. They can be weapons of satire and scorn, and also songs of love and hope.

Music does not arouse emotions that are specific or definite. It can only recall experiences that have taken place in our lives. Composers know well enough that certain musical passages will tend to excite and pacify us, suggest sadness or joy, and that the rest of the esthetic process must be left to us to complete for ourselves. The greatness of a composer [28] rests on how effectively he can charge our emotions, sustain our sense of exhilaration, carry us to the brink of a colossal climax which we never could have approached ourselves, give us time and courage to complete the experience, and then bring us back to where we started, exalted and refreshed.

Composers have no illusions about the power of music. It would be a rare score indeed that contained the seeds of revolt or rivaled the poet and painter in describing and commenting on life. A composer would not dare to presume that his music will draw a common response from those who hear it, unless it is a hymn or a patriotic anthem that is known around the world. Even then, there would be varied reactions to such a work although its purpose is clearly understood. A composer proceeds on the assumption that certain musical devices will affect listeners of a common culture similarly by eliciting from them responses stemming from their background and conditioning. The imagery that we envision when responding to music is similar to that in dreams. Musical images, like those in dreams, are relatively uniform and culturally significant if our religious and social backgrounds are the same. We cannot describe our musical images with words any better than we can those that we experience in dreams. There are very few poets among us who can translate our personal imagery into actual words.

The value of a musical work does not lie in its physical structure but in the affect it has on us. Aristotle noted that a man living in a house is a better judge of its value than the architect who built it. An architect knows what a substantially good house should have in physical characteristics, just as a composer knows what a musical score should possess, but the ultimate value of a house, as of a musical work, is what provisions it makes for our needs.

NOTES

[1] Psalm. 149:3, 150:3-5.
[2] Psalm. 137:4.
[3] Ephesians. 5:19, Colossian. 3:16.
[4] St. Augustine *Confessions,* trans. William Watts (London: William Heinemann, Ltd., 1925), Bk. X [Chap. XXXIII], pp. 167-169. ". . . sometimes, in the desire of having the melody of all pleasant music, to which David's Psalter is so often sung, banished both from mine own ears, and out of the whole church too: . . . I call to mind the tears I shed at the hearing of thy church songs, in the beginning of my recovered faith, yea, and at this very time, when as I am moved not with the singing, but with the thing sung (when namely they are set off with a clear voice and suitable modulation), I then acknowledge the great good use of this institution. Thus float I between peril

of pleasure, and an approved profitable custom: inclined the more (though herein I pronounce no irrevocable opinion) to allow of the old usage of singing in the Church; that so by the delight taken in at the ears, the weaker minds be roused up into some feeling of devotion. And yet again, so oft as it befalls me to be more moved with the voice than the ditty, I confess myself to have grievously offended: at which time I wish rather not to have heard the music."

[5] *The White List of the Society of St. Gregory of America,* Papal Documents on Sacred Music XII, Motu Proprio of Pope Pius X on Sacred Music (Nov. 22, 1903) (New York, 1951), II, 5, p. 8.

[6] Friedrich Nietzsche, *The Birth of Tragedy,* trans. Clifton P. Fadiman (New York: The Modern Library, Inc., 1937), p. 198. "... we must conceive the folk-song as the musical mirror of the world, as the original melody."

[7] The famous trouvère, Adam de la Halle, wrote *Le Jeu de Robin et Marion* in the thirteenth century.

[8] A. Z. Idelsohn, *Jewish Music* (New York: Tudor Publishing Co., 1944), p. 359.

[9] Peter Gradenwitz, *The Music of Israel* (New York: W. W. Norton & Company, Inc., 1949), p. 69. "It must be surmised that all or most of the motifs and melodies used in the Temple were folk songs (some of them may even have been of foreign origin) and the Levite music leaders only modified them and sanctified their use; this was the practice followed by clerical authorities throughout the ages, down to the Lutheran Protestant Reform."

[10] Kathleen Freeman, *The Pre-Socratic Philosophers* (2d ed.; Oxford: Basil Blackwell & Mott, Ltd., 1949), pp. 207-208.

[11] Plato *Republic,* Bk. IV. 424. "... the attention of our rulers should be directed,—that music and gymnastic be preserved in their original form, and no innovation made. They must do their utmost to maintain them intact. And when anyone says that mankind most regard 'The newest song which the singers have,' they will be afraid that he may be praising, not new songs, but a new kind of song; and this ought not to be praised, or conceived to be the meaning of the poet; for any musical innovation is full of danger to the whole State, and ought to be prohibited. So Damon tells me, and I can quite believe him;—he says that when modes of music change, the fundamental laws of the State always change with them."

[12] Plato *Laws,* Bk. III. 700-701. "... as time went on, the poets themselves introduced the reign of vulgar and lawless innovation. They were men of genius, but they had no perception of what is just and lawful in music; raging like Bacchanals and possessed with inordinate delights—mingling lamentations with hymns, and paeans with dithyrambs; imitating the sounds of the flute [aulos] on the lyre, and making one general confusion; ignorantly affirming that music has no truth, and, whether good or bad, can only be judged of rightly by the pleasure of the hearer. And by composing such licentious works, and adding to them words as licentious, they have inspired the multitude with lawlessness and boldness, and made them fancy that they can judge for themselves about melody and song. And in this way the theatres from being mute have become vocal, as though they had understanding of good and bad in music and poetry; and instead of an aristocracy, an evil sort of theatrocracy has grown up."

[13] Aristotle *Politics.* 1341b.

[14]*Plutarch's Lives,* III, trans. Bernadotte Perrin (London: William Heinemann, Ltd., 1915), p. 5.

[15] *Quintilian* Bk. I, X, trans. H. E. Butler (London: William Heinemann, Ltd., 1921), pp. 31-32. "... the music which I desire to see taught is not our modern music, which has been emasculated by the lascivious melodies of our effeminate stage and has to no small extent destroyed such manly vigour as we still possessed."

[16] Horace *Ars Poetica.* 202-219. (Albert S. Cook ed.; New York: Stechert-Hafner, Inc., 1926).

[17] John Milton, "At a Solemn Musick," *Oxford Book of English Verse,* ed. Arthur Quiller-Couch (Oxford: Clarendon Press, 1915), p. 319.

> *Blest pair of Sirens, pledges of Heav'ns joy,*
> *Sphear-born harmonious Sisters, Voice, and Vers,*
> *Wed your divine sounds, ...*

[18] Tchaikovsky, *Life and Letters,* trans. Rosa Newmarch (London: John Lane, 1914), p. 294.

[19] Kurt London, *The Seven Soviet Arts* (London: Faber & Faber, Ltd., 1937), p. 117.

[20] Igor Stravinsky, *An Autobiography* (New York: Simon and Schuster, Inc., 1936), p. 83. In his most recent book, *Expositions and Developments,* Stravinsky amends this view.

[21] C. P. E. Bach, *An Essay on the True Art of Playing Keyboard Instruments,* trans. William J. Mitchell (New York: W. W. Norton & Company, Inc., 1949), p. 152.

[22] Robert Schumann, *On Music and Musicians* (New York: Pantheon Books, Inc., 1946), p. 50.

[23] Stravinsky, *op. cit.,* p. 224.

[24] Reprinted by permission of the publishers from Paul Hindemith, *A Composer's World* (Cambridge, Mass.: Harvard University Press), pp. 142-143. Copyright 1952 by The President and Fellows of Harvard College.

[25] John Hospers, *Meaning and Truth in the Arts* (Chapel Hill: The University of North Carolina Press, 1946), pp. 96-97.

[26] George Santayana, *The Life of Reason,* IV [Reason in Art] (New York: Charles Scribner's Sons, 1937), p. 51. "A musical education is necessary for musical judgment. What most people relish is hardly music; it is rather a drowsy revery relieved by nervous thrills."

[27] Hindemith, *op. cit.,* p. 145. "This fact, namely to spend a life's work and, again and again, your heart's devotion and your mind's ambition in performances, with conviction that you did your best only when you and your work disappeared behind the piece performed: gone and forgotten the moment you climbed to the highest summit of perfection and self-denial—this seems to me the essential tragedy in the performer's existence."

[28] Leonard B. Meyer, *Emotion and Meaning in Music* (Chicago: University of Chicago Press, 1956), p. 161.

CHAPTER IV

THE RELATIONSHIP of MUSIC to the OTHER ARTS

FIVE SENSES

The fine arts make use of only two of the five senses that we possess: sight and hearing. The other three that we are endowed with—taste, touch, and smell—have been neglected for three reasons. One is that they are inferior because they cannot be organized as sensory responses as easily as sight and hearing. A second reason is that religion has probably been a factor in deterring their esthetic growth because of their sinful associations. The most fundamental reason of the three is that in the course of social and cultural evolution sight and hearing gained in supremacy and became the two most important senses of rational men. Taste, touch, and smell are now associated with animals more than with human beings.

⌣

Nature endowed us with five senses, but we only use two of them for the seven fine arts that man has created—dance, music, poetry, drama, painting, sculpture, and architecture. Touch, taste, and smell have been considered inferior to sight and hearing since the beginning of civilization. Sight and hearing were considered by the Greeks to be allies of intelligence, and the other three senses were associated with roving beasts of the forest.[1] The Christians believed that touch, taste, and smell aroused sexual passions and produced vulgar delights.[2]

Professor Prall in his book, *Aesthetic Judgment,* provides us with an explanation as to why the disparity between the five senses has remained to this day and will most likely continue into the future.

. . . smells and odors do not in themselves fall into any known or felt natural order or arrangement, nor are their variations defined in and by such an intrinsic natural structure, as the variations in color and sound and shape give rise to in our minds. Hence our grasp of them, while it is aesthetic very clearly, since they may be felt as delightful, is the grasp in each case upon just the specific presented nonstructural quality, which is as absolutely different, unique, simple, and unrelatable to furthur elements intrinsically through its own being, as anything could be. One smell does not suggest another related smell close to it in some objective and necessary order of quality or occurrence or procedure, nor does one taste so follow another. There are apparently more or less compatible and incompatible smells and tastes, but there is no clearly defined order of smells and tastes, or any structure of smells and tastes in which each has its place fixed by its own qualitative being.[3]

Music appeals primarily to our sense of hearing, but it does not altogether neglect sight or the three inferior senses. In fact, music indirectly uses the other senses to enhance her own existence as reigning queen of the arts. Of these she is more closely associated with sight and for that reason is at times more critical of it than of any other sense that man possesses. The Muse of song insists that reading a musical work is a different experience from hearing it. Music is not actually music, she points out, unless it is full blown sounds of varied tones and dynamics. Music was originally created to be heard, as poetry was, and the Muse of song is quite justified in holding that a musical score must be heard to receive its rewards instead of being read as a book, as some sophisticates take pride in doing. Music provides for our powers of vision in her own fashion. With sonorous tones and undulating rhythms, music generates visual scenes for our private needs. Music's sights are more imaginative than written words can describe, more satisfying than physical things in the actual world.

We cannot touch music as we can run our fingers surreptitiously over the surface of a painting or the contour of a sculptured piece. Yet, we speak of texture in music in the same way that we would describe our tactual delight on touching silk and soft velvet, or an object that is coarse and abrasive. Music by itself cannot evoke from us sensations of taste and smell, but with the help of a text it can make us feel as though we were savoring foods or smelling pungent perfumes almost as though they were real experiences.

SEVEN ARTS

Man created the seven arts to ward off seven evil afflictions: fear, superstition, lust, avarice, hate, vanity, and cowardice. These sins are interrelated, and so are the arts; each sin is deadly by itself, each art has its own power of catharsis to save us from ourselves. Without sin there would be no art. Indeed, art is born of sin as though it were a divine design for a form of human redemption. A world without sin would be Paradise. In Paradise art would be superfluous; virtue alone would reign.

Each art, like every profession and craft, has a vocabulary of its own. Certain words, however, are common to all the arts, but they have different shades of meaning among the arts. When words that are associated with music are used to describe some other art, or vice versa, they become mere artistic figures of speech.

Rhythm means a sense of movement in all the arts. In music, rhythm consists of patterns of sounds that emphasize and contrast one sound against another; and this is also true of poetry to a lesser extent. A dancer creates rhythm as a composer does. He stylizes and contrasts his movements so that an audience will associate these movements with experiences in their own lives, although the association may not be warranted. Sharp, blunt gestures and impulsive leaps will characterize an age of anxiety, and fine flowing movements, a soothing and pacifying experience associated with calmer days. But within these different dance moods motion is achieved in the same way—contrasts and resolutions, the ingredients out of which movement arises. The painter uses colors that are complementary and contrasting to produce rhythm. He may use two colors alongside each other to create the illusion that one is receding and the other is moving forward. These same colors, matched with different ones, might simply stand still or suggest very little movement. In the novel and the drama rhythm is the momentum with which the story is told, the manner in which actions and episodes are played off against each other. Spatial arts, sculpture and architecture, have rhythmic patterns ingrained in them—horizontal and perpendicular lines which suggest movement upward and sideways. Masses of stone and metal of different weights and strengths are arranged in such positions that they appear to lean and move away from each other, to reach down or up for one another.

Harmony in music consists of two or more voices simultaneously producing separate tones of an interval. In a general sense, it means satisfying relationships between the diversified parts of a work of art. It may be a repetitious passage in a poem that sustains a certain mood from the beginning to the end of the work. It may be the logical way in which a plot is developed in a play, and the consistency with which actors perform their parts. It may be the muted shades of a painting that hold all the colors together to convey the appearance of a balanced and unified work. Harmony may be the dominant motif in architecture, such as the rounded arches of Romanesque cathedrals and the pointed ones in the *Gothic*.

Polyphony in music consists of several voices performing simultaneously, with each voice retaining its own character. It is sometimes used in painting when patterns of color or objects recur at strategically placed parts of the canvas to suggest an appearance of "rhythmic intervals." The same concept appears in architecture in the way materials are arranged and relief is contrasted and spaced. Polyphony has been used in the novel to set one character off against another, just as the composer does with different musical voices.

A musical theme and variation is a rather loose form in which the composer states an idea and then embroiders it for as long as his ingenuity holds out. A painter can do this only in a meager way. His canvas is usually cut in size to fit a museum wall and unless he is a painter of extraordinary stature his variations have to remain modest and close to his subject. A theme and variation form is an artificial device for a virtuoso to exhibit his prowess. In painting and architecture, themes and variations are for practical reasons more limited than in music and dancing.

Gigue, bourrée, minuet, and an endless number of past dance forms are still used as musical forms. Originally the music was only the accompaniment; now the dances are forgotten. *Chorales,* originally the plain songs of the Catholic Church and, later on, the hymn tunes of the Protestants, are vocal expressions of praise to an Almighty God. A chorale can also be played without words of praise. We must be as careful about using musical terms in certain situations as lawyers are about words in their briefs. Musical terms keep changing as do the terms in all fields of communication.

Comparing musical styles and the styles of other arts is a risky enterprise.[4] There is very little similarity, on the surface, between the stone images and crude carvings of ancient man and his short simple tunes, and yet the spirit of that period in history is present in both these art forms. They are both quite elemental as artistic achievements; they do not possess elaborate designs and developed patterns as later forms of art do. Both baroque music and painting have ornamentation as a common quality. But this quality is not necessarily found in works of all the musicians and painters of the period (chronologically). El Greco created elongated figures similar to the architectural style of a Gothic cathedral. Rubens, the great representative of the baroque period, did not think in terms of perpendicular structure as the musicians did. His paintings have a diagonal quality which is associated with this era. Romantic art has been compared to a spiritual Renaissance, a period of history when the struggle for liberty and the dignity of man put its stamp on every creative activity of the age. A painting of Delacroix and the music of Beethoven express similar sentiments; both were champions of human freedom. It is also true that not every artist during the period had an interest in social problems or was very much concerned with the surge of individualism that marks the romantic age. Schubert kept to a private world of his own and Corot painted landscapes that had the other element we associate with the romantic period—sentimentality. Modern architecture features austerity, smooth surfaces, and transparency, but these stylistic characteristics differ from modern music with its *cacophony* and complexity. *Abstract* painters attempt to do the very thing that this type of music strives to do—primarily to express inner sentiments. We cannot group and arrange the arts in neat little packets or place them in arbitrary categories for the convenience of classification on the basis of dates and countries. Artists do not have common stylistic features among themselves even though they are of one period in history. Artists are men of varied temperaments and just as they are unlike in their own time, they are also unlike between each stylistic period.

Artists in every age use the materials that they have at their disposal in order to create. First came stone and wood, then iron and steel. Now we have alloys and plastics, with other materials on the way. The different arts lend themselves to working materials that are peculiar to their nature. Not every art is able to take advantage of the materials that exist in its time. At the present time electronic machines have opened new vistas for contemporary music but have no attraction for the poet or painter. The modern world of science does not spread itself equally among the arts.

Music is sometimes called a language of emotions and like the verbal arts has a grammar with a syntax for notes. Music and words do have characteristics in common, such as being sounds and having rhythm, and pitch, but that is as far as it goes. Music cannot express concepts, describe, or explain, and words do precisely this to fulfill their function in our exchange of ideas. With words we praise and blame, express admiration and disdain; with music we cannot be definite, but can only allude and suggest. Music cannot, as language can, convey specific ideas or detailed messages which are understood alike by all who hear them. The images that music arouses in us are related to our personal experiences. We may respond in common to the tune of a hymn, the call of an anthem, or the *Leitmotiv* in a Wagnerian drama because we have learned to know what a particular theme signifies; but even then our own imagery cannot be identical with that of our neighbor.

Painters speak of muted tones, soft and hard colors, as though colors could be heard or touched as musical tones and sculptured stone can. Poets sing about daffodils dancing with glee and how willow trees weep and bend their boughs to the ground, as though flowers had human qualities and trees expressed grief as women do when they can no longer restrain themselves. Sculptors compare the contour of an Apollonian figure to flowing lines of poetry to describe how an inert mass of clay generates an impression of movement. Musicians speak of colored tones, flat and sharp tones, as though they existed other than as similes.

The vocabulary of the arts is no more sacred than any other language that we have devised. It is good when artistic terms are used as imaginatively as the creation of art itself. But if artistic terms are to retain their definitive purpose, they must not be used so indiscriminately, and even fallaciously, as to destroy their usefulness. Critics are the most notorious offenders in the use of artistic language. Even when they do not like a work, or cannot understand it and do not know how to appraise it, or do not wish to say anything negative about it for fear they may be proven wrong eventually, they will safeguard their position by using artistic jargon that is applicable to all the arts to describe this particular work; in the end, what they have said means nothing. Words that are not clearly defined in the context in which they are used will be more apt to confuse than to explain and be meaningful.

Whether what is "natural" to one art can be expressed by another cannot be answered to everyone's satisfaction; the creative artists themselves are divided on this point. The romantic composers, Schumann, Liszt, and Wagner, believed that what is peculiar to one art can be expressed in another—perhaps not always as well but sometimes even better, depending on the stature of the artist. The poet, philosopher, and critic, Lessing, in his famous *Laokoon* stated categorically that what is peculiar to one art cannot be expressed by another with any high degree of success. Even suggesting movement and deep emotion in the faces of sculptured images is an incongruous example of the application of rhythm and feeling to stone. To him stone images must be stationary and lifeless in art, as stone appears in actual life. The poet Grillparzer, the music critic Hanslick, and the two philosophers Bosanquet and Croce, sided with Lessing against the three romantic musicians.

Poets have used onomatopoetic devices to infuse their words with musical elements. Rimbaud attempted to associate a particular color with each of the five vowels, hoping that his poetry would be like a musical instrument which produces sounds and colors simultaneously. Debussy sketched the visible world in musical tones with the shaded nuances of an impressionistic painter. Mondrian made a supreme effort to catch the tempo of modern jazz in one massive pictorial square, containing many colored squares that seem to dance with each other to vibrant and erratic rhythms. But however splendid each of these three endeavors were, one art cannot express as well what is "natural" to another art, and not to itself.

What is "natural" to one musical instrument is not to another. A composer, for example, is limited in what he wishes to convey by the nature of his instrument. Those who write for the voice as they would for brass instruments cannot bring out the best qualities and texture that the voice possesses and could well use with rare beauty if given the chance. A composer cannot even express with one instrument what he may be able to do very successfully with another. It would be impossible to achieve sublime effects with each instrument in the orchestra. Individual instruments can express a unique quality that cannot be imitated exactly by any other.

Artists and critics who claim esthetic omniscience and pass judgments on all the arts with equal authority are much too egotistical to possess the sensitivity that is required of any such superior mortal. Stravinsky noted that Gide wrote at length about music "without knowing anything about it," but what he had to say was taken seriously by the public because he was an author of great reknown. Artists are not always good judges of the work of artists in their own field, let alone of the works of artists in other fields.

VERSE AND PROSE

Greek   In its broadest sense music to the ancient Greeks consisted of melody, dance, and poetry. In its narrowest sense music meant what we ordinarily mean by the term in our day; but, traditionally, to the Greeks, music was inseparable from poetry. Some time after the Periclean Age poets and musicians went their respective ways in defiance of the tradition which Plato fervently championed. Roman poets and musicians continued the revolutionary trend that the Greek bards began and, although wandering minstrels still played and sang as their predecessors had done in former times, the inevitable result of this trend led to the independence of these two arts as individual expressive art forms.

Poetry was always chanted in ancient times, usually to the accompaniment of instruments and possibly gestures. The Homeric bard sang his ode and strummed his lyre simultaneously, as he told how Hector died, Troy was deceived, and a civilization fell because of man's impiety and greed. In another part of the ancient world King David chanted the psalms, to the accompaniment of a lyre, in praise of the God of Judea. Sometime during the Golden Age of Greece the "blessed sirens" of the arts were separated and, according to Plato's writings, instrumental solos were in vogue.

A song, wrote Plato in the *Republic,* must follow a prescribed set of rules. It should have three parts: "the words, the melody, and the rhythm; ... the melody and rhythm will depend upon the words." [5] The Greek musician's dependence on the words was so complete that each note was allied to each syllable of a word. Melody and rhythm were governed by the rise and fall, the tonal character of the word itself. Music without words, and music which did not follow the text in pulse and inflection, were "new" kinds of music which had begun to emerge perhaps a century before Socrates died. Innovations of this kind corrupt the soul, demoralize the State, and confuse the populace so that they cannot tell what is real from what is not, right from wrong, or good from bad, was Plato's contention. Such license usually begins in the arts. First it appeals to dissolute people and then it endangers all men and their institutions with notions of change and individual expression until there is nothing left that is stable or lasting.⁶ Music must, therefore, remain wedded to the text so that reason will prevail in music's appeal to us through the spoken word, otherwise music will become hopelessly irrational and base. Years later, writing in the *Laws,* Plato accused musicians of fraud and deceit because they had become more bold than they had been before. They were creating music without words for the sheer pleasure of hearing instrumental sounds.⁷ Bards were twisting and torturing the strings on their instruments so that they would produce tones that sounded like imitations of the human voice, reciting verse without musical accompaniment, and assuming the mannerisms of rhetoricians whose only interest is oratory.

Christians The Christians preferred that words and music should not be separated but this was purely for religious reasons and not esthetic ones.

⟶

"God established the psalms," wrote St. Chrysostom, so that Christians who give ear to sacred words will remain indifferent to the influence of the devil's licentious tunes. "Words purify the mind"; music, by itself, excites the flesh, which is what the evil demons want but is displeasing to God. God speaks to us through sacred writings. We praise Him in return, sometimes with His words and sometimes with our own. We embellish these words with song as best as mortals can to heighten our sense of exultation during worship.

St. Jerome believed that music with a sacred text will help us ward off evil. But music without sacred words "would make the house of God a popular theatre." St. Basil noted that God blended melody with "doctrines" so that "through the pleasantness and softness of the sound we might unawares receive what was useful in the words." St. Augustine's remorse over receiving pleasures from music that he would rather not hear was tempered by the thought that its infectious qualities could be used for teaching the Gospel of Christ. It mattered little if a Roman tune was wedded to a Christian text if, by this means, the holy words of Christendom were spread throughout the Roman world. Pagan tunes in time thus came to be associated with Christian texts, and what once was considered a pagan ditty has become associated with religious worship. The original character of the song itself was eventually subordinated to the text. But there are times, Augustine said, when Christians with justification sing to God with heart and voice but without any words. Words become inadequate in praising God, he wrote; one breaks forth in uncontrolled song, ecstatic and jubilant in praise of God.[8]

Calvin placed the same degree of emphasis on the relationship between sacred texts and their musical accompaniments as the Patristics did. He admonished Protestants not to be misled by the false pleasures that music could bring by pleasing and delighting the senses. Music which is composed only for enjoyment "is unbecoming the majesty of the church." Grace will not come to those whose ears are "more attentive to the modulation of the notes than the mind to the import of the words."

Renaissance to Romantic Age   An esthetic "war" between music and words kept going on from the Renaissance to the romantic era, with side battles fought by scholars, musicians, and poets. The trend was definitely toward the independence of poetry from song and equality between them; but the conflict had to run its full course until each proponent in the fight became exhausted. The climax was reached in the romantic period when an ultimate effort was made to remarry poetry and song, and to unite them with painting and architecture in one family of arts.

⌣

The Renaissance was literally a rebirth of the Golden Age of Greece. It was an era in which philosophy and the arts flourished as they had not done for a thousand years. While European philosophers pored over the original writings of Plato and Aristotle that had been brought to Florence by those fleeing from Constantinople, artists

Michaelangelo Amerighi Caravaggio (1560/5–1609), *The Musicians.* Oil on canvas, 36 1/4 by 46 1/2 in. The Metropolitan Museum of Art, Rogers Fund, 1952.

sought in vain among ancient ruins and precious unearthed vases and statuary for the canons of beauty that the Greeks used to achieve such excellence in their art. The poet Ronsard advised his contemporaries that, if they wished to equal the beauty of Greek poetry, they should insist that poems be accompanied by a musical instrument as it was performed in Plato's time. Poetry without music is as impoverished an art as instrumental music without singing voices.

The Florentine *Camerata* attempted to revive the Greek theater during the late Renaissance, as Ronsard had tried to bring the "blessed sirens" together, but their efforts produced the first Western opera and not an ancient play. They assigned greater importance to words than to music, precisely as the Greeks had done in creating for the theater, but Renaissance composers failed to achieve the element of unity in the opera between music, words, and plot, an element of the fullest importance in Attic tragedy. The members of the Camerata assumed that Greek actors sang their parts throughout the play; they had their performers do the same.

During the baroque period, Bach displayed the same genius in the battle between words and music that he did in developing the fugue. He could write an extended *recitative* to follow the inflection of words and he could compose music of breathtaking beauty for sacred words in a chorale. When it suited his purpose, he would chop and cut words asunder in fast-moving vocal fugues. If his text indicated descent from the cross, his music descended also. He would introduce snatches of familiar hymns into instrumental works when he wished his audience to associate certain words with melodic passages. Words were dissolved into musical elements; melodies drew nuances from a text that words themselves could not express.

In the classical era, Gluck wrote: "I have striven to restrict music to its true office of serving poetry by means of expression and by following the situations of the story." [9] Four years after he expressed these sentiments, he repeated them in a famous letter to the editor of the *Mercure de France*. Mozart took the position that poetry ought to be the "obedient child" of music; composers must think of melody primarily and let words take their course. Kant sided with Gluck's view, maintaining that music must be "a vehicle for poetry," "all music without words" is phantasy. Schopenhauer strengthened Mozart's position by writing that "if music is too closely united to the words, and tries to form itself according to the events, it is striving to speak a language which is not its own." [10] "The words are and remain for the music a foreign addition, of subordinate value, for the effect of the tones is incomparably more powerful, more infallible, and quicker than that of the words. Therefore, if words become incorporated in music, they must yet assume an entirely subordinate position, and adapt themselves completely to it." [11]

Words lost their historical importance in the romantic era among many outstanding creative artists and philosophers. Schopenhauer and Nietzsche became distrustful of the power of words and disciplined systems of philosophic discourse. They placed greater emphasis on the role of feeling, rather than logic, to guide humanity in its actions. Nietzsche wrote: "language can never adequately render the cosmic symbolism of music." Poets converted poetry into "verbal music," so that the meaning of the words would be lost in the beauty of the sounds they produced. Mendelssohn expressed his sentiments in this quotation:

> The thoughts which are expressed to me by music that I love are not too indefinite to be put into words, but on the contrary, too definite.... If you ask me what I was thinking of when I wrote it, I would say: just the song as it stands. And if I happened to have had certain words in mind for one or another of these songs, I would never want to tell them to anyone because the same words never mean the same things to different people. Only the song can say the same thing, can arouse the same feelings in one person as in another, a feeling which is not expressed, however, by the same words.[12]

Hanslick concluded for the critics: "What *instrumental music* is unable to achieve, lies also beyond the pale of *music proper;* for it alone is pure and self-subsistent music ... the term 'music', in its true meaning, must exclude compositions in which words are set to music ... music must leave out even compositions with inscriptions, or so-called programme music. Its union with poetry, though enhancing the power of music, does not widen its limits."[13]

Modern Bards and Narrators   Modern poetry is like a new shoot on a very old tree. It is endowed with the life essence of antiquity and the freshness of newborn life. Words arranged in mellifluous sounds and framed in structures modeled after musical forms are what modern poetry consists of. Some of it shocks, stuns, and grates upon the nerves, as so much of what is new in life does. Modern poets imitate musicians and, occasionally, flirt with painters and architects. They compare their poems to the structure of paintings and architectural forms; but the abundance of musical imagery in their work is wholehearted proof that music is the favorite art of the poet, after poetry itself.

⌐

When poetry and song were united, the melody grew out of the tonal quality, the inflection, the rise and fall, the actual sound of the words. After poetry and music were separated, poets retained their traditional practice of drawing upon the musical essence of spoken words. Poems without words do not exist except as symphonic phantasies; poetry without musical qualities is only a discourse in words. Poets have also used composer's forms and replaced notes with words to capture the spirit and organization of a musical work. There are parallels in Whitman's *Leaves of Grass* to the structure of operas and symphonies. Conrad Aiken has used musical effects perhaps more fruitfully than any other poet in our age. In the titles of his poems are found "nocturnes, tone-poems, variations, dissonants and symphonies." Striving for musical effects, trying to attain "an architectural structure in poetry analogous to that of music," was his goal from the beginning of his career. "What I had from the outset been somewhat doubtfully hankering for was some way of getting contrapuntal effects in poetry— the effects of contrasting and conflicting tones and themes, a kind of underlying simultaneity in dissimilarity. It seemed to me that by using a large medium, dividing it into several main parts, and subdividing these parts into short movements in various veins and forms, this was rendered possible." [14]

T. S. Eliot wrote in *The Music of Poetry:*

My purpose here is to insist that a "musical poem" is a poem which has a musical pattern of sound and a musical pattern of the sec-ondary meanings of the words which compose it, and that these two patterns are indissoluble and one. And if you object that it is only the pure sound, apart from the sense, to which the adjective "musical" can be rightly applied, I can only reaffirm my previous assertion that the sound of a poem is as much an abstraction from the poem as is the sense. [15]

The modern novel is a relatively new art alongside poetry. Novels are about two hundred years old, poetry more than three millenniums. Novelists emerged as story tellers without any association with music such as the bards originally had. Nevertheless, novelists have used musical forms, such as the structure of the *sonata,* and techniques, such as the Leitmotiv and counterpoint, to enhance their art. Aldous

Huxley in *Point Counter Point* constructed his novel as though he were composing a fugue. He has one of his characters, an author, describe how this is accomplished.

> The musicalization of fiction .... in the construction. The changes of moods, the abrupt transitions .... the modulations, not merely from one key to another, but from mood to mood .... How? The abrupt transitions are easy enough. All you need is a sufficiency of characters and parallel, contrapuntal plots. While Jones is murdering a wife, Smith is wheeling the perambulator in the park. You alternate the themes. More interesting, the modulations and variations are also more difficult. A novelist modulates by reduplicating situations and characters. He shows several people falling in love, or dying, or praying in different ways—dissimilars solving the same problem.[16]

Thomas Mann tells, with reference particularly to *Toni Kröger,* how music shaped the structure of his novels:

> Here probably I first learned to employ music as a shaping influence in my art. The conception of epic prose-composition as a weaving of themes, as a musical complex of associations, I later on largely employed in *The Magic Mountain.* Only that there the verbal leitmotiv is no longer, as in *Buddenbrooks,* employed in the representation of form alone, but has taken on a less mechanical, more musical character, and endeavours to mirror the emotion and the idea.[17]

Novelists are limited in the ways in which they can use musical techniques; they are even more limited than the poets. Novelists can use words, as poets do, to achieve musical effects, but they are restricted to grammatical rules which poets can, to a large extent, circumvent. Novelists can attempt to follow a musical form, but such efforts have met with dubious success. A novelist who is well-versed in music is able to instruct us and refine our esthetic sensibilities. James Joyce, perhaps more than any other modern author, has fulfilled this task. But writing about music and musicians does not produce musical effects. Using a character's knowledge of music in the novel as an index of his own character can only teach us how to take the measure of a man's value in real life. Novelists can educate us about music, but they have not yet been able, by using musical laws, to produce songs and symphonies with words governed by a grammatical syntax.

"Blessed Sirens"   Words merged with music turn into musical sounds. Words give music tonal qualities that instruments are unable to do. Music and words must be suited for each other or their merger will be as esthetically disasterous as an ill-fated marriage between a man and woman who are incompatible. Music can be composed for the most intellectually powerful text as surely as there is a woman for the most unusual man in the world.

⟶

In music, sounds alone evoke from us sensations of time and space. We create the sense of time within the duration of the musical piece by ascribing a temporal quality to tones that are rhythmically arranged because they suggest movement to us. The movement is as imaginary as the sense of time it creates, but it seems very real to us while we are absorbed in the musical sounds. Music does not give us an impression of space as architecture does or describe it as words do. But music can help us expand our spatial universe in imaginary flights of fancy to most distant places.

Music and literature are vastly different arts even though they have much in common. In literature words are definite aids which help us watch the passing of time as one event follows another. Time is an illusion in music; there are no events passing before us. Aural impressions and our background of experience, not vividly descriptive words as in literature, are the "stuff" of which musical time is made.[18]

Words added to music, whether they are understood or not, turn into music which is a combination of two different sounds, and this music is richer than pure melody or prose alone could produce. An absurd libretto can be woven into a musical gem that sparkles and delights, as in a Mozart comedy. The words of a famous poem, weighed down with conflict and tension, does not pale the music of a *Lied* by Hugo Wolf. A composer who is unequal to the task of translating a powerful poem into a musical illusion will produce a boring recitative instead of a flowing song. The more powerful and complete a poem is, the greater is the challenge to translate it into music. The weaker the text, the easier will be the task. There is no text so thoroughly complete, so fully satisfying, that it cannot be coaxed to give up its literary stature and enter into wedlock with song at the direction of a great composer.

Speech and music are both sounds with varied pitch and tempo, usually expressed in phrases and repeated for emphasis. Words and music have dynamic qualities in common; they can be expressed in soft or loud tones, and in intervals that are large or small. They are less alike in the time element. Musical notes have metrical values and markings, which is not the case with words. Another difference between music and words is that one art can express simultaneous ideas and the other art cannot. When several voices sing different texts to varied melodies, the effect is not one of conceptual clarity but a jumble of tonal pleasantries.

Words inform and enlighten us about facts and events in the world. Music induces introspection, suggestions to search within ourselves for the possible meanings its sounds may have. Words added to melody do make music articulate in a conceptual sense, but they diminish its mysterious elements. Music that is only a prop for words is weak indeed, incapable of standing independently. No matter how strong, erratic, and shocking a poem or libretto may be, there is music to match it. The opera *Wozzeck,* by Alban Berg, is an excellent example of how true this is.

Music merges best with those arts that are closest to it. It blends well with words because they are both temporal and tonal. Music favors the dance; both thrive on movement and suggestion. In its primitive beginnings music consisted of intoning words in rhythm to a ceremonial dance.

Musical affects and verbal emphasis can to a limited extent be achieved in the same way. A voice rising in pitch is like a melody going up the scale, engendering tension in us; and a voice coming down from on high has a calming affect. Poetic rhythms which take on momentum are expressive of aggression and forcefulness, and rhythms that are subdued we associate with feelings of calmness.

Rhetoric and music both make use of pauses, repetition, and emphasis for dramatic affects. Words can produce different tonal qualities, such as color and texture, almost as well as these qualities can be produced in music.

VISUAL AND AUDITORY ARTS

Dance   Adults observing works of art are like children playing games that are half real. Outstretched arms are not London Bridge, and children going under other children's arms locked at length are not ships sailing down the Thames. Of all the art forms, the dance is more a game than any other. It is unreal, imaginative, and incomplete; everything about it is purely symbolic.

The same impulses that cause birds and beasts to sing and dance are biologically inherent in us. But the difference is very great between animals and us concerning these two activities. Members of the wild-life kingdom do not sing and dance according to an artificial set of rules; they simply follow laws that are instinctive—they utter sounds and make gestures that are purely impulsive and uncontrolled. Man, the rational animal, has worked out artificial schemes to express, in an organized and disciplined fashion, the irrational desires that he has inherited from his animal ancestry. He first danced and chanted simultaneously in the service of religion, and worked off his excess energy worshipping unseen gods. Dancing in the modern world is a social activity, it is no longer part of religion. Its function, however, has not changed from that when tribal chiefs guided primitive men in dance. The dance remains a form of sublimation for us. All art, to some degree, helps us discharge our biological urges in a socially acceptable way.

Music's closest sisters are poetry and dance. The dance is as old as music; poetry was born somewhat later. At the dawn of time music and dance stretched their arms and created a magic circle to symbolize for primitive man that out of the womb of the world all life emerged.

The earliest form of religion was the fertility rite with dancers weaving a magic spell and drawing their viewers into the circle to infuse them with new life. The circle lost its magic spell when words were introduced into religious worship, but it reappeared as a Christian halo symbolizing eternal life; as late as the Renaissance, poets used the circle as a metaphor to describe God's perfect world.

Since the dance originally was a religious ceremony, the music consisted of words intoned by dancing men, and the rhythmic sounds from crude drums beat by women. In most primitive societies women were not allowed to dance. This privilege was reserved for priests and gallant warriors only. Medicine men, in their role of priests, through dancing, implored the gods for rain and food, to cure the sick, and to curse their enemies. Warriors, through dancing, asked that they be strong in the hunt, and for courage to overcome fear.

Dancing was used for secular activities of a joyous nature [19] and as part of the ancient religious service for the Jews. "David danced before the Lord with all *his* might." [20] And in the Psalms, God is praised with the timbrel and dance.[21] Dancing and the playing of instruments eventually became associated with secular activities and, except for occasional dancing with the Torah around the altar on festive holidays, so it has remained to this day for most orthodox Jews.

In Greece, the dance was associated with religion and the drama. The form of the dance became highly stylized; every movement a dancer made had a symbolic significance. Greek dance was delicate and precise, but it did not remain that way. During the demise of Greece as a power and the rise of Roman might, Greek religious cults, once dignified and austere, degenerated and became esoteric. Women, dedicated to Bacchus, replaced male priests in the performance of ritualistic dances.

Roman dances at the outset emphasized the erotic and were not as stylized as those of the Greeks. It was more an art of buffoonery than dancing in the classical sense. Later on, serious and comic pantomime were developed and brought to their highest peak of perfection under Augustus, and for a while they supplanted the older drama in the imperial theater.

In the early Christian Church special provision was made in the choir for dancing and, on feast days, the bishops led the dancing. In most countries dancing became discredited as part of the service and was forbidden in the Roman Church around the fourth century. However, traces of this practice were still found in churches in Spain and Portugal as late as the eighteenth century.

In primitive religion, dancing and intonation went on simultaneously as warriors of the tribe went through certain ceremonial motions. Greece and Rome included dancing as part of their religious services, and the Jews danced in their Temples. The dance and sacred music went with each other until the Christians separated them and no longer permitted dancing to the accompaniment of sacred music. What dancing was allowed by the clergy was performed with secular music outside the church.

Dancing in the modern world is associated with youth, romance, and fine art. Once it was primarily religious, a handmaid as it were; now, it is socially acceptable, free from Christian censure except by some very orthodox groups. In former times the different classes of society each had their own social dances. Aristocrats danced with dignified physical movements; uninhibited peasants were more natural in their feelings, less mindful of propriety in their colorful dances. These folk dances have not changed very much; they have remained quite the same in enthusiasm and camaraderie. Social dancing, however, is now a more democratic activity than it used to be. People of all classes are now apt to use the same popular dance styles, and listen to the same kind of music; there is no social significance attached to their cultural habits.

As musical composition and operatic forms expanded, they provided dancers with new ideas and materials with which to develop their art. Composers created special music for the dance, provided for a ballet in the opera, and also borrowed dance music from folk sources to include as sections in their sonatas and symphonies. Dance sections in many serious works eventually were little more than reminders of popular dances of former days.

The choreography for dancing as a fine art is worked out in different fashions. A dance may be developed to follow a musical composition, or may be worked out first and then music added, or dancers may perform without musical accompaniment, creating their own rhythm and continuity with physical movement and gestures. Some dances may have no story or plot but simply graceful movements that are pleasing to the eye, as puristic in their way as an abstract painting, as impersonal as a neoclassical musical work. A dance can begin and proceed in canon form as a composer constructs a musical fugue. A dance that is too simple may be boring; it needs an element of challenge to be interesting, and this is true for all the arts. A pause and period of rest in a dance has the same dramatic affect as silence in a musical work. The sense of movement does not cease, but continues psychologically. The dance can be highly creative when a musically unaccompanied dancer produces rhythm and phantasy through the force of bodily movements alone. Yet dancing without music is the same as looking at a play without scenery. It is a paradox that however wonderful and challenging such dancing is, somehow it is not as satisfying as the dance in its original form—bodily movements accompanied by music.

Dancing as a fine art imitates aspects of life with gestures that are incomplete and unreal. A dancer's motives are not acted out to a conclusion; they are deliberately left short of a final act, like a fighter "shadow boxing." The dance, as most of the arts, is a work of make-believe, a creation of phantasy, in which whatever takes place is once removed from actual life and, yet, is modeled on it. The dancers are alive, they perform before our eyes, their physical appearance is evident. Their movements are real, the suggestions that they imply by the gestures they make spell death and love; but no one dies, and dance partners do not embrace in an actual kiss, as men and women do in real life, but it only seems as though it were taking place. The dance is performed by real people going through unreal acts as children do in play.

The dance from its inception has been the most creative of the arts. The musician and the poet create illusion with sounds, the painter with pigments, and the architect with stone; but the dancer uses nothing but his body to achieve the same affects that his fellow artists do. Up until the last century stylized dance movements symbolized some activity in experience. In our century, dancers strive to create movements with gestures that we do not associate with events in life. We are asked to judge this type of dance on the basis of its ingredients alone (ingenuity, gesture, and movement) and not to equate the dancer's actions with sentimental associations of our own. In the process of searching for new gestures and movements, that we cannot directly associate with experience, the dancer creates new dances in the same way that composers, with an ear for new sounds, add tones to the musical repertoire such as we find in electronic music at the present time.

Painting   Painting has an affinity to mathematics, as music does, but to a lesser extent. In these two arts mathematical order rests on pictorial and tonal scales; one is natural and the other is man-made. Light refracted through a prism will bring out all the colors of a rainbow. A painter can blend certain paints on his palette to produce modified shades of colors and, although his arrangement of colors may be startling on canvas, the colors themselves appear in nature. A musician must be more ingenious than a painter. Nature provides him with tones only, and he must create his own scale and key relationships. A musician produces consonant and dissonant tonal affects in the same way that a painter complements and contrasts colors. But a fundamental difference exists between them in the character of their work. A painter begins with a ready made system of colors and uses nature as his model. A musician must create his own system of musical tones and do without the physical world as a model for his art.

⤳

From white light are derived all the colors of the rainbow when light is refracted through a prism. This spectrum of colors is nature s palette. Every color that a painter uses on his canvas has the possibility of existing in nature, but the way in which he arranges his colors may be unlike anything nature portrays. The musician also uses tones that nature provides him with, but he goes much further than the painter in the creative character of his work. The musician creates new tonal combinations and arranges them in ways that resemble nothing in the external world.

Music and painting have the common characteristic of being closely allied with mathematics, even though this may not appear obvious on the surface. Tones are distinguished from each other by their pitch, and colors are separated from each other by their hue. Musical tones are arranged into intervals, and man made scales and keys. The composer can only create within the confines of the musical system he invented. Colors fall into a scale that nature made, and rest alongside each other as they do in a rainbow in the sky after a summer shower. A painter mixes colors and then contrasts them; but whatever color he produces or effect he achieves goes back to nature's mathematical arrangement of colors. The musician was left to his own resources in this world more than the painter and thus he invented a scale of his own that even nature does not have.

Our emotional reactions to a painting can to some extent approximate the feelings that we experience in listening to music. A nonrepresentational painting may be somewhat like an instrumental musical work that is nonprogrammatic. We respond to patterns of color in an abstract painting as we do to the chamber music of an instrumental quartet; whatever emotions they evoke in us are usually not immediately and directly associated with our past experience. A painting with clear representation or music with well-structured words defines and limits our response within a prescribed orbit of feeling. A painting in which physical objects are transformed into patterns of colors is like a *Lied* in which words turn into musical expression, without giving up their complete identity.

Newton's analogy between the seven colors of the spectrum and the seven notes of the diatonic scale[22] caught the imagination of composers, and some of them have used it with the utmost seriousness. Mozart considered the key of A major to be a pattern of many colors and he employed it as though it were a stained glass window breaking waves of light into many shades and hues. "Rimsky-Korsakov interpreted the keys of C, D, A, F and F-sharp (all major) as white, yellow, rosy, green, and grayish-green, respectively, while according to Scriabin they represent red, yellow, green, red, and bright blue.... Obviously the whole matter of color-sound-synaesthesia is a largely subjective experience, comparable to personal likes and dislikes of smells and flavors." [23]

We speak of the golden tones of a tenor, the silver quality in a soprano's upper range. We describe the lower rumblings of the bass voice with the blackness of Mephistophele's life. The quality of a baritone voice we associate with the sensations that sombre browns give us in a painting. Blue was the color of early jazz, music based on Negro work songs and spirituals.

Painting and music, on the surface, do not have a great deal in common. One is a visual, the other a temporal art, and both are completely autonomous. Yet, the process of creation is the same for each of them and painters and musicians imitate each other in the styles of their work. Whistler created "nocturnes" and "scherzos" in an effort to convey musical qualities in his muted colored paintings. Composers have imitated painters, as Debussy has in his impressionistic moods (*Clair de lune, La Mer*), and Moussorgsky in describing a visit to a picture gallery (*Pictures at an Exhibition*) in which an exhibition was displayed. Painters have made ingenious attempts to capture, in visual design (Mondrian's *Broadway Boogie Woogie*), the qualities that we associate with a musical work, and composers have tried to incorporate into music the impressions we receive from viewing a painting.

Musicians and painters use similar themes and models for their respective mediums. Bach composed tonal images of Christ on the Cross (*Passions*), and Rembrandt portrayed the same theme in a visual image (*Descent from the Cross*). Bach composed baroque fugues which do not represent or imitate anything definite; and a modern painter, like Kandinsky, did the same thing with colored pigments that run over a canvas and then fall into place with the sense of completeness that we get at the conclusion of a musical masterpiece. Musicians and painters can also tell stories and describe events in their own way. Program music and representational painting serve similar purposes, and yet the esthetic merit of each art would not rest on how well one imitates the other but on the intrinsic value each has in comparison to other works in its own medium.

The history of our musical instruments has been visually portrayed in paintings and sculpture. Paintings on Greek and Roman pottery give us a picture of the instruments which ancient man used to accompany himself. Illuminations which were added to decorate the

Honoré Daumier (1808–1879), *Les Comédiens de Société*. Lithograph. The Metropolitan Museum of Art, Rogers Fund, 1922.

religious chants and pages of prayer books in the Middle Ages are one of our most authentic sources for acquiring knowledge of the type of instruments that medieval man used. Paintings and mosaics have enabled music historians to correct misconceptions regarding the performance of Renaissance music. It was supposed for quite some time that Renaissance singing was entirely *a cappela* until it was established early in this century, with the help of Renaissance paintings, that this theory was untrue.

Painters and musicians are alike when they take on the task of improving the world. Daumier's caricatures and Offenbach's satire sympathetically ridicule our foibles. Hogarth and Mozart exposed our social absurdities with affection and laughter, and not with malice, as our enemies do. Painters and musicians can be bitter, and shocking too, when they are incensed to a breaking point and can no longer contain their anger. The futility of war and the horror it brings is the theme of many of George Grosz's paintings. Romantic decadence, stripped of poetic metaphors, is the substance of Berg's *Wozzeck*.

Music and painting have their differences as well as their similarities. Musical tones move in succession; one emotional experience is succeeded by another. Music cannot express something all at once. It unfolds and progresses, arouses expectations, and induces apprehension, and, finally, draws to an end. Sometimes it ends with a resolution and, at other times, it is deliberately constructed to leave us beguiled and vexed. A musical work is like a human life, without certainty how events will turn out. A painting does not cover the span of a lifetime or unwrap one experience after another. It has a beginning and end only in a physical sense. A painting does not grow from small to large, as a musical composition does, and enjoin us in living through its development of pleasant and harsh experiences.

We do not listen to music in the same way that we look at a painting. A painting gives us an immediate, a complete visual experience, unless it is the size of Picasso's *Guernica*. Colors in a painting run, weave in and out, but, if we turn away and look back, they are just as they were. Music would pass us by if we turned our back on her to listen to something else and then returned to continue the emotion that she provoked in us originally.

Drama   As more actors were added to the plot of the Greek drama the role of the chorus diminished; music and the play began to go separate ways. Playwrights stopped writing their own music and hired musicians to do it for them.

﹏

The Greek drama was a play in which the actors, in oversized painted masks, declaimed their lines in rhythmic patterns based on the inflection of words that were allotted to them, and the chorus sang and chanted, all members singing the same melody, to the accompaniment of subdued instruments. The text of the play, the unraveling of the plot was never permitted to be blurred by the musical voices or instruments. The chorus explained in song-like fashion the significance of the dramatic episodes that took place on the stage, the consequences of what would follow because of what was happening and was, by fate, so decreed. Occasional solos were sung by individual members of the chorus (who later on became members of the cast, thereby diminishing the role of the chorus) but always as part of the tragic plot and never as a pure solo in which a singer starred. In time, the chorus was given a minor role in the action of the Greek drama and eventually lost its original purpose of being a rational observer, evaluating, predicting, and passing judgment on the events that went before it.

The Romans changed the physical appearance of the Greek theater and modified the role of the chorus. Early Roman religious festivals, in addition to sacred rites, consisted of both vocal and instrumental music, dance, and dialogue. But these were not dramas in the actual sense of the word. In Roman plays the chorus did not chant as a group and act as soothsayers in the background, but became like vaudeville actors, members of the chorus taking turns to sing solos which had little to do with the action taking place. Roman dramas did not ordinarily have a religious undertone; the emphasis was on the secular, and their dramas were not unified as those of the Greeks were. Playwrights hired musicians to write songs for them to fill in gaps in the plot; Greek playwrights maintained the continuity of their plot with dramatic action alone and the singers commented on this action but did not intervene. Music had a minor role in the Roman theater; in the Greek drama it was an integral part of the play. Greek plays were usually preceded by a religious ceremony which culminated in an offering to Dionysus. The Romans did not have a procession of torch-bearers and young girls placing offerings on the altars of favorite gods before a play would start. Eventually the Roman drama degenerated into a spectacle of sensual gestures and erotic dances; a chorus chanted a text while a single actor went through a series of pantomimes.

The Christians were forbidden to attend the Roman theater or to create any plays of their own. When the liturgical drama did arrive, it was more inadvertant than planned. It grew out of the art of music tropes, a device to explain the religious service to illiterate worshippers. A parish priest would read or chant a Latin passage of the service and other members of the clergy would repeat the passage in the vernacu-lar. Soon after, priests began to dramatize their roles, cultivate their voices, and add choirs of boys to their performance. The next step consisted of adding scenery and portraying religious mysteries in dra-matic form to establish a Christian drama. But these plays eventually became highly secularized and were cast out of the Church because of "profane" music and disrespectful actors.

The composers around 1600 assumed that the Greek actors sang their parts throughout the play and that the chorus was an adjunct, not an integral part of the play. In their operas they therefore at-tempted to balance music and words, and follow the stylistic precepts that they thought prevailed in the Greek drama. But this hope was never fully realized, however valiantly several composers tried. Drama has remained secondary in importance to music in the opera from its very beginning, and the likelihood is that it will remain that way. Even Wagner's romantic desire to bring the arts together on an equal basis in the music drama did not work out esthetically. His operas were successful because of the music he composed for them and not for the librettos he wrote, or the stage sets he designed.

Opera has been maligned from many sides, and not always with justification. It has to make artistic compromises, since it is a composite of several arts. Purists do not like this. Schopenhauer went so far as to say that people who are musically illiterate take well to opera. The im-plication is that opera lovers depend on words and actions to interpret the metaphysical significance of purely musical sounds. Another accusation, which is exceedingly superficial, is that singers do not often fit their parts and create a ludicrous spectacle on the stage which destroys the illusion of watching a unified art. Beautiful singing, and singing primarily is what opera thrives on, should be the sole criterion in making a value judgment about an operatic performance; if opera has inconsistencies that cannot be overcome, they bring it that much closer to life itself in which inconsistencies predominate.

Serious opera has changed format several times since the Renaissance, and music has kept pace with it. There is no modern tragedy that music cannot wed if she wishes. In the hands of a competent composer she can enhance any text that is suitable for an opera. She can serve several masters in the theatrical household when asked to, be it for a serious or comic opera, or an operetta, or musical comedy. Whether her talents be used for opera on the legitimate stage, the radio, television, or movies, she is equal to the challenge of enhancing a text.

Architecture   Architecture is visible and tangible, music cannot be seen or felt; and yet these visual and temporal arts have common qualities that stand out prominently. Principles of balance, contrast, unity, repetition, and variety are basic qualities they possess in common. These arts are so unlike in character that their differences and similarities are more obvious than those that arise when either is compared to other fine arts. But these distinctions are not actual, they are only similes. Architectural characteristics remind us of experiences that we associate with musical ones because they arouse similar emotions in us. The rhythmic lines of an architectural motif and the rhythmic pulse of a musical work evoke a sense of movement, agitation, and repose; these emotions which are aroused by architectural lines and musical rhythms are similar but not identical. The experiences of one art remind us of experiences in another art; the arts themselves are unique.

～

One of the many intriguing beliefs that the Pythagoreans maintained was that wherever certain mathematical components existed,

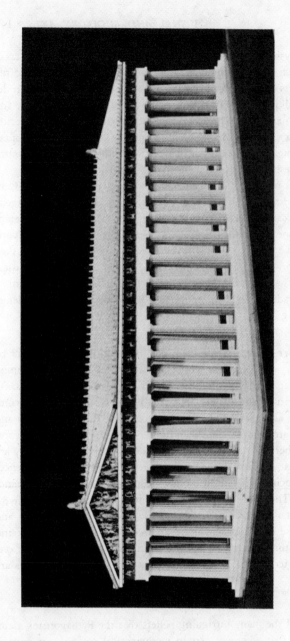

Model of the Parthenon in Athens. Fifth century B.C. The Metropolitan Museum of Art, Bequest of Levi Hale Willard, 1883.

harmony was certain to be present. These mathematical ratios and laws produced harmony, whether they were applied to music or to material things. They were as obviously present to a trained musician in a musical work as they were visually seen by an architect in the proportions of a portico or vestibule. These were the principles of mathematics which excited pleasure in a home owner because of the symmetry of the parts that prevailed in his house. Mathematical laws of consonance were responsible for producing the pleasant sounds that made music so enticing. The importance of mathematics in music and architecture is greater than it is in any of the other arts: music and architecture are also the oldest forms of artistic efforts based on principles of mathematics.

Greek architects emulated their gods perhaps more than any other mortals did. They built the Parthenon with stone and marble from nature's quarry; they called upon Phidias to plan and supervise the adornment of their edifice with statues, sculptured metropes and friezes. Greek architects and sculptors built their monuments and human forms according to standard canons of beauty that were presumed to be similar for all the arts. These laws were based on mathematical ratios and harmonies. Plato relates in the *Timaeus* that the gods created the world according to mathematical laws by using geometric forms and endowing them with order and motion through the principle of rhythm.

Harmony was the second principle which the gods followed in constructing the world. Harmony is to the gods and to their favorite, the musical bard, what proportion is to an architect. The architect must so arrange "the members of the works that both the separate parts and the whole design may harmonize in their proportions and symmetry," [24] wrote Vitruvius in the Roman era. He studied the rules of music so that he could duplicate the principles of rhythm and harmony in his buildings. He inserted a chapter on musical harmony in his treatise on architecture to guide the architects of the future.[25]

Greek music and Doric architecture were alike in mood and style; simplicity and grace were their dominant characteristics. Medieval music and Gothic cathedrals had much in common too. The *motets* of the School of Notre Dame and the Cathedral itself are pervaded by a similar spirit. Polyphony added a dimension to musical works and architecture acquired motion and contrast through contrapuntal techniques. Wölfflin discerns a musical pattern in the structure of a Gothic church. The sensation of movement and opposition of one part to another are like sensations that we associate with a musical work.[26] "... the quickening of the pulse is clearly indicated in the changed proportions of the arches and the intervals between pilasters. The intervals keep getting narrower, the arches slimmer, the speed of succession increases."[27]

Music and architecture do not progress artistically at the same rate of speed. They do not always express the spirit of their times in the same stylistic way. One is moored to the earth; and even when it thrusts masses of stone, steel, and glass upwards, its natural movement is downward. The other proceeds like a bird in flight horizontal to the earth. Yet, a jagged design in an architectural work will agitate us as a churning rhythm in a musical work does. Esthetic principles govern both these arts, however different they may be and whatever purposes they serve. Calvin S. Brown discerningly writes on this point:

Like repetition and variation, balance and contrast can be found in all the arts, on all levels, and on all scales. Perhaps the principle is most obvious in architecture, where the requirements of physical stability reinforce the aesthetic demand for a certain balance and symmetry of parts; but it is no less active in other arts. In the rhythmic structure of the temporal arts the balance and contrast between stressed and unstressed sounds is the basis of the foot and bar. In both arts the principle extends from this small beginning through balance of phrases, sections, and such larger divisions as books, acts, and movements.... with some slight reservations... precisely the same principles and the same kinds of examples are to be found in music.[28]

SUMMARY

The superiority of sight and hearing over touch, taste, and smell, with reference to esthetic problems, first appears in the writings of Plato and Aristotle. St. Augustine and St. Thomas compared the gradations of perfection among the senses to the different kinds of knowledge that human beings can develop under guidance. St. Thomas summed up the Christian view: sight and hearing appeal to reason and therefore are of a higher order than the other three senses. "We speak of beautiful sights and sounds but do not give the name of beauty to the objects of other senses, such as tastes or smells." Schopenhauer even suggested that, as far as the seven arts are concerned, the sense of hearing is above that of seeing in importance. Plastic and literary works reveal the "eternal forms of the world"; in music the universal *will* is immediately rendered, it "speaks" to us directly. In his classification of higher and lower senses as they refer to esthetic experience, touch is third, the sense of smell comes next, and taste is the lowest of the five.

Homer implied in the *Odyssey* that the poet-musician and not the religious priest had influence or could intercede with the gods. The poet-musicians were taught their art by the gods; the priests, alas, were not. Poetry and music, "blest pair of sirens," were inseparable sisters to the early Greeks. Aristophanes was dismayed because they were becoming separated, each going its own way. He feared that bards would become either proficient technicians on instruments or orators, instead of poets.

Aristophanes' fears were borne out. Musicians vied with each other to see who could add more strings to the lyre, and introduce novel sounds. Some musicians even learned how to produce tones on their instruments that imitated the sounds of words. Since bards no longer confined accompaniments to the style of the poem, they found that rhythms could be more lively and vivacious than those the Greeks had known before. But in time the once-inspired musician strayed so far from his true mission that he became a competing technician and was no longer a minister of the gods. Horace wrote that in Caesar's reign the sons of Orpheus no longer sang sweet songs but strained their throats at Roman festivals to win a paltry prize, sometimes "a shaggy goat."

Man is the only animal, wrote Aristotle, with the power of speech. Language he created himself so that he could express his ideas with the gift that nature gave him. Now man is at the mercy of the language he invented. He thinks in terms of words, sentences, and rules of grammar which act like binders on the imagination. His experience is limited to what language can express. There is no way to break the bounds in which words hold him except, when the imagination demands it, to use rules of language that are different from those to which he is accustomed. But most of us are held fast and cannot free ourselves from the rules of language, the limitations of logic, of speech, and literary composition. The combined strength of grammatical rules and principles of proof which logicians use to test whether what we are saying is valid, prohibits us from certain kinds of experience and knowledge. It is a paradox of our making that we created words and language to express ourselves and now we are confined and even hindered by them in our thinking and practical experience.

Man's first serious dancing was in religious ceremonies. Eventually the dance developed into a secular activity and, in time, into a fine art. Dance and music were inseparable from the beginning and up until now the dancer was dependent on the musician even though his art is an autonomous one. A dancer gives physical embodiment to the imagery a musical work suggests to him. He cannot imitate the music with physical gestures, for that would be an impossibility. He can only act out the music as he conceives it. The dancer uses the musician's score, just as the painter uses nature as his model, to create a visual image of his own.

Painting and music ordinarily serve a similar purpose in our lives as forms of deception or phantasy, and at times they can even help us in a practical way in industry and medicine. There is an ancient story that Zeuxis painted grapes that looked so real that the birds tried to eat them. The Etruscans attracted birds into their nets by using music that sounded like their own songs. In the modern world painting and music still perform a function of deception; but no one is hurt or led astray, even when these arts provide us with flights of fancy into rarefied atmospheres.

Music and the dance were integrally united with the plot in Greek tragedy, but this was not so in Roman drama. Watching a single actor playing the part of a buffoon became the Roman's idea of a well-spent afternoon in the theater. Music, dancing, and acting had very little in common with each other as far as a unified work of art, in the classical sense, was concerned. The art of well-integrated drama died in Rome. Comedy not only survived but it actually thrived up until the Catholic Church acquired so much power that it was able to close the Roman theaters altogether.

Certain esthetic principles are basic to all the arts, such as balance and contrast, unity and variety. The different parts or aspects of a work of art must be consistent with and relevant to each other and be in keeping with its form and style. This may not be obvious on the surface, but the principles are present nevertheless. These artistic principles are more evident when music and architecture are compared because they contrast with each other so sharply that they display their differences and similarities more obviously than when either is compared to any of the other arts.

NOTES

[1] *Greater Hippias*. 298. Plato has Socrates say that by the beautiful "I do not mean all pleasures but that which makes us feel joy through hearing and sight." Aristotle in *Problems*, Bk. XIX. 29. 919b: "Why do rhythms and tunes, which after all are only voice, resemble moral characters, whereas savours do not, nor yet colours and odours? Is it because they are movements, as actions also are?"

[2] *See* Thomas Munro, *The Arts and Their Interrelations* (New York: The Liberal Arts Press, 1949), pp. 136-139.

[3] D. W. Prall, *Aesthetic Judgment* (New York: Thomas Y. Crowell Company, 1929), pp. 62-63.

[4] Meyer Schapiro, "Style" in A. L. Kroeber, *Anthropology Today* (Chicago: University of Chicago Press, 1953), p. 295. ". . . the various arts have different roles in the culture and social life of a time and express in their content as well as style different interests and values. The dominant outlook of a time . . .does not affect all the arts in the same degree, nor are all the arts equally capable of expressing the same outlook. Special conditions within an art are often strong enough to determine a deviant expression."

[5] Plato *Republic*, Bk. III. 398.

[6] Plato *Laws* [*See* footnote [12], Chapter III].

[7] Plato *Laws,* Bk. II. 669. "For when there are no words, it is very difficult to recognize the meaning of the harmony and rhythm, or to see that any worthy object is imitated by them."

[8] Patr. Lat. xxxvij, 1272 in Peter Wagner, *Introduction to the Gregorian Melodies,* trans. Agnes Orme and E. G. P. Wyatt (2d ed.; London: Printed for The Plainsong and Mediaeval Music Society, 1901), Part I, p. 32. "He who sings a *jubilus,* speaks no words, but it is a song of joy without words; it is the voice of a heart dissolved in joy, which tries as far as possible to express the feeling, even if it does not understand the meaning. When a man rejoices in his jubilation, he passes from some sounds which do not belong to speech and have no particular meaning, to exulting without words; so that it seems that he rejoices indeed, but that his joy is too great to put into words."

[9] Alfred Einstein, *Gluck* (London: J. M. Dent & Sons, Ltd., 1936), p. 98.

[10] Schopenhauer, *The World as Idea* (New York: The Modern Library, Inc., 1928),p. 207.

[11] Schopenhauer, *The World As Will And Idea,* III, trans. Haldane and Kemp (London: Kegan Paul, Trench, Trübner & Co., Ltd., 1896), p. 233.

[12] Felix Mendelssohn, *Letters,* ed. G. Selden-Goth (New York: Pantheon Books, Inc., 1945), p. 314.

[13] Eduard Hanslick, *The Beautiful in Music,* trans. Gustav Cohen (London: Novello & Co., Ltd., 1891), pp. 44-45.

[14] Calvin S. Brown, *Music and Literature* (Athens, Georgia: University of Georgia Press, 1948), p. 202.

[15] T. S. Eliot, *The Music of Poetry* (Glasgow: Jackson, Son & Co., 1942), p. 19.

[16] Aldous Huxley, *Point Counter Point* (New York: Harper & Row, Publishers, 1928), pp. 293-294.

[17] *Stories of Three Decades,* trans. H. T. Lowe-Porter (New York: Alfred A. Knopf, Inc., 1946), p. vi.

[18] *See* Susanne K. Langer, *Feeling and Form* (New York: Charles Scribner's Sons, 1953), pp. 134-138.

[19] I Samuel. 18:6. "... the women came out of all cities of Israel singing and dancing, to meet king Saul, with tabrets, with joy."

[20] II Samuel. 6:14.

[21] Psalm. 149:3. "Let them praise his name in the dance: let them sing praises unto him with the timbrel and harp."

[22] Sir Isaac Newton, *Optics,* Bk. I, Part II, Prop. 3.

[23] Willi Apel, *Harvard Dictionary of Music* (Cambridge, Mass.: Harvard University Press, 1945), p. 161.

[24] Vitruvius, *On Architecture,* trans. Morris Hicky Morgan (Cambridge, Mass.: Harvard University Press, 1914), Bk. III, [Chap. I], p. 75.

[25] *Ibid.,* Bk. V [Chap. IV].

[26] Walt Whitman, *Poems* (New York: The Modern Library, Inc., 1921), [*Leaves of Grass*], p. 186.

*All Architecture is what you do to it when you look upon it
(Did you think it was in the white or grey stone? or the lines
of the arches and cornices?)
All music is what awakes from you when you are reminded
by the instruments,
It is not the violins and the cornets, it is not the oboe nor the
beating drums, . . .*

[27] Rudolf Arnheim, *Art and Visual Perception* (Berkeley: University of California Press, 1954), p. 347.

[28] Calvin S. Brown, *op. cit.,* p. 114.

CHAPTER V

THE RELATIONSHIP of MUSIC to SCIENCE

METAPHYSICS

The Greeks had two metaphysical theories about the origin of music. One was theological and the other philosophical; both had strong poetic overtones. The older belief was that the gods created all musical instruments but that the Muses created beautiful singing and chose Orpheus as their earthly representative. The later belief, which evolved out of the researches of the philosopher and scientist Pythagoras, was that music emanated from the harmony of the spheres. The Pythagorean theory was so fascinating and convincing that, as late as the Age of Enlightenment, Kepler gave "scientific" reasons and Father Mersenne offered theological arguments that there is a metaphysical relationship between music and astronomy.

⌣

A poetic allegory, which ancient bards once created, became the explanation that the Greek philosophers used to account for the status of man in the world. Homeric minstrels sang of man's frailty and destiny; even the gods could not intervene to save Achilles from destruction. Hesiod's priests chanted: the gods are supreme; they can intervene in human events; they do so when they please. But man himself, Homer and Hesiod concurred, stands to the world as a child to a parent, each child sharing the spiritual soul and physical appearance of his parents.

The first organized school of philosophers, the Pythagoreans, put the poet's fancy to an empirical test based on ancient mathematics and physics. They verified, in their esoteric way, that the human soul and the universal soul are united and that man's thoughts and actions are imitations of the thoughts and actions of divinities in heaven. Philosophers, as different as Democritus and Plato, later added that the bard, poet-musician, was chosen by the gods to reveal to man in a rapturous moment that the world is a harmony and all is one.

This harmony which binds the human soul to the soul of the world is made plain to us, even more firmly than in logic and science, by the art forms themselves. Of all the art forms which exist, music is the most faithful reproduction of the laws of nature; its rhythmic character more accurately approximates the rhythm and order in the world than all the arts which men make. We discern these qualities in the art of song only because we have an affinity for rhythm and order and logic in our souls. Otherwise we would respond to the ways of nature like irrational animals, and remain impervious to our calling.

The Pythagoreans believed that natural law functions according to uncompromising principles. The same laws that govern the rhythmic movement of the stars and space them apart also govern rhythm and tonal relationships in music. The octave, fifth, and fourth are inherently consonant because they are spaced on the strings of the lyre as the stars are arranged to each other in the heavens. Rhythm in music is akin to the grace and measured movement of the celestial bodies; never are the stars erratic and frivolous in their ways. "Numbers are the whole Heavens" and the numbers that explain the heavens also explain the earth.[1] But one number is the source of life for all the other numbers—it is the secret of the universe. Mathematics is the key to understanding the universe and all that nature embraces, for nature and the world were synonymous to the Pythagoreans. But the number of numbers ceases to be pure mathematics; it is a metaphysical cause guiding the universe, a number of such immeasurable mystery that it transcends all understanding. Music too is mathematically constructed; but in listening to music, as in pondering the mysteries of the physical world, we intuit the existence of some power which exceeds mathematics in importance, a revelation of an ultimate metaphysical cause.

Plato's theory of music is essentially the same as that of the Pythagoreans, but in Platonic metaphysics numbers are replaced by Ideas. Music may be mathematically constructed, but it is an imitation of the moral order in the world. The worth of music can be measured only by a moral rule based on metaphysical laws of order and truth as they exist in the realm of Ideas. Plato's musical views are governed by transcendental principles, a metaphysics of eternal values. Numbers are only symbols once removed from the Ideal World.

In the philosophy of Aristotle the gods replace Platonic Ideas, and Pythagorean numbers. Nothing exists without a purpose, everything that comes into being does so to serve some divine end. The gods made us according to their will and they would not have made us as we are if they had not wanted to. Each man is created for the purpose of performing a specific task. Thus it is that one man is a physician and another a musician, one man is a philosopher and another a soldier. Music is not mathematics alone, or a faithful copy of nature; it has a metaphysical origin like everything else in the world.

The Greek atomists scoffed at the popular belief of the average Greek that gods intervene in human affairs or make arrangements for divine music to be brought to man. Gods are figments of the imagination and we are victimized by the very fancies we created. This was the view of the more ardent ancient materialists. These theories were softened by Lucretius for Roman consumption, but even in his theories the gods and music have a naturalistic basis and not a transcendental origin. Each man's esthetics of music stems from his metaphysical conception of the world, and Greeks and Romans were as divided among themselves and intolerant of each other's philosophical positions as we are among ourselves. The pleas of the "empirics," as Plato derisively called them, not to read into music what does not properly belong to it, fell on deaf ears for Greek and Roman alike. Men are given to wonder and fear throughout their entire existence. They have created many things, both physical and imaginative, and read into their own creations wonderous things. Ancient men endowed their gods with their own attributes and those they would like to have; and, according to the materialists, they also created music and read into it their own psychic needs, just as they did when they created the gods. How futile it all is, mused the cynic; man can do without gods and music, they are both useless things.

The Romans created gods of their own, fashioned more after the poems of Homer than Hesiod's theogony. The fondness of the Greeks for mysticism turned into Roman naturalism. The preoccupation of the Greeks with pure mathematics gave way, in the Roman world, to the practical application of mathematics to material things. The philosopher Boethius evolved a theory of music that was a mixture of Plato and Aristotle, poetic myth and ancient science, which he reconciled as a Roman would. The Romans were not attracted to metaphysical abstraction; in utility and function lay their strength for success. The hidden power of music as a mental discipline and a molder of character was accepted as a truism by the Roman philosopher but not the Roman engineer. The fact that music could soothe the mind and relieve the body of fatigue and sickness was more significant to the average Roman than any theorizing about the origin of music.

Aristotle claimed that music was a gratuitous gift from the gods of Greece. Music was created by man, the gods were only the Muses, was the Roman belief. Music, like bridges and roads, had no counterpart in the heavens. Neither was it modeled after Ideal archetypes, nor formalized mathematics. The Roman did not ask what is beyond mathematics. Is it some vague metaphysical cause? What interested the Roman primarily was the practical applications to which mathematics could be put.

When Solomon married Pharaoh's daughter, she brought a thousand instruments of assorted types with her as a gift to the Jewish people. Some of the instruments that the Egyptians used in their own religious services were used by the Jews in arranging the sacred music in Solomon's magnificent Temple. The Egyptians defended the moral worth of their music, according to Herodotus, with the same metaphysical reasons that the Jews and Greeks used. All three believed in the existence of a supernatural realm from which life emanated. The Egyptians and Greeks had a polytheistic religion, the Jews a monotheistic one. Theologies based on idealistic beliefs, with perhaps some exceptions, seem to share a common view of music no matter how they differ among themselves. This common belief is that wherever gods reign, be they one or many, the physical character of music is indeed based on mechanics and explained by mathematics, but its origin is in the heavens.

The Christians placed Aristotle's God in the Platonic realm of Ideas. The God of Christendom was made the ruler over a finite Aristotelian world in the same way that the Pythagorean number or numbers was the source of mysterious life and ruler of all the other numbers in its command. The Guardian of Guardians in the Platonic Republic and the God of Gods in Christian theology are like model citizens in comparison to the Angelic Hosts. In music, as in theology, the Christians borrowed from the Greeks and Jews and then qualified what they borrowed to fit in with their own beliefs. Augustine's *De Musica* reads like a treatise of a Pythagorean who was converted to Christ. Music is numbers, numbers are symbols, and symbols lead us to an understanding of God's harmonious world. The mechanics of music, like the mechanics of the physical world, are ample evidence of God's handiwork, so wonderful are they to behold, one to the ear the other to the eye. Christian metaphysics and theology cannot be separated, and so music and morality must be accepted as coming from a higher source, the source from whence all that is good emanates.

How the Catholics Christianized the writings of the Greeks is an old story. St. Augustine carried on the tradition of Plato; St. Thomas, in the late Middle Ages, that of Aristotle. Scholars of such rarity as Scotus Erigena, who could read the ancients in Greek, in the ninth century adapted the picturesque theory of the harmony of the spheres to the theology of his day. In his *Divisione Naturae:*

. . . the beauty of the whole universe of similar and dissimilar things has been built up in a wonderful harmony from diverse *genera* and various forms in different arrangements of substances and accidents, compacted into an ineffable unity. For an organized melody composed of diverse qualities and quantities of voices is discerned, note by note individually, to be separated by different proportions of high and low, yet they are mutually co-adapted in accordance with established and rational rules of the art of music . . . rendering a natural sweetness.[2]

With the revival of Greek scholarship during the Renaissance, a humanistic strain began to make itself felt in learning and the arts. Music, as every other art, was assumed to be governed by common laws. The canons of beauty with which a composer created a musical work were identical with the laws that an architect and a sculptor used to create a cathedral or a monument to a saint. These laws were based on mathematical norms and not on theology disguised as metaphysical principles. The Catholic Church eventually withdrew from many facets of Renaissance life, in which naturalism was replacing supernaturalism. Behind thick walls, that housed nuns and priests, the purity of Catholic belief remained firm. The sanctity of liturgical music had to be preserved until the outer world would be freed from its musical heresy. The admonitions of Augustine regarding music would then hold sway once more and the observation of Thomas, that Christ and music are one, would be recalled again.

In order to do away with the ritual of the Catholic service the Protestants downgraded the importance of music in worship as a partial means of achieving their purpose. Calvin went beyond Luther's intentions to such an extent that a composer like Bach felt, later on, that he had a God-given mission to beautify the Protestant service with more colorful music than it had. But Protestant orthodoxy gave little ground. The loyalty with which they kept faith in their religious beliefs carried over into all their worldly activities. Music had little place in their worship and so it had little place in their lives. Music had no profound theological overtones and so it had no metaphysical status in their thinking. Music was something nebulous, a source of pleasure and an irritant. It was not worthy of serious thought and might consume time taken from more serious matters. If music had any serious significance, the Bible would have said so.

Philosophic rationalism emphasized mathematics as a healthy antidote to the theological dogmatism with which the Catholics and

Protestants tried to destroy each other. Descartes and Leibniz gave mathematics the task of bolstering their religious notions; that of itself was revolutionary in a world in which faith and not reason was the beginning of any scholarly discussion. Francis Bacon and Thomas Hobbes were of sterner stuff, declaring that empiricism was a more trustworthy interpretation of the world than any fanciful attempt to argue that God exists according to the ontological argument. Rationalism is more satisfying esthetically than empiricism; for in a rationalistic system nothing is irrelevant to anything else in it, and it is, therefore, like a mental work of art. Descartes and Leibniz had much to say about music and the place that it had in the world. In the works of Bacon and Hobbes there is little reference made to music and, where there is, it is considered as a source of "agitation" which affects the nervous system and should be judged solely by the pleasure or pain it affords.

Descartes began as the empiricists did, but he would not allow facts to fall where they would. Our musical reactions begin as sensations, he declared, in response to external rhythms and tonal sounds. These sensations affect the body, as sensations will, in a pleasurable or negative way. Consonant tones please us and dissonant tones are usually displeasing. Mathematics accounts for consonance and dissonance in music, as it does in the ordered regularity or disorder of human physiology. Proper musical ratios, and the synchronized functions of the body produce consonance in one and order in the other, in the same way as proportion and the arrangement of parts in an architectural structure produce a harmonious balance. But now Descartes, goes beyond the empiricists with the metaphysical belief that on the strength of what he has already established as knowledge there is a reasonable assumption that a correlation exists between the rhythm of music and the rhythm of the soul. The *doctrine of affections* which musicians use to evoke certain moods with certain music, like begetting like, explicitly demonstrates what is implicit in mathematics itself. Mathematics is subject to laws emanating from God, otherwise how could it govern the soul as well as the body of man.

"Nature must always be explained mathematically and mechanically," wrote Leibniz, "provided it is remembered that the very principles or laws of mechanics or of force do not depend on mathematical extension alone, but on certain metaphysical reasons." [3] Music too, continued Leibniz, must be explained according to mathematical and physical laws but, like nature, music has its source in the same ultimate metaphysical "cause" by which God provides us with a plan for the best of all possible worlds. Just as teleology reigns supreme in God's magnificent world, so music has its purpose for being, even if this purpose evades us. Intuition, more than reason and logic, will unfold this truth to us. We would no more say that God's perfect world is wholly reflected in one spiritual monad than we would insist that one pleasant sound makes music. Rhythms and tones, like monads, achieve the purpose God proposed for the best of all possible worlds when their individual potentialities are fully realized and they emerge as a complete and self-sufficient formal work. Whether this formal product be the world itself or a musical composition, the laws of God are the same for both. Leibniz spiritualized the atoms of Democritus and arranged them into a hierarchy. He re-created the world as Plato had in the *Timaeus,* but he did it more imaginatively. He repeated Aristotle's theory that form is only matter realized and that the purpose of art is to serve a useful end. He converted the naturalistic world of Spinoza into an idealistic one, thus making a novel contribution of his own, both in philosophy and mathematics. The art of music he endowed with a supernatural origin and a divine purpose, more so than any other philosopher since the time of the Greeks.

"In the charm and mental movement produced by Music, Mathematics has certainly not the slightest share," wrote Immanuel Kant in his *Critique of Judgement.* Mathematics is only the indispensable condition for arranging tonalities into harmonious sounds and holding the musical form together. But music is after all, especially music without words, phantasy which has no place in the "kingdom of ends." Pure music is like decorative relief on the wallpaper of a room, a purely sensual attraction. A rational man must go beyond mere sensory gratification in appraising music. There are universal predicates which must be applied in evaluating music, predicates based on esthetic judgments that all men share in common. Although music is mathematical and affects each man differently, its final value must rest on a universal judgment. We determine the esthetic value of music on the grounds of reason alone. All men by nature possess an innate capacity to discern what the beautiful is. If a man can share his concept of beauty with all other men in the world, he has overcome his subjectivity and achieved universality in his judgment.[4]

God is the state marching through history [5] in the totalitarian world that Hegel created. God is the spirit which directs the everchanging forms the arts must take as expressions of the level of the cultural development of the state. The inevitable laws which proceed with unfailing logic and determinism are just as evident in the history of music as they are in the history of the state. The dialectical process is all-embracing, nothing can escape its purposeful direction. Music emerges from a simple chant to a complex symphony as a primitive state rises to a civilized one—both by divine design.

The first musical forms came into existence, according to Hegelian logic, to fulfill a need in the development of man and the state. No sooner did this elementary musical form make its appearance, in a world that cannot stand still, than it partially outlived the purpose for which it arrived. A static musical form in a dynamic world creates a contradiction between the two. A new form must emerge to comply with the changing needs which the first form could not fully fill and, even then, the process of movement does not cease or the struggle between static forms and dynamic change come to an end. The old form and new form are synthesized into a third form, by man, which embodies the salient features of its predecessors and also contains new features expressive of a cultural need. This new form soon becomes an old form and so the story never ends. The Hegelian dialectic is progressional and neverending. One musical ideal will be replaced by another, more perfect than the one that preceded it and less perfect than the one that must follow it. This is the law of God.

Reason strained beyond its proper limits will either erupt into ugly thoughts or turn into muted feelings of disenchantment with the world. Rationalism will turn into irrationalism when logic is pushed to a breaking point in striving for the Absolute, as Hegel so ably did. Schopenhauer's philosophy is the inevitable pessimism that follows overcertainty; there is nothing unusual in this turn of events, it is as old as Ecclesiastes, and older even than that.

Schopenhauer pointed out that music is not God calling from on high but the *will* in every one of us chanting a litany of despair.

In its struggle with the other voices in a musical work which would destroy it if they could so that they might each be heard as individual voices, a musical melody is like a human life striving to survive. Escape and negation are forms of salvation; music can aid in both. Through music we can achieve a union with the universal *will* and thus be released from ourselves.[6] In all such mystical unions individuality disappears, the personal *will* is made will-less, desire ceases to exist. As soon as the magic spell is broken, for music gives only periodic relief, the world of torment reappears, the world of hopeless despair.

Science has demolished the poetic image of the harmony of the spheres and left us to our own resources in this century. The stars that we have added to the collection already in the sky are characteristic of man, the artist, improving the world, no matter under what label he creates. Ancient notions of celestial bodies producing divine harmonies as they move through the heavens is as much a myth as the belief which persists even in our day, that musical consonance and dissonance follow ordained mathematical laws.

Metaphysics, in the traditional sense, is no longer applicable in our automated world. Schools of taste, rules of politics, and straightforward religious decrees have replaced such allegories as the morning stars singing together with doctrines of their own. Esthetic criteria are not referred to as metaphysical[7] any longer, except by some few scholars of Maritain's bent, and they are small in number compared to the other estheticians in the world. Instead of "integrity, proportion, and clarity" we now speak of "significant form." In place of the "harmony of the spheres," we now use such a term as "ideologically sound." We have replaced the supernatural association with metaphysics with a naturalistic one and given it a different name.

MATHEMATICS

The Romans were more practical people than the Greeks. They considered music a mathematical means to give both sensual delight and to steel the mind. The Greek conception of bards as intermediaries between gods and man was too fanciful for the Romans to accept. Music was man made. It had no supernatural overtones. From the early training of Roman children to advanced studies in English universities in the late Renaissance, music and mathematics went hand in hand as educational disciplines.

᠆

Musicians and mathematicians have much in common, however their temperaments differ. They have been in alliance with each other since ancient times. Greek mathematicians provided the musician with the necessary knowledge that was required to add additional strings to the lyre and to improve the flute. They worked out ratios between intervals and arranged the modes on which our own music is based. Now mathematicians are building machines that produce electronic music.

The first important mathematicians to concern themselves with music were the Pythagoreans. The school split after the death of Pythagoras, each group going off in a different direction. One group was the "empirics" who were interested mainly in arithmetic problems and in investigating physical phenomena, such as the relationship of tonal sounds to each other, and in the construction of musical instruments. The other group spent their energies studying the galaxies and drawing moral analogies between the rotating bodies in the skies with the behavior of the human soul and musical harmonies.

Plato, originally a poet, never strayed too far from his first love. He may have had harsh things to say about the poet's fancy and erratic temperament, but he was hardly any kinder to empirically minded philosophers who could not see that there was an Ideal realm beyond atoms, matter, and mathematics. Plato's *Timaeus* was a poetic conception of a world in which mathematics and God go hand in hand, paving the way for a perfectly constructed geometric Ideal. Mathematicians "who tease and torture the strings and rack them on the pegs of the instrument" give too much importance to the senses. They neglect the intellect and intuition with their emphasis on numbers only. Plato had little in common with those Pythagoreans who "investigate the numbers of the harmonies which are heard, but they never attain to problems—that is to say, they never reach the natural harmonies of number, or reflect why some numbers are harmonious and others not." [8] Plato's sympathies were with the Pythagorean faction that envisioned in number and ratio a moral significance that transcends research. Music, in essence, he maintained, is modeled after laws that cannot be discerned through physics and numbers alone.

The "empirics" had their champion too, Archytas of Tarentum, a remarkable ruler, almost the equal of Pericles, a mathematician who was a worthy rival of Euclid. A letter to him from Plato has survived, but his mathematical writings, unlike Euclid's, have come down to us only in fragments. He paid more attention to music than any of the other members of his Pythagorean group. He did not hold that numbers contain a "religious or magical admixture." "The rational attributes of Number and Harmony are sufficiently wonderful in themselves." [9] Plato's admiration for him was not lessened by this empirical attitude toward music or by his democratic practices as a ruler of a Greek state. Perhaps Archytas was a more exact model of the philosopher-king than Dionysius who could not master geometry, even under Plato's guidance.

Aristotle described the Pythagoreans in the *Metaphysics:* "They saw that the modifications and the ratios of the musical scales were expressible in numbers;—since, then, all other things seemed in their whole nature to be modelled on numbers, and numbers seemed to be the first things in the whole of nature, they supposed the elements of numbers to be the elements of all things, and the whole heaven to be a musical scale and a number." [10]

Aristotle considered the Pythagorean theory of the harmony of the spheres equal in credulity to an old wives' tale. The magic with which they clothed numbers he dismissed as an import from the East that had already lingered much too long in Greece. He concurred that rhythm and melody have moral value because they can mold the malleable soul of a child for better or worse by affecting the rhythm of the soul itself. But musical modes do not have any archetypes in the heavens; this is one more Pythagorean myth which Plato honors, but there is no evidence for it. [11] Aristotle joined the side of the "empirics" as his mentor, Plato, originally labeled them. Both philosophers are excellent examples of poet and scientist following separate

Pythagorean schools—schools which originally began with Pythagoras, a religious mystic, asking: "What is the meaning of existence?"

In the *Problems,* after experimenting with pitch and vibration, Aristotle reported his own findings and listed conclusions which are wholly mathematical in character. "In the reed-pipe an accord in the octave is obtained by doubling the length, and this is how flute-makers produce it. Similarly they obtain a fifth by means of a length in the ratio of 3 to 2, ... and a fourth by means of a length in the ratio of 4 to 3." [12] The shriller notes are caused by more frequent impacts upon the air and "strings which are tightly stretched give a shriller note, for their movement is quicker." [13]

One of our most authentic records of music in ancient Greece is *Harmonics,* a book by Aristoxenus of inestimable importance to historian and theorist. Philosophers, observed Aristoxenus, read too much into musical modes and rhythms. He could not find the obvious affinity between music and morality of which Plato was so certain. Mathematicians who treat music altogether as a science of acoustics go to the other extreme, in his estimation. There is more to the art of song than "asserting that height and depth of pitch consist in certain numerical relations and relative rates of vibration." Mathematicians, such as the empirical Pythagoreans, tend to concern themselves with studying simple tones only, dispense with reason in their research, and confine "themselves to isolated dogmatic statements." Our method, concludes Aristoxenus, "rests in the last resort on an appeal to the two faculties of hearing and intellect. By the former we judge the magnitudes of the intervals, by the latter we contemplate the function of the notes." [14] Aristoxenus, a student of Aristotle, avoided the extreme views of the "empirics" and the mystics. His own position is a shining example of the Golden Mean applied to the art of music.

In the Greco-Roman era a mathematician named Ptolemy accomplished for astronomy what Euclid had achieved for geometry. Ptolemy began by synthesizing the theories of his predecessors and eventually became the best informed astronomer of the Greco-Roman age. He also had a lively interest in music and did quite a bit to improve its physical structure, more than anyone else since the death of Aristoxenus. With this ideal combination of astronomer and musician he was in a most favorable position to answer the enigma: Does the harmony of the spheres exist? But there is no evidence that can be gleaned from his writings that a correlation between music and the stars could be given any credence; if anything, the obverse is true. Ptolemy noted that music and astronomy have little in common except when compared as poetic metaphors, and, at that, with considerable license. If he had any idea that the colorful myth of the harmony of the spheres would soon disappear because of his learned pronouncement, he was mistaken indeed. In ensuing centuries the theory of the harmony of the spheres repeatedly appeared in scholarly treatises of scientists and philosophers, not as often, however, as in poetry. Even in the findings of Kepler, more than a thousand years later, allusions to music and the stars are numerous, as though there were an affinity between them.

The close bond between music and mathematics is not limited to the fine arts alone. Music and mathematics have had a traditional courtship in the liberal arts as well. In Greek education music was considered a form of mental discipline—disguised mathematics—to be studied prior to and in preparation for philosophical dialectic. During the Roman era, Boethius and his contemporary, Cassiodorus, included the study of music in the educational quadrivium which also consisted of arithmetic, astronomy, and geometry.

The capabilities, inherent in music, to steel youthful minds and induce disciplined patterns of mathematical thought were taken seriously by the Greeks and Romans. A student exposed to the proper kind of music could acquire commendable habits and qualities of thought. Music, a science of numbers, could encourage straight thinking and a precise use of logic. A musical work follows a systematic pattern. It could therefore be suggestive of how to follow an argument with consistency to a satisfying conclusion. Music demands concentration from its listener. Thus powers of absorption and tenacity can be developed, and at that, in a most delightful way. Music has eloquence of expression, greater than any other art, from which a student's rhetorical abilities could well profit.

The early Fathers of the Catholic Church were of one mind that God had given us the gift of song so that children would learn the words of the psalms more easily. In the late Middle Ages the Franciscan monk, Roger Bacon, wrote: "...children learn mathematical truths better and more quickly, as is manifest in singing."[15] The educational value of music was used to full advantage by the ancients and Christians in the belief that it could help a child master a difficult chore with a minimum of effort.

During the Renaissance, Cardinal Cusa, a more astute mathematician than Bacon, noted that lower animals cannot learn music because they do not have a mathematical faculty as rational men possess. A child can, therefore, profit from studying music, but lower animals could never be taught to measure intervals or effect a transfer between the mathematical order in music and their irrational selves. Mathematics and music are of extreme importance in molding the mind of a child. The mathematical order, inherent in music, acts like a magnet drawing from the child a love for balance and wisdom without the child being consciously aware of it.

During the Renaissance, the mathematician was the patron saint, not of the musician alone but also of the artist. Even before the fall of Constantinople, scholars fleeing from the Near East brought writings of Plato and Aristotle, uncensored and in their original purity, to the Florentine Academy which was begun by the Medicis. Up until then European men of letters had been acquainted with versions of the Greek writings that had been censored for the needs of the Church and translated into Latin. Now, with faithful copies of what the ancients wrote before them, their reverence for the Greeks spilled over into their art and education. Every creative artist, whatever his medium, turned to the philosopher and the mathematician imploring for the canons of beauty that existed in ancient Greece.

In the liberal arts, the courtship of music and mathematics developed into a marriage in English universities during the medieval and Renaissance periods. At Oxford, students preparing for a higher degree were permitted to take their examination on Boethius' theories of music under the supervision of a mathematics instructor. In Cambridge, students preparing for the Master's degree were required to spend three years studying arithmetic and music. On occasion a lecturer in mathematics was hired to teach music along with advanced mathematics.[16]

Mathematicians are able to break down into measure and figure what musicians do intuitively. Aristoxenus for the Greeks, and Boethius for the Romans, did precisely this, just as Pythagoras had before them. The relationship is not, however, one-sided. Mathematicians with their findings have enlarged the physical world of music in which the musicians can wander. But, in an ever so rare musician song and number are merged in one, as in the great Zarlino, man of the Renaissance, after whose theories Descartes fashioned his own book on music. Rameau, one of the major contributors to our modern system of harmony, was both a gifted and accomplished composer and a perceptive writer about the relationship of music to mathematics. He expressed the view that music is a science which "can scarcely be known to us without the help of mathematics." The fugues of Johann Sebastian Bach are the equivalent of a monument by Vitruvius in which mathematics and perception are joined and cannot be separated by ordinary logic.

The measured thought of eighteenth century philosophical rationalism had its influence on the era of musical classicism. In the following century the philosophy of both Schopenhauer and Nietzsche turned *voluntaristic,* and music became romantic. Music is not an unconscious process of counting numbers, but the expression of desire, countered Schopenhauer, in refuting Leibnitz's best of all possible worlds. Musicians like Wagner and Berlioz, idols of the romantic age, broke the rules of mathematically contained classical forms, bringing near chaos in their wake. Out of the esthetic revolution which followed at the close of the romantic period new musical concepts emerged to shape the music of our age. The experimental research of German scientists into the mathematical components of consonance and dissonance, particularly by Helmholtz and Lipps, have been challenged by the results of modern research.[17] The ancient idea of music as a preparation for philosophy and as a rightful member of the quadrivium passed into history in this age of specialization. Our universities keep music and mathematics apart: music to insure our comfort on earth, mathematics to take us to the stars.

Whether there are basic patterns in the arts which have a similarity to natural objects has been a lively problem throughout the centuries. In the visual arts certain ratios produced the perfect forms. Be it in painting or architecture, the ideal pattern was modeled after the proportions of natural objects, including the human form. Canons of beauty and objective criteria have also been evident in the esthetics of music from the time when the first minstrel was punished by the temple priest for changing the form of a time-honored song. In our day matters have not much changed in the relationship which music, as a fine art, has to morality and mathematics. Theologians have held fast to their traditional demands,[18] but the mathematician has both vacillated in his interest in music, and given ground when the evidence warranted it. If a mathematician with esthetic inclinations intuitively or on the basis of inadequate research thought that he had arrived at a canon for visual beauty and if it could be demonstrated with additional evidence whether his conclusions are just or faulty, he would be expected to accept the outcome of the additional evidence. The fact that a norm for beauty which mathematicians of repute have set down may become the subject of derision by their future colleagues illustrates that mathematicians do not perpetuate a mutual admiration fraternity. If anything, they are ever challenging each other's findings. In our modern world, the mathematician has been drawn to music again by way of machines and engineering. What will become of music in this mechanized age?

The proverb, "the more things seem to change the more they are the same," is quite applicable at this point. The modern theorist, Schillinger, rivals Pythagoras in explaining how music develops out of mathematics. "Nature produces physical phenomena, which reveal an esthetic harmony to us"; this harmony embodies mathematical principles—it is there for everyone to see. According to Schillinger, the composer re-creates this harmony by imitating nature; "this process of reproduction involves mathematical logic," whether the composer is aware of it or not. He maintains that our earliest composers intuited the wonderful harmony in the universe, and with these insights formed the musical systems that we have come to take for granted. But now we must replace intuition with science. The laws of musical composition must be mathematically regulated. The creation of music, since it involves construction based on mathematics, should be considered a branch of engineering. Machines will replace the unpredictable composers. A trained mechanic, under the Schillinger system, will be able to graph a musical composition, plot pitch versus time on one graph, intensity versus time on another. Our responses will be uniform according to mathematical norms. The norms will be based on statistical means. Esthetic criteria will lose their amorphous character and music will become a science, reaching new heights that it could not do otherwise except as a discipline based on mathematics.[19]

Children can be taught how to create music as easily as they now can be taught how to add and subtract simple numbers, according to Schillinger. Systems of numbers associated with consonant and dissonant tones can be memorized as the rudiments of mathematics are memorized in its earliest stages of development, and then intuitively applied. The norms for consonance and dissonance will be standardized on a hedonistic basis, a calculus of esthetics as it were. As children taught according to this system become more sophisticated in their choice of mathematical combinations in producing musical affects, so much more will their scores become increasingly mature and worthy of accomplishment, a sign of proficiency and discernment. A musical work will be limitless in its use of mathematical combinations. Schillinger held that if his system for a science of music is accepted, it will do away with romantic notions of divine inspiration and amorphous standards of value judgments.

Learning how to create music will become like learning any other science. The exceptional composer, like the unusual scientist, will be able to do more with his material than his predecessors and colleagues. In the chemistry laboratory a many-colored chart displays the elements indigenous to diversified chemicals. Just as students memorize this chart to be able to produce the compounds they wish, so a student can memorize the Schillinger table of numbers to produce specific harmonies by formula. The unique status of the orthodox composer will become archaic when the public acquires literacy in the Schillinger method. As the chemist replaced the alchemist, the musical scientist will replace the subjective composer.

MUSIC MACHINES

Now that the scientific age is upon us, electronics has added one more technique to the process of creating music. Tape recorders and computer machines, manipulated by human brains at present, have brought a revolution to the art of making music, perhaps greater than we are yet aware of. Tones and rhythms, dynamics and varieties of musical affects never before conceived by the most imaginative musical minds are within the province of these lifeless machines. The esthetic, social, and economic effects which this may have on the creator, performer, and listener to music, as well as the music industry, have some frightening aspects. It also bears promise of enriching rewards. The chances are that in the future traditional music and mechanized music will exist side by side as they do now, but to a greater extent.

⤳

The physical sciences grew out of ancient techniques, cures, and even feats of magic. As technology increased, the technical arts were helped by the sciences to produce practical things for human needs in greater abundance than was ever possible before. The fine arts went to the other extreme, remained exclusive and contemptuous of mass production. Now science beckons to the art of music, by way of the machine, with a promise of automation in keeping with the times. A merger of music and science would bring the fine arts and technical arts together again. The arts were divided by science, now brought together by science; whether art can be made a science is a question to be answered in the twentieth century.

Electronics is as great a boon to music as the transition from musical neumes to fixed notes on a five line staff. But in electronic music, the musical ideas of a composer can be conveyed to us without the necessity of musicians; the machine, with the aid of an engineer, usurps for itself the function of interpreting the composer's intentions. The live performer is replaced by a mechanized and lifeless instrument. The music machine accommodates itself to other machines, such as the movies and television. Of late, it has been used to accompany the ballet and to take a leading part in an opera. With a minimum of help from us, machines can give a concert of their own or replace an orchestra in the pit for a theatrical production. Its range of musical possibilities is endless. The electronic machine is so expansive in nature that it may well lead to the invention of new artistic forms and conceptions in the process of fully expressing itself.

If there ever was any chance, as the philosopher John Stuart Mill

The RCA Olson-Belar Sound-Synthesizer in the Columbia-Princeton Electronic Music Center. Courtesy of Milton Babbit, Princeton University.

feared, that the diatonic musical system would eventually become bankrupt because of a limited supply of tonal combinations, the invention of the electric computer and magnetic tape recorder will keep anything so ominous from happening. With the help of the tape recorder a composer can produce and manipulate musical tones and combinations of harmonic sequences that he could never possibly have included in a musical score previously because of the range and nature of the human voice and orchestral instruments, not because of the musical system itself. Rhythms and tempi can be contrived which human beings could not by themselves produce but which machines would be able to do. Musical dynamics and harmonic possibilities have endless opportunities for variety and extension with this new medium. A new range of musical affects, which traditional composers could not envision, will be introduced into human experience by this machine. A composer will have to study the techniques of the machine, as composers originally studied and performed on each instrument in the orchestra before composing for the public.

Traditional musical notation falls short of the needs of the electronic composer, so he has introduced new symbols that will, themselves, soon become traditional. The electronic composer is a far cry from a frenzied Beethoven in the throes of creation. By contrast, the creator of an electronic musical work sits with punch cards, dials, and circuits. He produces sounds that register on tape. When these are played back they have a grandeur of their own which the past could not have known.

Electronic composers are as varied in their creative roles as traditional composers are in theirs. One type of composer writes music through the use of digital computers. Since the structure of music is mathematical, the machine can be given instructions in mathematical terms to form sequences of random numbers, to select, to reject and to hold for future use in the musical composition. Further instructions are then given regarding the composition itself, and when this is formed the results are punched out on paper tape, run through a teletype machine to transpose into letter-number combinations, and then transposed into formal musical notes to be played on regular musical instruments.

A composer can use the digital computer not only to compose music for regular instruments to play, but also to perform the music it creates. This is possible because the sound waves of the various instruments can be described by a series of numbers. In this method the sound of each instrument is translated into numbers which the machine can use. These are processed and an orchestra "set up" in the machine. The machine is then given instructions to produce the notes of the composition with the various instruments. This produces waveforms which represent the combined sound of the various instruments in numbers. These are reconverted so that they can be played on an ordinary tape recorder. As new techniques of programming are developed, the composer's work becomes more and more simplified. In fact, since the compilation of an orchestra is a complicated process, this can be done by a professional programmer and the results used by the composer. With different instructions the machine could also be used to compose the music, or the composer might arrange the overall structure of the composition and have the machine fill in the details.

At the present time music produced by these expensive machines is in the experimental stage. The composer is not primarily interested in how his score will sound or what emotions it will evoke. If the music that he produces turns out overly mechanical, too complex, or just plain uninteresting sounds, he is not too greatly disturbed. Composing music in a traditional sense is not his objective; experimenting with new methods is.

Composing music by a mathematical formula on a computing machine is not the only electronic inroad into the art of song in the second half of the twentieth century. Several schools of electronic composers have mushroomed into existence in a relatively short time with ideas and methods equally as ingenious and with more artistically successful results than those of the composers who replaced the Muse with mathematics. Magnetic tape recording machines and electronic devices are their stock and trade. They record natural and mechanical sounds on tape. These sounds are then rerecorded through electronic devices that distort and modify them in a thousand different ways, and the resulting sounds are then used to construct the final product.

One type of electronic composer will record the songs of birds, the roll of the surf, the speech of an animated child—any number of sounds, whatever their source, that may interest him. After he has reproduced these sounds on tape he distorts, blends, and sets them against each other with the passion used in composing a fugue. Sometimes he is content to retain the original sounds that he has recorded on tape; at other times he will convert these sounds into something else; or, he may do both of these, blending them to get his results.

Another electronic composer will hold that once a sound has been recorded on tape, like the rumbling of thunder before a storm, the sound of thunder should be exhaustively exploited through electronics, but not distorted beyond a recognizable state. To hear a familiar sound electronically expanded and yet know what the sound is, is like looking at a painting that idealizes some facet of our life. An electronic composer who uses the magnetic tape technique may create according to the first method that we have described, or to this one; or he may create, at different times, using one method or the other; or, he may use both methods in a single composition if he so desires. He may even decide to combine natural sounds with instrumental sounds and, on occasion, use electronic music as an accompaniment to the human voice in a live recital before a traditionally conditioned audience.

An electronic composer of a puristic bent may insist that only sounds that emerge from a device such as the electronic tone generator should be used for music. Only music based on such sounds will forge new frontiers of musical experience. To him electronic music that culls from us associations with conventional musical instruments and tones is esthetically inferior to that produced from pure mechanical sounds.

The element of inspiration is just as much present in the creations of the electronic composer's scores as it is in those of traditional works. He achieves his results differently, but the manipulation of the revolutions of a tape recorder to speed the flow of sound or retard it is not unlike the use of notes of long and short duration which the conventional composer employs so that his music will flow fast or slow. Turning a dial this way or that to heighten the volume or diminish it it like the dynamic markings that a traditional composer includes in his score for the performer to manipulate himself. Staccato, pizzicato, syncopation, and vibrato are as important to electronic music as they are to conventional music. Splicing a tape, repeating and transplanting it in a number of ways is comparable to the traditional form of a theme and variation, and the polyphonic inversion and augmentation of varying voices in a fugue.

The musician, like the scientist, is only as far advanced in his medium as are the tools which he has at his command and with which he investigates, probes, and exploits his ideas to the fullest possible extent. The electronic composer is not limited to musical instruments, tonal sounds, and tonal rules, as well as key relations, in the same way that the conventional composer is. But with all his freedom and knowledge of acoustics he can produce music that is esthetically of merit only if he is a man of imaginative means.

Electronic music which is produced by machines brings serious social problems with it, as all forms of automation must. What is to become of choral groups and instrumental ensembles that have been coming together as mere amateurs to perform for their own pleasure and the enjoyment of friends? Man's gregarious nature cannot be altered in a short span of time by a music machine. Man by nature is a social animal and would soon die culturally if left in isolation by being cut off from his fellow men. Coming together to sing and play is a social event like going to church and shopping in the market place. Whether electronic music in the future can replace this gregarious human need is very doubtful indeed. The likelihood is that traditional music and electronic music will both exist a long time from now, side by side.

Will ready-made music machines replace the incentive to produce our own music? Making, creating, and exerting ourselves are vital functions for our survival. The electronic music machine is not the only machine that has clouded our lives by reducing us to mere listeners without an opportunity for participation. The spell of the machine wears off in time, and then our normal impulses to express ourselves return. If we do not allow ourselves to become victimized by our own inventions, we will make music, as well as listen to it, for a very long time to come.

What will become of the performer and the relationship that we have had to him as the intermediary between the composer and us? The chances are that the performer will not be done away with any more than we will submit to complete depersonalization. The performer is one of our secret idols who actualizes the potential ideals that we nurture within us. To watch and exult as he brings to life our deepest hopes, however vicariously, are experiences that can never be brought forth by a machine. Electronic music is unable to fulfill the psychological need that a performer of traditional music provides us with simply because its performer is too far removed from us. The psychical distance between the audience and engineer is too great to be esthetically bridged. We cannot, at the present time, effect an emotional transfer to the manipulator of an electronic machine as readily as we can to the traditional type of performer.

Musical interpreters sometimes are technicians only; they are like orators mouthing words without understanding their meaning. Composers have no assurance that their creations will be executed by performers as they may wish to have them done, either during their lifetime or long after they are dead. Some composers, rather unjustly, have considered performers simply as their faithful lackeys who are to carry out commands clearly marked in the score. Through electronics such composers may have their way, the machine will send the music out just as it went in, with the precision of mathematics. But most composers are aware that performers of stature are capable of reading into their score subtleties and nuances that they themselves were unaware of and to which a machine would be altogether impervious. An electronic machine could not elaborate on a composer's intentions unless a rational being arranged for it to do so. The machine would be a faithful recorder and reproducer of the created work but, like a phonograph record or the background music of a movie, it could function only in a mechanical way unless a human being intervened.

In the electronic music that has had the greatest esthetic impact on us up until now, the musical engineer has replaced our traditional concept of the performer. Sometimes the performing engineer is hidden from the audience, as when he is directing the music for a ballet. At other times he may be part of the action on the stage, such as guiding the activities of an electronic "actor" playing a role alongside living ones. The musical engineer will become our idol too in time. Engineers are no more stereotyped than creative performers are.

Electronic music not only creates an esthetic and social problem, but also an economic one. In the electronic age a composer will be able to write a work that outdoes Berlioz in its demand for instrumentation and size without fear that economics will keep it from ever being heard. Once his score is recorded it can be electronically played. New forms that may be created for machines, unlike even the most elaborate traditional score, will with their expansive orchestral colors be more wonderful than we can now imagine. Archaic practices like sitting in a group, playing from a printed page, and being directed by a leader will be associated with music of another age.

Music machines are now used in opera and ballet with extraordinary success. In the first opera, *Aniara,* a Swedish work set in outer space, an electronic brain named Mina sings a heroine's tragic role. Mina is constructed like a huge hourglass and endowed with a mind, soul, and conscience. Her arias consist of electronic harmonies and snatches of human speech recorded on tape. As she sings to the passengers and crew on a spaceship zooming between Earth and Mars, an engineer, taking part in the action on the stage, stands very near her watching over her every utterance. Mina, distressed at man's folly in this world, laments that we are exterminating ourselves with poisonous radiation. Now man has turned nomad again and must look for new homes in outer space in order to survive. After Mina concludes her musical warning to mankind, she dies. The spaceship, deflected from its course by a swarm of shooting stars, pursues an endless journey through outer space with a cargo of corpses, both human and machine.[20]

The first important electronic music for the ballet was presented in West Germany, then was brought to New York [21] and performed with new stage sets and choreography. The sounds for this electronic score were mechanically produced and registered on tape in their purity. These sounds are purely electronic, having no relation to natural sounds or musical tones of conventional instruments, but time factors are controlled by a performer in the normal fashion. During the performance the composer, much like the traditional performer hidden in the pit below the stage, "monitored" the electronic device. The sounds that come out of this machine are relayed through "speakers" well-placed throughout the theater so that the overall effect upon the audience is that of being completely surrounded by these sounds, instead of having them come from one source. An audience engulfed by electronic sounds that are eerie and odd, extraordinary in their dynamic dimensions, can quickly become tense and expectant, as well as experience delight at new tonal experiences. Electronic music that seems to be ubiquitous, unnatural in tone and dynamics, needs choreography and stage sets as dramatic and expansive as the music is to realize its full esthetic potentialities.

A musical engineer may be able to construct an electronic machine and from an analysis of a large number of the works of one composer be able to set up instructions for the machine to produce music of the style of that composer. The machine may thus be empowered to mix, scramble, and rearrange what is fed into it to produce a musical work which would not only have all the earmarks of this certain composer but be superior to anything that he had ever produced himself.

It may even be possible to construct a machine in the future that would be able to feed on itself as a composer, in a figurative sense, feeds on his unconscious. It might, under these circumstances, create an original masterpiece, but the chance that such a thing would occur is not likely. A composer uses judgment in the employment of his material; a machine has no judgment of its own. The machine can produce only what its "brain" permits. Such a masterpiece would, therefore, be an accident, not a creation. But assuming that the "brain" in the machine could develop its creative capacities and make decisions, it would produce music that is peculiar to its own nature, not to ours. If ever such a time should come, we would have to educate our esthetic responses to what the machine produces. Our actions and tastes would be gauged by machine standards. These standards would have little to do with human needs or emotional tolerance, and the general public would be expected to measure up to the machine, instead of the machine catering to it. When a composer expects us to measure up to his standards, there is a man-to-man relationship which basically has human values in it. But there is no reason why we cannot adjust to the music of the machine in the future as we do to that of the avant-garde composer now. True, the machine would not express human sentiments, and the sounds that it produces might not be music in the traditional sense. It would be a new type of music, alongside the kind we are now accustomed to hearing. In time we may even endow these mechanical musical sounds with the attributes that we now bestow on traditional music.

Electronic music is a new voice in the modern age. Some of its advocates claim that traditional musical styles have worn themselves thin; composers writing in the traditional vein have run out of ideas, and what meager ideas they have are expressed in the same old ways. Electronic music is a complete break with the past. It has a new approach, new methods, and styles to create a new musical language for the machine age. The attraction that it holds for young composers is great. It offers them a new tonal universe in which to search out new tones and experiences that their predecessors could not have known. Electronic music is scarcely fifteen years old, but it already has a compendium of clichés and mannerisms that can be found in its styles and performances. The monotony and agony of repetition that electronic composers ascribe to traditional works is already present in their own.

SUMMARY

A metaphysics of music, such as the Greeks were imbued with, could have thrived only in a mental climate in which poetry was more important than science. In the Roman world ideas like the harmony of the spheres were disdainfully passed off as archaic notions of Greek theorists. The theologians of the Middle Ages were more like the Greeks than the Romans. The harmony of the spheres became the angelic realm where peace and harmony dwelt and from whence all good things came. The philosophers, particularly after Descartes, took separate ways in interpreting the world and the place that music had in it. Rationalists were like the fanciful Greeks, and empiricists like the practical Romans. In our scientific age the overwhelming evidence is that a metaphysics of music in a traditional sense is an anachronism. It simply does not fit in with our "facts." But some men, nevertheless, even in this time of material accomplishment, find more reason to believe the metaphysician and the poet than the mathematician and the scientist.

Mathematics and music are inseparable. This is difficult for many people to accept. Even musicians at times become frightened by the word "mathematics," using it as an epithet against one of their own as the most condemning thing that can be said about his music. The Russian Five, according to Rimsky-Korsakov, believed that Johann Sebastian Bach, perhaps the greatest contrapuntalist that ever lived, "was held to be petrified, yes, even a mere musico-mathematical, feelingless and deadly nature, composing like a very machine." Composers are more critical of each other than critics are of them. Quite often they are critical for different reasons from those which a critic might decide on; but they can be just as contemptuous in their attitudes and wrong in their views as critics can be about creative persons. Not all composers dread mathematics and baroque masters, such as Bach, as much as the Russian Five. Paul Hindemith points out that "the basic fact of our hearing process reveals to us how closely related are numbers and beauty, mathematics and art." Hindemith has a very deep reverence for Bach.

The philosophers were the first to declare that music is numbers arranged in certain patterns and forms. First Plato and then Aristoxenus rejected the Pythagorean theory that music is only numbers converted into sound patterns. They also shunned the "empirics" who relied solely on the ear in tonal matters. Augustine and Boethius believed as Plato did that music is a mathematical manifestation of the moral order in the world and not just numerical sound patterns to be judged by the sense of hearing alone. Descartes and Leibniz brought their mathematical skill to every branch of knowledge and the arts. Their application of mathematics to music is particularly fascinating: in the science of numbers they saw a sign of God, through the symbol of music this sign was revealed to all mankind. Hegel called music the second of the romantic arts, painting was lower and poetry higher. The laws that allow music to develop from the simple to the complex, from a primitive cry to a romantic form are mathematical, inexorable as the dialectic that pervades all the activity in the world. Just as the dialectic is inherent in the cyclical dynamism of nature, so does mathematics reside in music. Man's progressive development of musical forms is a spiritual unfolding of his inner self. If we would judge the progress of the world by its history, we would find that the inevitable logic underlying the growth of music is a mathematical development. Rational man, Hegel maintains, is striving toward an ideal, and an ideal beyond the last one; but this is only to be gained through strife and conflict, in music as in everything else in this life.

Structured music and mathematics are very closely allied. From the simplest interval, the most elementary rhythm, to *polytonality* and *polyrhythm,* mathematics reigns supreme in ruling over their structural being. Key relationships are mathematically arranged on the physical basis of our diatonic scales. Notation is measured by mathematical values. Rhythm and tempo are dependent on mathematical signs, symbols of guidance as it were. Harmony, counterpoint, and the tone row technique of the atonal school are mathematical constructs very much like the geometry which gives a Greek vase its physical shape or Steuben glass its rare elegance. Mathematics is present in a primitive folk song and in the most elaborate score. In one it is used unwittingly and in the other deliberately, but not necessarily consciously as a mathematician would in working on a problem. The musician goes about his task unmindful of the mathematical nature of his art. His creations fall into a mathematical pattern just as creative ideas of poets take shape in a grammatical context. He develops his score as an architect builds a house, according to prescribed laws of logic. His work takes form in the style of a mathematical norm in keeping with the tenor of his time. If he should introduce a revolutionary advance by altering the physical character of the music of the past, it would mean that he is using mathematics in a way that it had not been used before to produce new musical ideas, as a scientist would to create new conceptions of the world.

A composer is aware that certain musical patterns will evoke some fairly definite responses from listeners, but he goes about his task unmindful of the mathematical character of his work. A mathematician with the aid of machines might be able to reduce a composer's intuitive use of tonal combinations to mathematics, but this would not explain why the composer chose the combination that he did. It would be an impossibility to do so on the basis of mathematical calculations alone. If a mathematician could prove, as some think they have, that music is explicable in mathematical terms, then music could be properly considered a science, as exacting as a geometer's theorems for studying the properties of a triangle or a square. The composer could express musical moods in a standardized way and, with certainty, expect stereotyped responses in return, just as baroque composers employed the doctrine of affections to a lesser extent. Composers may have "built in number tables" that give them a propensity for order and expression while composing, which the rest of us have to a smaller degree only. But a composer's method of creation is never so thoroughly conscious that he can be explicit about what he does. Those who maintain that his motives and unique style are analyzable, according to scientific standards, are mistaken. Modern technology still cannot give us the answer to the problem of creation.

There is no reason why machines will not be able to arrange random numbers and then rearrange them according to some lawful means of musical composition, as students of elementary harmony now work out a daily exercise in the classroom. But to set up the machine so that the process it follows will not only lawfully follow the present musical forms but also create new forms of itself out of the old forms fed into it, is like asking the student of harmony to create new musical forms out of his exercise on the basis of what he has learned about the rules of composition and his knowledge of existing forms. He may well be able to do it by chance, so may the machine; the probability is not great, but there is always the possibility present. It has been said that a monkey could have written *Hamlet* by just such chance too, painted an abstract work, or devised a rambling poem. The student of harmony will grow into a mature composer if he is sensitive and gifted, the monkey will acquire new habits, the machine will be weighed down with additional gadgets, but the monkey and the machine are by the nature of things in this world destined to imitate man, not to create for themselves.

If ever man can build a machine that can profit by its experience, sublimate, procrastinate, cry out in anguish at frustration, then that machine will be able to give us something more than duplication of patterns formed by human beings. Thus far we have brought our experience to machines and expect them to do with it what we have been able to do ourselves; this is how it will probably remain for a long time to come. Music can be composed on computing machines and it has much merit in it. Music can be composed from the songs of birds and the cries of wild beasts, and there is no reason why it should not be done. The music of the future will be as different as the world itself will be; there is no way of knowing precisely how it will come about and what music will be like. But a science of music in our time in an anachronism. To make a science out of music, in the sense that we accept music as an art, is to negate the very nature of its personal qualities that make it all things to all men.

NOTES

[1] Aristotle *Metaphysics*, Bk. I. 986a.

[2] Henry George Farmer, *Historical Facts for the Arabian Musical Influence* (London: William Reeves, 1930), pp. 350-351.

[3] Leibniz, *Philosophical Writings*, trans. Mary Morris (London: J. M. Dent & Sons, Ltd., 1934), p. 74.

[4] Kant, *Critique of Judgement*, 53, "Comparison of the respective aesthetical worth of the beautiful arts," trans. J. H. Bernard (London: Collier-Macmillan, Ltd., 1914), p. 218. "Thus as modulation is as it were a universal language of sensations intelligible to every man, the art of tone employs it by itself alone in its full force, viz. as a language of the affections, and thus communicates universally according to the laws of association the aesthetical Ideas naturally combined therewith."

[5] G. W. F. Hegel, *Philosophy of Right*, trans. T. M. Knox (Oxford: Clarendon Press, 1942), p. 279.

[6] Arthur Schopenhauer, *The World as Idea*, ed. Irwin Edman (New York: The Modern Library, Inc., 1928), p. 201. Music is "*as direct* an objectification and copy of the whole *will* as the world itself, nay, even as the Ideas, whose

multiplied manifestation constitutes the world of individual things." Music is not an unconscious counting of numbers as Leibniz wrote, but metaphysics itself, unconscious philosophizing.

[7] Jacques Maritain, *Art and Scholasticism,* trans. J. F. Scanlan (New York: Charles Scribner's Sons, 1946), p. 125. "So music perhaps more than any other art gives us an enjoyment of being, but does not give us *knowledge* of being; and it would be absurd to make music a substitute for metaphysics."

[8] Plato *Republic,* Bk. VII. 531. "The teachers of harmony compare the sounds and consonances which are heard only, and their labour, like that of the astronomers, is in vain."

[9] Kathleen Freeman, *The Pre-Socratic Philosophers* (Oxford: Basil Blackwell & Mott, Ltd., 1949), p. 239. "In particular, he worked out the numerical ratios corresponding to the intervals between the notes of the tetrachord for three different types of scale: the enharmonic, the chromatic, and the diatonic." —p. 238.

[10] Aristotle *Metaphysics,* Bk. I. 986a.

[11] Aristotle *Problems,* Bk. XIX. Chap. 38. 920b. "We enjoy different types of song for their moral character, but we enjoy rhythm because it has a recognized and orderly numerical arrangement and carries us along in an orderly fashion; for orderly movement is naturally more akin to us than one without order, so that such rhythm is more in accordance with nature."

[12] *Ibid.,* Chap. 23. 919b.

[13] *Ibid.,* Chap. 35. 920b.

[14] *The Harmonics of Aristoxenus,* ed. and trans. Henry S. Macran (Oxford: Clarendon Press, 1902), pp. 188-190. Macran writes: "Thus they [Pythagoreans] missed the true formal notion of music, which is ever present to Aristoxenus, that of a system or organic whole of sounds, each member of which *is* essentially what it *does,* and in which a sound cannot become a member because merely there is room for it, but only if there is a function which it can discharge."

[15] *Selections from Medieval Philosophers, The Opus Majus,* trans. Richard McKeon (New York: Charles Scribner's Sons, 1930), p. 49.

[16] Nann Cooke Carpenter, *Music in the Medieval and Renaissance Universities* (Copyright 1958 by the University of Oklahoma Press), pp. 187-188. Oxford: A traditional alignment between music and mathematics existed. A candidate could "lecture on any book of Boethius" for a bachelor's degree and "the bachelor created doctor or *inceptor* by the Savilian professor of mathematics." pp. 188-189. Cambridge: "Although not mentioned specifically, music is probably to be understood in accordance with the traditional teaching of mathematics.... bachelors seeking the master's degree must spend the first three years in the study of arithmetic and music." p. 190. Trinity College, Cambridge: ". . . it is stated that the *lector mathematicus* teach music along with the other mathematical disciplines."

[17] Theodor Lipps, *Psychological Studies,* II, trans. Herbert C. Sanborn (2d ed.; Baltimore: The Williams & Wilkins Company, 1926), pp. 138-265.

[18] *Basic Writings of Saint Thomas Aquinas, The Summa Theologica,* I [Part I, Question 1, Article 2], (New York: Random House, Inc., 1945), p. 7. "Hence, just as music accepts on authority the principles taught by the arithmetician, so sacred science accepts the principles revealed by God."

[19] Joseph Schillinger, *The Mathematical Basis of the Arts* (New York: Philosophical Library, Inc., 1948), pp. 4-5, 9, 46. Also: *The Schillinger System of Musical Notation* (New York: Philosophical Library, Inc., 1946).

[20] The opera, *Aniara,* is based on a group of poems by Harry Martinson. It is composed by Karl-Birger Blomdahl, and the libretto is by Erik Lindegren.

[21] *Electronics,* composed by Remi Gassmann in collaboration with Oskar Sala; choreography by George Balanchine.

CHAPTER VI

THE PRACTICAL
APPLICATIONS *of* MUSIC

THERAPY

Historical   Music was used in very ancient civilizations to cure physical and mental disease. Primitive societies often placed more importance on magical chants and ritual dances to cure the sick than on herbs with medicinal value. Of all the arts, even more than dance, music has been used to cure sickness of body and mind.

Perhaps the three oldest stories in which music is used as medicine to cure a distraught mind, a sick body, and even to propitiate Apollo so that he would stop a plague are found in the three greatest books of antiquity: the Bible, the *Odyssey,* and the *Iliad.* In the Bible there is a description of how David cured Saul of his black moods with soulful music.[1] In the *Odyssey,* Homer noted that when Ulysses suffered a knee injury during a boar hunt on Parnassus, the "chanting of lays" helped ease the pain and heal the wound.[2] In the *Iliad* Greek youths "with sacred hymns and songs that sweetly please" delighted Apollo so that he brought to a halt the fury of a deathly plague.[3]

The origin of music as a therapy goes back to incantations and dances performed by primitive tribal magicians to drive evil spirits from the bodies of their people. The Greeks undoubtedly learned

188

about the healing power of music from civilizations older than their own. The Pythagoreans, with their ardor for science and mystery, believed that music could alter moods and cure the sick. To them, the human soul and the world soul were united and governed by similar harmonious laws.[4] Since music is an imitation of the divine harmony it can, through rhythm and melody, instill a harmonious balance in a human soul that has become untuned. Music can produce in others the mood that it expresses itself, and thereby modify the character of its listener and alleviate the ills of the mind.

Plato observed that women who were highly agitated responded to exciting music with excellent therapeutic results.

Bacchic women are cured of their frenzy . . . by the use of the dance and of music. . . . The affection . . . of the Bacchantes . . . is an emotion of fear, which springs out of an evil habit of the soul. And when someone applies external agitation to affections of this sort, the motion coming from without gets the better of the terrible and violent internal one, and produces a peace and calm in the soul, and quiets the restless palpitation of the heart, . . . and making the Bacchantes, although they remain awake, to dance to the pipe with the help of the Gods to whom they offer acceptable sacrifices, and producing in them a sound mind, which takes the place of their frenzy. And, to express what I mean in a word, there is a good deal to be said in favour of this treatment.[5]

Aristotle traced mental illness to a deficiency in the soul brought on by overindulgence, and bodily disease to excessive fatigue. Following the Golden Mean is the best guarantee against falling sick. Aristotle considered the body and soul as inseparable; disease in one would infect the other. Music and the drama could restore a balanced functioning to an afflicted soul and body, and make them healthy again.[6]

Aristotle's theories on the value of music as a therapy were not original. He systematized the views of the Pythagoreans and Plato, and made some observations of his own. He concurred with the views of his predecessors that since music affected the mind more powerfully than any other art, it could be used as a *homeopathic* remedy. Music of a passionate nature could cure a turbulent mind as though it were purged by a drug. The Phrygian mode is orgiastic and frenzied; it can be used in the treatment of highly agitated mental cases. Lydian airs are soft and sad; they can be used for those who are melancholy and depressed. The Dorian mode is like a tonic for the sick and well alike; it is the essence of simplicity and purity. Aristotle extended his knowledge of the therapeutic value of music to theatrical tragedies. His conditions for undergoing catharsis through drama and being cured through music are based on a similar principle, homeopathy.

Roman physicians and temple priests used music as a therapy up to the time when the Empire was completely Christianized. As late as the sixth century Cassiodorus, in a letter to Boethius, wrote about the medicinal value of music and the effect that the different modes had upon the general welfare of a person. Since Christian physicians of the Middle Ages have not left us any serious references on the value of music in treating the sick, we may assume that they had a low opinion of this ancient practice. Arabian physicians, who were still reading Aristotle and Galen in the original Greek, were known to be using music as a therapy for several types of mental disorders in the thirteenth century. Roger Bacon may have had this difference between Christian and Moslem physicians in mind when he recommended that music should be used in the cure of mental patients, as was done in former times by the Greeks and Romans.

That children with speech impediments were helped by music was known in antiquity. Roger Bacon comments, what a blessing music is to Christian children with stammering difficulties. This would illustrate that music was used for remedial purposes in his day. Henry Peacham, in the seventeenth century, wrote that singing was an aid in correcting bad pronunciation as well as stammering.[7]

Renaissance scholars and artists tried to imitate the Greeks in order to achieve their high degree of formal beauty. Renaissance physicians, thinking of themselves as full-fledged scientists, scoffed at any notion that the Greeks could have been very successful in using music to cure disease. A Renaissance physician might prescribe music to dispel melancholia or to exercise tubercular lungs, but he did not ascribe any lasting cure to this medicinal application of "sweet harmonies."

In some seventeenth century virginals and harpsichords, "Music, the medicine of men's minds" is inscribed on the inside lid of the instrument. This is probably more the doing of an enterprising business man than the view of the medical fraternity of that time. There is a story that the famed philosopher, Hobbes, would take time from his writings to practice singing in order to exercise his lungs. He would shut the doors of his rooms so that his neighbors would not be disturbed by his loud singing. Because he showed such thoughtfulness towards his neighbors while looking after his health with diligence, Providence granted him life until the age of ninety-one.[8]

People with mental diseases fared very badly in the Western world during the past thousand years or more. A mental disease was a stigma, something to be ashamed of. Insane people were thought to be possessed by the devil, and sometimes burned at the stake. Others were treated like criminals and housed with criminals. Townspeople were known to visit these institutions, as they would a zoo or circus, to watch and laugh at the antics of these unfortunates. Music was used primarily to amuse mental patients. On Easter and Christmas, church choirs would come to sing hymns and chorales to them in the same spirit that they performed for the inmates of the prisons. Little, if any, effort was made, to reclaim these unfortunates with music or any other form of therapy. Once lodged inside prison walls, they were considered hopeless. Mental patients of a borderline type were not much more fortunate than those who had more serious disorders. They were forced to wander from place to place; and wherever they went they were ridiculed, scorned, and even, at times, flogged, and forcibly sent on their way.

Modern Practice For all the remarkable things that music can do to help the sick and weary, its powers to cure, unfortunately, are very limited.

Music is useful as a background of familiar and assuring strains in a hospital ward; its soothing affects are of inestimable comfort to the sick. On occasion, music is used as a mild anesthesia for minor surgery and dentistry. It is not improbable that in the near future electronic machines will be able to produce rhythmic sounds at certain pitches and intensities that will make music an even more effective anesthetic device than it is so ably proving to be at present in medical surgery and dentistry.

Group singing among ambulatory patients in mental hospitals lessens their dread of isolation and sparks their gregarious instincts to function normally again. Music is extremely effective where other therapeutic devices have failed to get patients, who have mentally withdrawn from society, to participate in group activities. Learning how to play an instrument is the equivalent of acquiring a skill, achieving something very definite for all to see, a sense of assurance—a feeling the patient may never have known before. All these things music does very well, but it cannot cure mental illness by itself.

Music can be used in the same way that psychological tests, such as looking at pictures or ink blots, are employed to determine the nature and depth of an emotional disturbance. Although music has been used as a diagnostic aid for unraveling mental and emotional problems, no one has yet been successful, to the same degree that has been achieved with painting, in correlating and standardizing patient responses that are elicited by certain musical works and themes. Music, more easily than any other art, can instill a mood in a patient that encourages free association. A patient can then be asked to relate his passing thoughts to the examiner or write them down, either while the music is being played or after it is finished. Which procedure is used would depend on the patient. But the difficulty is that examiners and their patients do not share the same musical symbolism to the extent that they both do when looking at a painting or a patterned splash of black or colored ink. Nevertheless, music's potentialities as a diagnostic technique for mental and emotional disease have not been exploited. The average psychologist is not trained in music and, if he is, there is no standardized test for him to use. If he devised his own, complete with scoring procedure for evaluating responses to varied rhythms, individual tones, intervals, and entire compositions, it would still be extremely difficult to validate such an examination so that it could be considered as scientific as objective type examinations. Even, if the near-impossible is achieved and a musical test for the mentally ill is developed, it could never by itself be anything more than one strand of a cord that leads to an understanding of the patient's illness. In this respect it would be like any other technique that psychologists employ in their testing.

With the aid of music, emotionally disturbed people can be encouraged to act out their difficulties, in the presence of a trained examiner, as though they were taking part in a drama or a dance. This can be done in the same way that the psychodrama is being used, with such excellent results, in modern therapy. Music can create an environment that lessens inhibitions and prompts a person who might be highly restrained and tense to "act out" or "dance out" his feelings, thereby not only discharging surplus energy but perhaps allowing his observers to detect some possible sources of hostility or fear that may go to the root of his neurosis. This type of therapy cannot achieve lasting cures, as the Greeks surmised, or eject the poison of a snakebite by dancing the highly erotic tarantella, as inhabitants of southern Italy once believed.[9]

How do insane people respond to music? Their responses are even more varied and bizarre than those of normal people. Those who are too far gone will not respond at all, others may find the music totally irritating, and some few, who are still able to be reached, will respond as though it were their last chance at salvation. A motionless catatonic, a supercilious hebephrenic, a deluded paranoic, who remain mute to the prying questions of psychiatrists and cannot be brought out of their private world with accepted remedies, may, over an extended period of listening to music, show signs of being communicable. Music which can induce a stream of mental associations in a patient may encourage him to take the next step in human relationship, relating to his benefactor, the music therapist, what grievances he harbors against the world. Establishing rapport with a mental patient by means of music, so that he will give up his madness, is a hit-or-miss affair. There is no possible way, at the present time, to know which types of music to use for specific mental ailments as can be done with medicines. Music, at the present time, cannot cure or diagnose. It is only one more means by which we try to reach a mind which has divorced itself from us. The affects which music has on mental patients is no more lasting than it is for the rest of us. Even a hopeless psychotic, deluded and hallucinating in his private world, may respond to a musical stimulus, speak coherently for a brief moment about some tragedy, joyous moment, or insignificant detail which he has nurtured and developed into major proportions in his warped mind; but a moment after the music ceases, or even while it is going on, he might become distrustful and return to the world in which he lived before the music began. If he has not deteriorated seriously, music may be of some use in helping him to communicate with others.

It would be as illogical to think that a tonic could cure an organic disease as it would be to assume that music could bring a schizophrenic patient back to normalcy. Music can be used with excellent effect as a soothing agent and to bring cheer to sick people. It can also be a pleasant distraction from pain; but while music can alter the chemistry of the human body, it cannot do so to such an extent that it could induce a lasting cure in a patient racked with discomfort from a pathological condition. Music alone cannot erase a mental illness, nor can it be a substitute for surgery.

Music can definitely change metabolism, affect muscular energy, raise or lower blood pressure, and influence digestion. It may be able to do all these things more successfully and pleasantly than many other stimulants that produce these changes in our bodies. Nevertheless, music has some decided drawbacks that would exclude it from the category of scientific therapies. Music is a cultural phenomenon and not a "drug" that can be expected to affect everyone in the same manner. Responses to music are personal, cultural, and varied beyond description within cultures themselves. This is not true with medicines. With them, we may expect fairly similar results.

WORK

The Laborer   Peasants who once sang as they worked would be astonished at the modern means by which music is employed to minimize boredom and fatigue. Recorded music emanates from a central source. It consists of types of music suited for the time of day and character of work, and is piped into factories and offices throughout the land. Laborers rarely sing at their work any more, either to themselves or in groups. Now the singing is done for them by other workers. Occasionally, one may hear fishermen, who have been at sea for several days, singing chanteys, as fishermen did before them; but even this practice is fast disappearing.

⌣

Music eased the physical burdens of slaves building pyramids for Pharaohs obsessed with immortality. Greek seamen sang chanteys as they pulled at their oars with rhythmic precision. Stevedores sang as they weighted down barges with products for other lands and unloaded cargoes from distant shores. Fishermen sang while they spread their nets in a calm sea before the morning sun arose, and farmers sang as they worked their fields to offset the heat of the rising sun as it beat down on them from above.

Aelian, a Roman teacher of rhetoric, has given us some wonderful stories regarding the use of music in ancient times for hunting, fishing, and domesticating wild animals.

There is an Etruscan story current which says that the wild boars and the stags in that country are caught by using nets and hounds, as is the usual manner of hunting, but that music plays a part, and even the larger part, in the struggle. And how this happens I will now relate. They set the nets and other hunting gear that ensnare the animals in a circle, and a man proficient on the pipes stands there and tries his utmost to play a rather soft tune, avoiding any shriller note, but playing the sweetest melodies possible. The quiet and the stillness easily carry (the sound) abroad; and the music streams up to the heights and into the ravines and thickets—in a word into every lair and resting-place of these animals. Now at first when the sound penetrates to their ears it strikes them with terror and fills them with dread, and then an unalloyed and irresistible delight in the music takes hold of them, and they are so beguiled as to forget about their offspring and their homes. And yet wild beasts do not care to wander away from their native haunts. But little by little these creatures in Etruria are attracted as though by some persuasive spell, and beneath the wizardry of the music they come and fall into the snares, overpowered by the melody....[10]

Those who hunt Crabs have hit upon the device of luring them with music. At any rate they catch them by means of a flageolet (this is the name of an instrument). Now the Crabs have gone down into their hiding-places, and the men begin to play. And at the sound, as though by a spell, the Crabs are induced to quit their den, and then captivated with delight even emerge from the sea. But the flute-players withdraw backwards and the Crabs follow and when on dry land are caught....[11]

Those who live by the lake of Marea catch the Sprats there by singing with the utmost shrillness, accompanying their song with the clash of castanets. And the fishes, like women dancing, leap to the tune and fall into the nets spread for their capture. And through their dancing and frolics the Egyptians obtain an abundant catch.[12]

Work songs have kept pace with industrial tools. Crude instruments and back-breaking toil are apt to encourage rough and bitter songs; machine tools and electronic brains call for soft background music to soothe the nerves and disrupt the monotony of mechanized work. Music has been used as a "tool" itself by the laboring class, from ancient times into the modern industrial age, to help complete a day's work.

Industrial music, filtered into modern plants, is carefully planned so that it will not distract employees from their work. It is "guaranteed" to soothe and relax, not to annoy or irritate. Industrial music is specifically tailored for types of work and fitted to the mood and time of the working day. Employers are assured that music, emanating from a distant studio and wired into their establishments, will diminish objectionable noises, fill in extended periods of silence with pleasant melodies, thereby lessening fatigue by keeping monotony at a minimum. With the help of music an employer can keep production from lagging as the day wears on.

Music employed for industry must not be used throughout the day without letup because it loses its power to stimulate, becoming more enervating than helpful. It should be introduced periodically, for a limited time only. Those whose work is mental will profit less from music than physical laborers. Office workers may not be able to think while listening to music. Men who work in a thoroughly mechanical fashion are not faced with this problem. Following the words of a new tune may be distracting, except in the most repetitive kind of work.

Industrial automation has decreased the physical hardships that laborers were once forced to endure. But, by the same token, man has weakened his physical capacity for arduous work by having the machine do what he formerly did himself. His dependence on the machine is gradually depersonalizing him. Music can, to some extent, introduce a human element into his work, even if the music itself is mechanized. It is possible that music can help a man affirm his existence as a person when he is surrounded by machines.

Industry Musicians are more practical than we think. They have always made use of any new media, such as materials for the construction of new instruments, and devices which would help them to communicate their music to the public. In our time the phonograph, radio, television, and movies have turned the music industry into big business.

⤳

The activities of the laborer and the sounds of machines have been sources of inspiration to creative composers. They have described peasants working in the field and the sounds of locomotives rumbling across the land. They have invented machines of their own and have collaborated with other builders of machines. During the Middle Ages composers worked with clockmakers whose masterpieces may still be found in European cathedrals and town halls. Mechanical figures appear on the hour, dance a bit to a musical motif or act out a scene, and retire behind the face of the clock. Composers at times supervised the construction of church organs as bishops oversaw the construction of cathedrals. Musicians were called upon to help with the construction of hurdy-gurdys, and mechanical gadgets, such as singing birds and music boxes, to amuse the aristocracy.

Composers not only helped to create mechanical figures that danced to the tune of an organ-grinder or the movements of a clock, but they helped to invent, and invented themselves, mechanical figures that could play a musical work. The most ingenious of these musicians was probably Johann Maelzel, whose fame rests primarily on his invention of the metronome. He constructed "an automaton instrument of flutes, trumpets, drums, cymbals, triangle, and strings struck by hammers, which played music by Haydn, Mozart and Crescentini, . . . His next machine was the Panharmonicon; . . . with clarinets, violins and violoncellos added. . . . He next constructed a Trumpeter, which played the Austrian and French cavalry marches and signals." [13]

It is somewhat paradoxical that in an era which emphasized the supremacy of feeling over reason so strongly, such as the romantic one, that the mechanical piano was perfected and used extensively. Composers gladly gave their consent to have their soul-searching creations reproduced on mechanical machines. Famous performers vied with each other to record the works of the composers.

The phonograph has done for music what the printing press has done for books. The printing press has carried the written word almost everywhere on earth; the phonograph has brought both great and commonplace music within the grasp of practically everyone. The phonograph reaches out to more people than books, odd as it may seem. Recorded music has an appeal to illiterates and primitive people in far-away places whom books cannot reach. With the phonograph we can also leave to posterity an authentic musical document of our world in the twentieth century.

The phonograph has brought harm and good to mankind, as every invention has. Where men once played for a livelihood, now mechanical records are used. Men and women who once enjoyed singing together are now apt to listen to highly trained, recorded artists instead. The phonograph has invaded our lives to such an extent that there is no escape from it. Even in our homes, the sanctuaries of civilized men, privacy is disturbed by mechanical musical machines. We are subjected to our neighbor's musical tastes, and they are forced to put up with ours.

Radio and television have brought us mixed blessings too. They have become the modern patrons of the arts. Composers write for these two media, and for the movies as well, as they once accepted commissions from popes, kings, and millionaires to produce music for specific occasions. Radio and television carry the music of the great and near-great to every part of the globe; there is no place in the world that these media cannot reach. They bring us music that we could not hear unless we had a record library as vast and varied as those in the radio and television studios.

For all the good that they do, radio and television are often crass and corrupting. Music is sold and music is used to sell other things in a most undignified way. Downgrading music to a serious jingle to sell a commercial product may have economic advantages as a memory game but does not help raise the cultural level throughout the land. Using music to deceive, glorify the "commercial lie," as part of an advertising scheme is to debase a noble art. Breaking into a recorded concert so that a barker can sell his wares is closer in mood to a carnival than a concert hall.

Although the movies technically improve from year to year, the music written for them remains at a low grade. Most of the music which is used as a backdrop for action on the screen is a patchwork of musical ideas, hardly anything creative. This is even more pronounced on television. For all the splendid films that can be remembered, very few musical soundtracks equal them in merit.

We have become so accustomed to living with noise that many of us feel psychologically insecure when we are left to ourselves with our thoughts. Business people make the most of this weakness and provide us with pleasant "noise," in the guise of music, to draw us into their establishments. Music is provided for shopping and banking so that we feel relaxed among people whom we do not know. Music accompanies us when we travel, up or down in the elevator, on a bus ride across town, or on a plane trip around the world, alleviating our fears and reducing anxieties so that the element of danger is diminished by listening to pleasant sounds. The physician, like the business man, has music in his waiting room to offset any anxiety the patient might have. Music, when used for any of these purposes, must not draw attention to itself, nor distract or intrude. If it does, it fails, as it so often does, in the purpose laid out for it.

Listening to music when we please is usually a pleasurable experience; but when we are compelled to hear music while we shop or travel in public conveyances, it is an invasion of our rights. Business men do not provide this music for cultural reasons but only to advertise to a

captive audience. Music also loses its magic qualities if it is used indiscriminately and without letup throughout the entire day.

The music industry is ruled by economics, as every industry is.
Music, a commodity, is an art produced by a composer and sold to a
consumer. Some composers produce music to suit the taste of the
public. They make sure that it elicits from their audience such pleasant
responses that they are assured of immediate success. Their financial
returns for services rendered to the public need is most rewarding
indeed in terms of the actual labor given and the remuneration received for it. Composers of sterner stuff will produce what they think
the public ought to have, even if they are not ready for it. This may
mean biding one's time and putting up with economic austerity,
but that is not the whole story. Dedicated composers differ from
manufacturers and tradesmen as night does from day. They usually
follow their inclinations, not their pocketbooks, in what they produce
for the public good. Although they are affected by the reaction of
the public to their music, they will not compromise, they will not
cater; many of them would rather starve and some of them almost do.

Musicians who travel from place to place selling their wares are
like salesmen in other forms of business. If a performer does not please
and excite his audience with the commodity that he carries wherever
he goes, he will lose his concert route to someone more successful in
pleasing the public than he. Musical concert bureaus which arrange
itineraries for artists have their eyes on a budget primarily. They are
not in business to promote music but to make money with it. The same
is true with radio and television networks; it is business to the bitter
end. The concert musician differs from the salesman however. The
musician owns his product, but the consumers must be provided for
him by a managerial staff. The ordinary salesman makes his own audience, but he has no product of his own; he carries the product of someone else wherever he goes. A salesman solicits orders for a product;
his success depends on the number that he can amass. A concert artist
who caters primarily to public taste is not worthy of our trust. His cardinal obligation is to be faithful to those he musically represents,
particularly to the Muse of song, even if it means ostracism by many
and the acceptance by the few who make up his audience.

Music festivals are like conventions where consumers of music come to hear different artists and a variety of orchestral and choral groups. In ancient times such festivals were contests in which prizes were given for excellence of performance or creativity. During the Middle Ages wandering minstrels gathered at festivals to entertain and amuse the populace. Now music festivals have become commercial ventures primarily, selling culture at a fair rate of exchange. Festivals have always had their commercial side, but never to their present extent.

EDUCATION

Historical   Children find music extremely helpful as an aid in learning. Music aids in the education both of the mind and of the emotions. Music sharpens a child's sensibilities and familiarizes him with his emotional resources. Music intensifies his capacity to feel and probe. Music gives him a sense of order which the outside world does not supply. Music converts the animal in him and transforms him into an affectionate child, sublimates his feelings of hurt and revenge into love and devotion. Education is the sensitizing of the whole child, not of the mind alone.

The Greeks used music to educate in a more serious way than we do. Plato believed that music could strike a balance between gymnastics and letters. During half of his training period, the education of a child in his formative years of development should consist of dancing, singing, and listening to myths. The other half of the time devoted to his education should be spent learning mathematics and dialectics. Although Plato speaks of the musicians as our "fathers and authors of wisdom" [14] he is careful about the kind of poetry and music that he will allow in educating the young.[15] Music enables a child to construct a formidable character, mathematics and dialectics make him as knowledgeable as his neighbor. Music is a powerful aid to help a child find himself, and to prepare him to live with everyone else.

Aristotle believed, as Plato did, that education is a sensitizing process, not just a gathering of facts. Education tempers the emotions as it steels the mind. If emotions can be disciplined to obey the commands of reason, then men will do what is right, act according to the Golden Mean, and strive for the "summum bonum," the highest good that can be attained. Music, Aristotle maintained, is an educational discipline that is empowered to mold emotions and instill virtuous habits in the malleable soul of the child.[16] Each musical mode has a character of its own, such as steadfastness, courage, or gentleness, to which a child will easily respond. A child will retain what he hears, especially if it is repeated and if he listens to certain modes over a period of time. He will imitate the mental dispositions expressed in the music. These ingrained habits he will retain throughout his adult life.

How much musical education should a Greek child receive? "The right measure will be attained if students of music stop short of the arts which are practised in professional contests, and do not seek to acquire those fantastic marvels of execution which are now the fashion in such contests, and from these have passed into education."[17] To what lengths should the musical education of Greek children be drawn out? ". . . until they are able to feel delight in noble melodies and rhythms, and not merely in that common part of music in which every slave or child and even some animals find pleasure."[18] What instruments should be used in education? Plato insisted that only the lyre, simple harp, and the shepherd's pipe were suitable for educational purposes. Aristotle differed somewhat on this point. "The flute [aulos] or any other instrument which requires great skill, as for example the harp, ought not to be admitted into education, . . . the flute is not an instrument which is expressive of moral character; it is too exciting. . . . the impediment which the flute presents to the use of the voice detracts from its educational value."[19]

The low estimate which Aristotle had of the aulos is symbolic of the educational conservatism that he shared with Plato. Their dislike for this instrument is associated with the corruption of Greek civilization. This trend began about four hundred years before they both tried to stem the tide of dissolution, as they saw it. Greece was great and respected when Apollo, the god of patriarchs and aristocrats, reigned supreme. There was dignity in his rule, the lyre was his symbol of classic strength and order. But a wave of unrest, which came as a result of political transitions, brought a democratic surge to Greece. The masses "imagined" that they were equal to the privileged classes. They imported a god from the East, Dionysius, and a foreign instrument called an aulos, to rival the god of the aristocrats. The children of the aristocrats had not yet acquired the prejudices of their parents; and when they heard the noisy and orgiastic music coming from the Dionysian temples, they became as fascinated with this foreign music as the children of the lower classes. Very soon the aulos appeared in the temples of Apollo; a musical instrument had broken down a social barrier. This is precisely what Plato and Aristotle feared would lead to further amalgamation and then compromise until the merchants and artisans ruled Greece instead of the aristocrats. A young Greek would, therefore, not develop into a model patrician if he was indoctrinated with democratic ideas and introduced to musical instruments that were the symbol of a social group inferior to his own.

We know very little about music's place in Roman education except that it was part of the quadrivium which, besides music, included arithmetic, geometry, and astronomy. Roman educators were not as concerned as the Greeks were with the moral and political aspects of music. They probably used music in the education of young children as we do in our kindergartens and in the elementary grades. In more advanced stages of schooling, music was considered a mental discipline in the liberal education of a Roman.

The Christians gave no importance to music in their liberal arts education, but it was used in religious education. St. Basil believed that music could help children learn the psalms more easily than if they tried to memorize the words alone. Teaching children biblical writings with the help of music is like "the practice of wise physicians, who when they give bitter draughts to the sick, often smear the rim of the cup with honey." Musical tropes and liturgical dramas were important forms of education during the Middle Ages. They explained the Mass and Holy Scripture to the Christian populace which could neither read, nor write, nor understand the Latin used in church. In the late Middle Ages, Roger Bacon expressed the view that music helped children learn mathematics because they were both constructed on numbers; music should, therefore, be used for secular as well as religious studies. Luther considered training in music to be important for Protestant children. He maintained that it should be used in education to help a child make social adjustments, such as learning how to sing and dance with other children of his own age group. Educational training was under the aegis of the Church during the Renaissance. Children were taught how to read music and, if they had fair singing voices, were trained for choir service. Practically every composer of the period had sung in a church choir as a child. Higher schools of learning placed music on the level of mathematics as a discipline of the mind. An educated man in the Renaissance could sight read madrigals and motets with the ease of reading a book.

Friedrich Schiller kept the thought alive during the classical and romantic eras that music can reconcile impulse and reason and be effectively used in training young children.[20] He thought that music harmonizes conflicting forces in a child: his impulsive animalistic drives, and a need for order and social adjustment. Music permits a child to discharge his primitive drives in infantile forms of phantasy, and music also serves as a base for instilling patterns of discipline into his life. Music education can reconcile the breach between law and impulse, help an adolescent become a model citizen of society. Through the ordered character of music a child can express his infantile needs which he might otherwise repress out of fear of punishment. The impulsive drives which he may fear to express openly he can express through music in the same manner that he does in play.

Function   Music educates with rules of its own. The composer takes the place of the teacher, and the classroom disappears. There are no other students to compete with for grades of excellence. We achieve success or fail very much alone.

⌐

There is no such thing as a tone-deaf or unmusical child, unless some organic deficiency is present. Some children may have to be taught more slowly than others, with unorthodox methods of pedagogy, how to recognize one rhythmic beat from another and how to carry a tune. Teachers of remedial reading have aptly demonstrated that children who in former years would have been classified as hopelessly incapable of becoming proficient in reading, only needed some psychological guidance to help them become literate beings. A similar situation existed in the past as far as children and music were concerned. The damage done is inestimable when we stop to reflect how many children were embarrassed by their teachers and fellow students because they could not readily carry a tune. These children, now adults, have retained a feeling of inferiority in musical matters which they have never overcome.

Our potential capabilities are not alike at birth, and we all cannot therefore achieve the same level of understanding of music, no matter how hard we try. But our inborn capabilities can be influenced by training and perseverance to a greater degree than is ordinarily believed. In order to reach a high level of musical achievement an intelligence which is above the norm is necessary. But even if we cannot all become virtuosi, we can learn how to read and understand music as we learn to read and write and do arithmetic. We may not all be able to become composers or accomplished performers; but then how many of us become successful poets, even though we know how to read and write?

Nature and democracy present a paradox to a musically educated person. It is natural to feel superior to a neighbor who is not as far advanced as we are musically. Attending concerts is limited to an elite minority and is not taken up by the general public. Education does create social divisions as well as intellectual ones. It would be foolhardy indeed to think in any other terms. But the mark of an educated person is tolerance to new ideas; and if a person well-versed in music should allow his superiority to make him intolerant of other people's musical values, then the purpose of his education is misused. Purists, in this respect, fail the democratic test; they are generally intolerant of their neighbor's musical values.

There is a difference between the way we learn through music and through the regular disciplines. Through music we acquire insights; each bit of knowledge that is revealed to us is a mystical experience. Rhetoric and logic acquaint us only with facts and appearance. Music also educates as dreams do, teaching us to resolve conflicts that are irreconcilable during the waking day.

In music we purge ourselves of the malice and envy in our souls, and dispel the greed in us. Those whom we have bullied and those who have baited us are depersonalized and pass out of our lives in rhythmic sounds. Drives that make us slaves of passion, engender hatred, envy, and greed, are put to sleep by the Muse of song. Learning how to discipline ourselves is an educational enterprise.

Some musical works are like puzzles in life.[21] We take pleasure and delight in filling in gaps that the composer deliberately contrived, so that psychologically we complete the work. It is a sense of achievement or fulfillment which we may not have in real life. Unraveling contrapuntal themes, following a musical line as it weaves in and out and comes to a logical end, is a form of personal accomplishment. Our curiosity is aroused by certain turns the music may take; our inquisitiveness is satisfied when temporary digressions come to rest. Music lends itself well to exercising the mind and emotions simultaneously. Using our faculties to solve puzzles, unravel complex problems, stretch and satisfy the imagination, develops astuteness, assures fuller use of the potentialities nature has given us. Educating the emotions through music will not destroy the animal in us or lessen feeling, any more than becoming literate and discriminating in letters would make us inhibited and jaded in our tastes and responses.

ENTERTAINMENT

Graces and Demons Boredom, ennui, and melancholia are evil demons that torture the mind, twist the body and weigh it down to the ground. Certain types of pleasures are the good graces who often save us from these demons with the help of the arts. The demons are not altogether alike in the intensity of their evil ways, any more than the graces are alike in the amount of good that they do. Boredom is a state of being annoyed, listless, and satiated. It can be any one of these ailments or all three with variations. Ennui is something more serious. Weariness, despondency, futility, and hopelessness are some of its worst symptoms. Melancholia is the darkest of the evil agents. It is like black bile that has driven out the red blood in our veins, turning our moods into dreary darkness. Morbidity, gloom, dejection, and even suicide are examples of its work. The more intelligent, the more sensitive a human being is, the more easily does he fall prey to these three demons of night. And yet, without these afflictions to plague us there would be less art in the world.

⌐

Well-bred gentlemen of Greece pursued a course of noble leisure consistent with their station in life. They studied philosophy and dabbled in the arts for their personal pleasure. A Greek citizen who used his talents for monetary profit was grouped with common laborers and excluded from his social class.

About the time of Plato, members of privileged Greek families began to appear at public contests to vie with professionals in feats of musical skills. It had become quite obvious that music, which was originally a sacred art, was turning into a form of amusement which, according to Plato, was sure to bring ruin to Greece. Music which amuses, as "jugglery" does at a community fair, is evidence of the moral decay that has crept into this ancient art. Musicians who think that their sole purpose is to amuse are no better than grotesque clowns at traveling circuses whose task is to make children laugh. "The excellence of music is to be measured by pleasure,"[22] but of a type that appeals to virtuous and educated persons.

Plato thought that using music to amuse by arousing the emotions was as bad as taking stimulants to offset boredom; a man could become addicted to both. The music which Plato condemned was in his estimation a symptom of the disease which plagued the moral life of Greece. Music that watered the emotions or only amused could have no lasting cure. Throughout his vast writings one theme is stressed: censorship of the arts, particularly music which enervates and only delights the senses.

Aristotle did not agree with Plato that music which is performed essentially for amusement is intrinsically immoral. However, he thought it was improper for aristocrats to compete at public musical contests. He taught his student Alexander moderation, the philosophy of the Golden Mean; a monarch must be wise enough to know how proficient he may be in performing on musical instruments. He must not be as proficient as a professional musician. A man is judged by the task which he performs; a slave works with his hands, a musician performs on instruments, a sovereign rules. Therefore, if a sovereign wishes to perform on an instrument, he must do it in a limited way so that he does not detract from his status. Aristotle thought that emotions charged by amusement are worked off in harmless fancy in the same way that children diffuse excess energy as they play at different games. Amusement in moderation is a moral stabilizer for intellectuals and slaves alike. Music which entertains and pleases because of its mental attraction is more desirable than the kind that amuses by titillating the senses. "And therefore our fathers admitted music into education, not on the ground either of its necessity or utility.... There remains, then, the use of music for intellectual enjoyment in leisure ... this being one of the ways in which it is thought that a freeman should pass his leisure." [23]

Art exists essentially to give us pleasure, Aristotle noted.[24] We derive pleasure from imitating nature; even things which appear ugly to us in their natural state give us pleasure when produced as art. The musician, like the painter and poet, receives pleasure playing the role of a god, creating a more perfect world than the model he copies from. But the musician's task is not fulfilled until his musical creation serves its final purpose, to give pleasure to the listener who must re-create the musician's music for himself.

The Romans became so hopelessly addicted to amusement that it eventually was one of the major causes for their cultural demise. Games and races became as important as politics and military campaigns; their values were the same for life and play. The hippodrome replaced the forum in importance. Moderation gave way to such excess that the average Roman resorted to more and more amusement, as sick men take heavier dosages of medicine as they grow weaker and require opiates to move about. The function of music in the Roman world was primarily to amuse and please, and not as a form of serious entertainment.

Music did not affect Christians in the same outgoing way that it did the Romans. Pious believers used music as though it were fuel to fire their emotions in the service of their religion. They prided themselves on doing without such pleasures as enjoying pleasing musical strains. Both St. Augustine and St. Mary of Egypt confessed how troubled they found themselves when enjoying musical strains that they associated with their youthful days.

There are people in the modern world who respond to music as the early Christians did. Some Christian sects do not permit singing in their church or allow themselves to receive pleasure from secular music. Other Christians will not listen to an "infidel's" sacred music any more than they would visit his church. There are Jews of such orthodoxy that they will not listen to a Mass because of its association with Gentiles. They derive much pleasure from their own music, but not from that of "disbelievers."

Modern man is bored with his newly acquired leisure, and that is a dangerous thing. If art and play, the two safety valves of this mechanized age, cease to serve as outlets for our excess energies, there is very likely to be an explosion. Boredom can come from the monotony of work as well as misused leisure; but however anxiety may accumulate in excess the end result is the same. Boredom can make a well-behaved child into an unruly brat, and turn an adolescent into a delinquent. Boredom will drive men to drink and gambling. It will even tempt them to overthrow a state when the insatiable need for variety in their lives cannot be restrained. Boredom is no friend of man, is the moralist's complaint.[25] Boredom does lead to sin and revolution, as moralists and statesmen claim, but boredom is also the source of much of our music. Music born of boredom is a cure for boredom itself. The danger begins when music ceases to entertain and becomes boring itself.

Music coordinates reason and impulse, the rational and the sensuous in our beings, by stimulating the imagination. In listening to music, as in playing games, we are free to experience in phantasy what we are restrained from doing in society. We substitute the rules of life with rules of our own creation, free of moral obligations and social taboos. Conflicts between reason and desire are temporarily calmed, freedom and necessity momentarily stayed, as we mediate between a world of reality and a world of make-believe which musicians provide, as Morpheus does in dreams, and children experience in games.

Music is like so many other games that we consciously enter into and with which we deliberately deceive ourselves, knowing full well every minute of the game what we are up to. But in order to deceive ourselves we must observe certain rules which nature stipulates and which we cannot circumvent with rules of our own. We play solitaire rather than tennis when we are tired; one would be normally pleasant under such circumstances and the other would be taxing so that it might well be unpleasant. We derive pleasure from music that we are familiar with when we are mentally fatigued. Listening to new and intricate music when tired and weary would exhaust us all the more. Nature is specific on this point; we can only be as tolerant and receptive as our health permits. Listening to complex music is not any more restful than playing chess after a day's energy has been expended. We have come to associate rest with pleasantness, tiredness with unpleasantness, in the course of our lives. Music which is likely to sound pleasant to us when we are rested and fresh may well lose this quality for us when we are exhausted and would rather rest.

All entertainment simulates actual life in phantasy, and music is no exception. Our anxieties and fears of the practical world are transferred to entertainments which amuse and sadden us. But in entertainment our actual anxieties are diffused into wistful make-believe in the manner of a catharsis. Entertainment will not completely erase our difficulties, but only bring them into the open so that we may see them from a different perspective, detached and more objective. Since ancient times music as entertainment has been medicine for men's souls.

Entertainment furnishes us with imaginary excursions to places that we cannot get to physically, or are frightened away from for moral reasons. Music as entertainment can sketch far away places in our imagination that we are not able to reach bodily, and can blot the moral censor out of sight so that we have no shame for our mental escapades. Such illusory adventures only partially satisfy our romantic needs which we miss in actual life. But it is because we can work out this need, in this deceptive way, that we are capable of remaining more stable and moral in life than we might be if this outlet were denied us.

Jazz   Jazz is an American creation that has spread around the world. Its appeal is so strong that it has worn down the vigilance of bureaucrats in foreign lands who would keep this "alien" music from making cultural inroads into the lives of their youth. Moralists in our own country attribute vice and corruption to this art. Of late, jazz has been used to accompany a religious service so that people coming to church would hear music in the idiom of their day.

⌐

Jazz began as amusement; only on rare occasions has is risen to heights of serious entertainment worthy of being performed in our finest concert halls. In a little more than half a century it has traveled from bawdy houses, saloons, and minstrel shows into our living rooms and houses of worship. Jazz dominates the air waves as though it were the cultural barometer of the times. It has a primitive and immediate appeal for both young and old. There is no escape from its ubiquitous presence. It may never become a serious art form. The sensations that it arouses in us are all too fleeting because of the brevity of its traditional forms. When it is used in ballets, sonatas, concertos, and operas, its melodies are short-lived, its rhythms are monotonously alike. Its sustaining power is weak and appeals more to the feet than to the heart and head. Nevertheless, jazz has enriched the musical world by its appeal to all classes of people. Our youth consider jazz their private medium that separates them culturally from their elders. Many serious composers have directly or subtly introduced jazz rhythms and instrumental techniques into their works. Jazz influences in serious musical works are like alcoholic stimulants in medicinal tonics which teetotalers would ordinarily avoid but thoroughly enjoy when they are disguised.

Ragtime is the precursor of jazz. It dates back to the end of the last century. Its source of life comes from songs that were performed in minstrel shows, spirited country dances, and marches. The earliest ragtime musicians played mostly by ear and improvised as they went along. The blues came after ragtime, early in this century. Its source of inspiration came from spirituals, and Negro work songs. The lamenting qualities of the spiritual, pleading with the Lord for love and understanding, are transferred to a human lover in the first songs of Negro blues singers.

Jazz was born in the brothels of New Orleans; its parents were ragtime and blues. From one parent was derived syncopation, from the other, melody. A handful of illiterate Negro musicians were its first nursemaids and they nourished jazz so well that in a decade it went from New Orleans to Chicago and New York. Trained musicians soon adopted jazz and introduced it to the legitimate theater and movies; after that they brought jazz to the concert stage and eventually to the finest opera house in the land.

Jazz became refined. Its original melodies were sickeningly sweetened and erotic rhythms were tempered by white arrangers for standardized commercial musical works. A small group of Negroes who did not believe that jazz should be completely written out and rehearsed in detail, as symphonic music is, retained its original improvisational character. Their music was personal, free, and not confined to what a commercial arranger set down for them to follow. They improvised in a personal style for as long as they wished; each man in the small band took his turn as soloist to show his prowess. They made no attempt to play sustained melodies, follow rules of harmony, or bother with different keys. One man led and the other members of the band followed. At times it seemed like a religious revival, so great was the spiritual dedication to music, so ecstatic was the mood of the performer and audience.

Swing's contribution to jazz was meager. There was little about it that was original. It shook the sensibilities of the music public with its disrespectful "swinging" of classical works. True, ragtime and blues had done so too, both for bands and symphonic orchestras, but they did it with dignity and out of respect for the classics, not to deride them as swing enthusiasts did. Rock 'n' roll is the musical aftermath of a terrible war. Of all the popular forms that have existed, it has been attacked more fiercely by moralists and statesmen than any of the others.

A noted psychiatrist compared it to a "communicable disease" which appeals to "adolescent rebellion and insecurity." He made this diagnosis on the basis of a youthful "disturbance" in a local theater where a "name band" was appearing. In another part of the world statesmen complained that decadent, bourgeois jazz from the capitalist world incites their youth to rebel against party discipline. A segregation "leader" in our own country charged that enemies of the status quo in the southland are demoralizing "Dixie" youth with "cannibalistic and tribalistic" music. The English press carried the news that the kind of music that has been provoking near riots in the United States is having a similar and unsavory influence on the young people of Britain. The board of censors in a South American country banned "all public demonstrations of Rock 'n' roll" to protect the public from this insidious medium.

It is true that jazz, particularly music as primitive and crude as rock 'n' roll is, brings out the worst in our youth and incites them to riot. Adolescents are often so carried away by this earthy music that they work out their hostility and anger in actuality instead of phantasy, as is usually the case. Jazz is an outlet for repression and the sheer bitterness that young people harbor within them; its value goes far beyond simple amusement in dance halls and jam sessions.

There is good jazz and bad jazz just as there is good and bad serious music. Jazz has its own criteria for determining values. A good jazz piece has an energetic rhythmic beat if it is danced to, and a short endearing melody if it is sung. The rhythm must be easy to follow and the melody learned without difficulty. It must have elements of tension and release, however simple the music may be. It must not become technically involved or elaborate in size. It should please for the moment and soon be forgotten, as light forms of amusement are expected to. Most jazz tunes are so alike and lacking in originality that they do not long endure. But jazz tunes do appear on rare occasions that are so refreshingly new and infectious that they take their place in our folk music. When jazz is used in classical musical forms it must be judged by the standards employed in serious music.

Jazz is "hot" and "cool" and very much like a woman of many moods. It can rage like a scorching fire and ignite everything around it. It can blow like a soft south wind and then gently move on to another mood. When its temper is "hot" it revels in dance halls and jam sessions, and when in this torrid state its enemies compare it to a woman of the street. "Cool" jazz is found in the soulful improvisations of languid piano players, refined orchestrations and symphonic jazz. Jazz, on such occasions, is like an elegant lady notwithstanding its shady past.

Jazz has fared so well economically and socially of late that it has even taken to going to church, not as a performer at weddings and funerals as in former days, but as an accompanist to the liturgy itself. It is simply repeating an age old practice of bringing secular music into the house of worship. Its claim for a place at the religious service is based on the supposition that jazz is more representative of men's feelings in the modern world than music that was composed for other ages.

However well jazz has fared it cannot rise to full maturity as an art and must remain content to be a less than serious form of amusement. Jazz is still on the level of a sultry child for all its niceties, though its age be more than a half century. Its potentialities are limited, and when invited into the concert hall it appears awkward in presence. Its forms are ragged, melodies all too short, and rhythms, even when crossed and compounded, remain jungle beats. When jazz is "sweet," it is like a coy and flighty adolescent. Jazz is at its best when itself—ludicrous when miscast as an intellectual.

Jazz has made many contributions to our lives, not all of which have been good; but it has not greatly developed. Jazz has taught the world to sing and dance more freely than ever before. It has enriched serious music with its syncopated rhythms and instrumental colors. Its musicians revived the practice of improvising instead of playing mechanically and following a conductor as in the symphony and opera. Jazz has been our American ambassador; it has made friends with people in lands that our diplomats could never reach.

SUMMARY

Music has accompanied mankind in his daily chores from the earliest stages of civilization. Music helped women at their household duties and farmers in the field. Music eased the burden of captive slaves constructing monuments in Egypt and Greece. Now, mechanization of industry is so advanced, laborers are no longer treated as beasts of burden. Modern workers are plagued with boredom and fatigue because of the nature of their work. They no longer sing as they perform their tasks, but have machines do it for them.

The Greeks considered the production of music a craft, such as weaving, building, and making shoes. True, the musician was divinely inspired, but like all craftsmen, he was a skilled producer of his art, creating for a purposeful end. Music was, for the Greeks, an art of making (techné), an industry devoted to human needs as every other industry is.

The Church was the primary consumer of music during the Middle Ages. Composers of serious music had very few outlets aside from the Church. Some minstrels were employed by Church dignitaries and aristocrats to produce secular music, but most of them earned their livelihood wandering and performing from place to place. The rise of publishing houses industrialized music during the Renaissance. The invention of the phonograph revolutionized the music industry in the twentieth century.

Our earliest descriptions of using music as a therapy comes from Greek literature although the Greeks themselves said that it had been known long before their time. Greek Bacchic priests were reputed to have made periodic excursions throughout the land to assemble women who were mentally disturbed and bring them to the temple for treatment. The priests would presumably cure their patients by playing flutes in a Phrygian mode with such fury that the "wild" women would respond to the "wild" music by taking to dancing and singing. This treatment continued until it took on the aspects of an orgy. The more frenzied the music became, the more frantic the dancing and singing became. In time the mentally deranged women would fall to the ground from exhaustion and enter into a deep sleep. Upon awakening, their irrational behavior would have subsided and they would return to their families cured.

The Greeks and Egyptians looked upon the insane as sick individuals. Egyptian priests used music and occupational therapy as part of their treatment for the mentally ill, the Greeks used music and "kindness," but these methods of handling the insane were forgotten. In the Middle Ages the insane were thought to be possessed of the devil. These devils must therefore be exorcised by moral or spiritual means. Pilgrimages to shrines were used for the mildly insane but those who were considered a menace to the community were either expelled from the towns or locked up in the jails to be chained, starved, tortured, and even burned.

Real hospitals for the insane, not just retention places, were established in the nineteenth century. Before that, there had been mention of an asylum in Jerusalem in the fifth century, and in England and France abandoned monasteries were eventually used to separate the insane from the criminals. Bedlam, for example, was originally founded as a priory and later used for the insane.

The impressive advances which clinical psychology has made since the turn of this century is almost equalled by those of the academically trained profession of musical therapists. They have gone as far beyond the aulos-playing temple priest as the psychiatrist has from the medicine man who used music and a magic wand to exorcise evil spirits lodged in a sick patient's mind or body. We have, however, retained many of the linguistic expressions which connected music with medicine.[26]

Music was used to educate long before formal schools existed. Primitive children learned about their ancestors through songs and tribal chants. In music their ancient mores and religions were preserved. One generation taught another the ceremonial songs and dances that went with hunting and fighting. Tribal chieftains and medicine men eventually were replaced by professional teachers who instructed the young. The most colorful dispensers of knowledge, but not always the most respected, were the wandering minstrels who sang historic odes wherever they went. In Greece, minstrels kept alive the glories of the past through their songs and recitations. They did not have the prestige of sophists who taught rhetoric and dialectic, and who instructed mainly for money. Bards wandered throughout the far-flung regions of the Roman Empire singing of battles and the deeds of heroes. Minnesingers, troubadours and trouvères carried on this work throughout the Middle Ages.

Music, dancing, and sports were part of Greek education. All three contributed to the building of character and a strong body. It was traditional with the Greeks to have music performed during sport festivals. They were considered religious events; both the musician and the athlete dedicated their talents to the gods. Roman educators followed in the footsteps of the Greeks in using music to accompany young children in dancing but they stopped using music in their sports. Plutarch believed this was because Roman musicians gave up composing for the gods and turned to the theater for inspiration and a livelihood. Roman contests lost their religious character and qualities of character training and became gruesome exhibitions of brute strength.

The Christians used music to teach the psalms; music added to words helped a child memorize more easily. Their educators taught children to distrust the body in contrast to the importance that the Greeks assigned to it. Although the Church did not officially disapprove of dancing, we do not know how seriously it discouraged its use in education. The Church Fathers insisted that only sacred music should be taught; dancing to sacred music was not permitted. If a child, therefore, were allowed to dance to secular strains he would become acquainted with secular music and the whole purpose of a Christian education would be defeated.

Roger Bacon was quite advanced in his musical ideas, both in the application of music to the treatment of the sick and in physical education. He saw no harm in music and dancing and even encouraged Catholic educators to use music and dance in training children. Luther, later on, advised Protestant educators to emulate the Greeks by using music and dancing in the education of the young in order to produce Christians strong in body as well as fervent in spiritual matters.

In the Renaissance, music had an importance almost equal to mathematics in the two most famous universities in England, Oxford and Cambridge. Music and mathematics were considered to have similar powers that could be used with good profit to discipline the mind. English educators, in the Age of Enlightenment, used music as the Greeks had done, to discipline bodies as well as minds. John Locke considered dancing a vital part of a child's education. He pointed out that the effects of dancing give children "not mere outward gracefulness of motion, but manly thoughts and a becoming confidence."

Locke thought that dancing to music would build character and body, and transform an awkward child into a well-coordinated one.

In our schools of today, music is used to accompany calisthenics as well as the dance. It can help a child develop a sense of rhythm in a direct way. Music used in this fashion gives a child an opportunity to harmonize his physical actions with others in a group. Music has very definite psychological effects, as well as physical ones, even when it is used as an adjunct of another activity, such as calisthenics.

The education that our children receive is often parochial and narrow. Wherever this is true, the amount of time spent on the emotional needs of a child is inadequate in comparison to the time that is spent on mental and physical exercise. Music will have to accompany the scientific revolution taking place in our schools or the emotional life of our children will be limited to solving mathematical problems. Music educates in ways that factual knowledge and technical skills cannot.

When we use music with school sports it is only as amusement and relief from the tensions of the game. Music that is marched to has a high disciplinary value in physical education. But it can be a social catalyst when used at athletic events. People who are unknown to each other, in number by the thousands, will sing as one with unfettered gusto at the beckoning of a single cheer leader.

Music's prime functions are entertainment and amusement now but it has not always been so. In ancient times music was used to worship, hunt, and cure the sick. Entertainment and amusement were its least important functions. Only after primitive man developed skills and knowledge that helped him to survive with less effort than he had expended previously did he find that a new factor had entered into his life—leisure. Singing to himself and in groups during leisure time became an accepted way to live. In time, music as entertainment and amusement became as important as music for the hunt and ceremonial rites had been. Now the latter two are almost gone from our lives, and we have more leisure than we can use.

The additional leisure which the machines have brought us seems to increase our boredom, most of us are so ill-prepared to entertain ourselves. Our insatiable craving for amusement increases proportionately to the monotony of mechanized labor and not knowing what to do with ourselves when we are alone. In this kind of climate music is judged by its qualities to amuse and quite often these qualities are esthetically very poor.

If the level of musical amusement should sink to a low point throughout the land, as some moralists think it already has, it will be a bad omen for us. The crosscurrents of our time, the anxiety of the day are reflected in the erotic character of popular songs and the harsh, biting music of the serious modern composer. But if ever our music should become so boring for lack of esthetic substance that it is no longer emotionally satisfying, we will require music that appeals to the jaded tastes that we associate with those who are satiated with pleasure. Deterioration of taste leads to a loss of discrimination and intelligence in the kinds of decisions we make. The usual direction that such events take is to drift lower and further away from a healthy mean.

Jazz is a form of amusement, not serious entertainment. It is possible to make it into a classical art form by complicating and extending its melodic line and changing its simple rhythmic structure to a more varied one. But when this was done, by composers of repute, a hybrid musical art emerged that was neither amusing nor worthy of serious attention. Jazz is at its best when it is raw, vibrant, and partly improvised. It is beautiful and endearing in musical comedies, but often out of place when turned into serious compositions and performed in a concert hall.

NOTES

[1] I Samuel. 16:23. "And it came to pass, when the *evil* spirit from God was upon Saul, that David took an harp, and played with his hand: so Saul was refreshed, and was well, and the evil spirit departed from him."

[2] Homer *Odyssey*, Bk. XIX. Athenaeus relates this story of how music was used to cure sciatica: "That music can also heal diseases Theophrastus has recorded in his work *On Inspiration*: he says that persons subject to sciatica would always be free from its attacks if one played the flute in the Phrygian mode over the

part affected."—*The Deipnosophists,* VI, trans. Charles Burton Gulick (Cambridge, Mass.: Harvard University Press, 1950), Bk. XIV, 624.

[3] Homer *Iliad,* Bk. I. 472.

[4] Sir John Hawkins, *General History of the Science and Practice of Music,* I (London: T. Payne and Son, 1776), Bk. III, p. 318. Hawkins quotes Boethius: "And so well was the power of music known to the ancient philosophers, that the Pythagoreans, when they had a mind to refresh themselves by sleep after the labours and cares of the day, made use of certain songs to procure them an easy and quiet rest; and when they awaked they also dispelled the dulness and confusion occasioned by sleep by others, knowing full well that the mind and the body were conjoined in a musical fitness, and that whatever affects the body will also produce a similar effect on the mind; which observation it is reported Democritus, whom his fellow-citizens had confined, supposing him mad, made to Hippocrates the physician, who had been sent for to cure him." Poets throughout the ages have kept alive the thought that music brings balm and surcease to a tortured mind. Aeschylus, *The Complete Greek Drama,* I, *Agamemnon* (New York: Random House, Inc., 1938), p. 167.

> *And if at whiles, for the lost balm of sleep,*
> *I medicine my soul with melody*
> *Of trill or song . . .*

Shakespeare, *The Tempest,* Act I, Scene ii.

> *This music crept by me upon the waters,*
> *Allaying both their fury, and my passion,*
> *With its sweet air: thence I have follow'd it,—*
> *Or it hath drawn me rather, . . .*

[5] Plato *Laws,* Bk. VII. 790-791.

[6] Aristotle *Politics,* Bk. VIII. 1342a. "For feelings such as pity and fear, or again, enthusiasm, exist very strongly in some souls, and have more or less influence over all. Some persons fall into a religious frenzy, whom we see as a result of the sacred melodies—when they have used the melodies that excite the soul to mystic frenzy—restored as though they had found healing and purgation. Those who are influenced by pity or fear, and every emotional nature, must have a like experience, and others in so far as each is susceptible to such emotions, and all are in a manner purged and their souls lightened and delighted."

[7] Henry Peacham, *The Compleat Gentleman* (London: Clarendon Press, 1906), p. 98.

[8] Thomas Hobbes, *Leviathan* [Introduction by A. D. Lindsay] (London: J. M. Dent & Sons, Ltd., 1931), p. xi.

[9] Hawkins, *op. cit.,* p. xxx. "What an implicit assent has been given to the reports of the sovereign efficacy of music in the cure of the frenzy occasioned by the bite of the Tarantula! Baglivi, an eminent physician, a native of Apulia, the country where the Tarantula, a kind of spider, is produced, has given the natural history of this supposed noxious insect, and a variety of cases of persons rendered frantic by its bite, and restored to sanity and the use of their reason; and in Kircher's Musurgia we have the very air or tune by which the cure is said to be effected."

[10] Reprinted by permission of the publishers from Aelian *On Animals,* trans. A. F. Scholfield (Cambridge, Mass.: Harvard University Press), Vol. III; XII, 46. Copyright 1959 by The President and Fellows of Harvard College.

[11] *Ibid.,* Vol. II, VI, 31.

[12] *Ibid.,* 32.

[13] *Grove's Dictionary of Music and Musicians,* III (3d ed.; New York: The Macmillan Company, 1946), p. 284.

[14] Plato *Lysis.* 214.

[15] Plato *Republic,* Bk. X. 607. "Homer is the greatest of poets and first of tragedy writers; but we must remain firm in our conviction that hymns to the gods and praises of famous men are the only poetry which ought to be admitted into our State. For if you go beyond this and allow the honeyed muse to enter, either in epic or lyric verse, not law and the reason of mankind, which by common consent have ever been deemed best, but pleasure and pain will be the rulers in our State."

[16] Aristotle *Politics,* Bk. VIII. Chap. 5. 1340b. "The whole subject has been well treated by philosophical writers on this branch of education, and they confirm their arguments by facts.... Enough has been said to show that music has a power of forming the character, and should therefore be introduced into the education of the young."

[17] *Ibid.,* Chap. 6. 1341a.

[18] *Ibid.*

[19] *Ibid.*

[20] Friedrich Schiller, *On the Aesthetic Education of Man,* Letter 23, trans. Reginald Snell (London: Routledge & Kegan Paul Ltd., 1954), p. 108. "... there is no other way to make the sensuous man rational than by first making him aesthetic."

[21] *See* R. G. Collingwood, *The Principles of Art* (New York: Oxford University Press, 1958), pp. 84-88.

[22] Plato *Laws,* Bk. II. 658-659. "Thus far I too should agree with the many, that the excellence of music is to be measured by pleasure. But the pleasure must not be that of chance persons; the fairest music is that which delights the best and best educated, and especially that which delights the one man who is pre-eminent in virtue and education."

[23] Aristotle *Politics,* Bk. VIII. Chap. 3. 1338a.

[24] Aristotle *Niomachean Ethics,* Bk. X. Chap. 4. 1175a.

[25] *A Kierkegaard Anthology,* ed. Robert Bretall (Princeton: Princeton University Press, 1947), p. 24. "Boredom is the root of all evil," wrote Kierkegaard in *Either/Or.* "Idleness is not an evil," he continued, "indeed one may say that every human being who lacks a sense for idleness proves that his consciousness has not yet been elevated to the level of the humane.... Idleness is by no means as such a root of evil; on the contrary, it is a truly divine life, provided one is not himself bored."

[26] William Fleming, *Arts and Ideas* (New York: Holt, Rinehart and Winston,

Inc., 1955), p. 32. "The importance attached by the Greeks to the role of music in health and life is found in certain linguistic images that are still in current use. To them a happy person was like a well-tuned lyre. When the body and soul were in a proper state of attunement, a person was well and health thus meant being in a harmonious condition. Muscles, when the body was in good form, were said to have the proper tone, and physicians today still speak of a quality of 'muscular tonus.' When individuals were too tense they were said to be 'high strung'; or when too relaxed or depressed, they were 'low' and needed a 'tonic' to tone or tune them up. When things reached a really critical state, the patient was said to be all 'unstrung.' Still another Greek word connected with health was *katharsis*, which Aristotle used in reference to the function of art as a purging of the emotions through the experience of music and the drama."

CHAPTER VII

BELIEFS and MYTHS ABOUT MUSIC

TRADITIONS

An institution or art without tradition is like a fruit still green on the vine; tradition that outlives its usefulness is like an overripe fruit that goes to rot. Every tradition which exists was once an innovation whose coming was fought against just as hard as men fight, later on, to abolish it. Whether it be in art or life, the new and the outmoded rarely come and go without a struggle. Certain traditions are necessary for stability; complete anarchy would turn the human kingdom into a jungle. It is as necessary to have traditions in music as in the practical world. They are similar to the basic mores and customs of a society without which that society could not exist. If music is to retain its character, then whatever innovations are introduced, however avant-garde they may be, the music must have some resemblance to traditional concepts of tone and rhythm.

~

The history of music is a story about an interminable struggle between men with new ideas and men who cringe at the thought of permitting anything different to enter into their lives for fear that it might have an adverse effect on their security. Traditions and accepted beliefs are comforting; something new and revolutionary brings uncertainty and even fear to timid souls. Traditions are not determined by fixed laws such as those, for example, which cause night to follow day; but changing traditions are inevitable, as inevitable as the physical changes that take place in the world. New ideas are as necessary to our spiritual existence as food is to our bodies. But not all new ideas and changes are necessarily good for us. Some may be forms of retrogression that we could well do without.

Our knowledge of Greek music is based mainly on what philosophers have written, not on what musicians have left us to peruse. Among the handful of precious fragments of actual Greek music that we have in our possession are two *Delphic Hymns to Apollo* which were carved in musical notation on a wall of the Treasury of the Athenians at Delphi and part of a selection from the *Orestes* of Euripides. These musical works do not have the same emotional appeal for us as they had for the Greeks, however sympathetic we may be when listening to them. Time and ethnic differences play havoc with our emotions. Traditions in one's own life span that are very different cannot be easily assimilated, let alone those with a difference in time of almost three thousand years.

If we could be transplanted into ancient Greece with the wave of a magic wand, we would find that the musical scene was not unlike the kind we have in our time. Musician attacked musician over stylistic changes. Aristophanes tangled with Euripides; Euripides favored the new, Aristophanes agreed with Plato that playwrights such as Euripides were ruining the country with drastic innovations. After the magic wand that took us to Greece waved us back home, we could reflect on what we saw and heard and see for ourselves whether Aristophanes and Plato were justified or whether Euripides lent his name to a cause that died or altered the musical world.

The Romans were practical people. They built roads and bridges that are still used, constructed aqueducts that carried water for many miles, and created new techniques of warfare with which they conquered a large part of the world. Unfortunately, they did not show the same genius for developing the art of music as they did for constructing monuments and a political empire. Their musical writings have not survived, and songs that they passed down to each other by rote have long since disappeared. We know about Roman musical traditions from poets and philosophers, such as Horace and Boethius.

Roman music was not staid and dignified in comparison to Greek musical styles. Music contests in the Roman world encouraged novelty instead of perpetuating tradition as the contest judges in Greece insisted on. Romans did not possess qualities of moderation in their daily habits, such as the early Romans and early Greeks took such pride in following. This element of excess was reflected in their music and was satirically noted by Horace in scathing poetry which dealt with the cultural degeneration that was taking place in his own lifetime.

The Christians did not excel in such engineering feats as the building of roads and aqueducts, as the Romans, or in drama, as the Greeks; but in the process of Christianizing the Western world, they did develop the physical structure of its music. St. Paul, in his sermons to the first groups of Christians, set the moral tone for their musical traditions. He preached that the original Greek ideal of moderation is noble but impracticable. He noted that moderation is a form of compromise which eventually leads to excess in earthly pleasures, as was the case with the Romans. A Christian life must be based on abstinence and obedience, thus self-denial and blind faith became the Christian virtues. Penance replaced Roman pleasure. Moderation was frowned upon by the Patristics so that a pious Christian became as extreme in practicing abnegation as a Roman was in searching for new sources of amusement. Tertullian, the zealot, called the theater Satan's residence. St. Augustine experienced guilt from hearing music that gave him pleasure. Pope Gregory banned secular knowledge. As late as the thirteenth century, St. Thomas wrote that scholars who are dedicated to the study of the liberal arts are more enslaved than free. It was his contention that the only liberating writings that exist are found in the Bible.

Shortly after St. Thomas died, the composer slipped out from under ecclesiastical control and very soon after changed the style and emphasis of his compositions from the kind that the Church expected of him. He set secular poems to music in great abundance, restrained the words so that they would not mar his musical line, and endowed his scores with flowing rhythms that gave them elegance and grace. He kept all the voices in his work equally balanced and, throughout the score, a modal quality prevailed.

The baroque era consists of three different musical periods: the early, middle, and late baroque. It began toward the close of the sixteenth century and ended with the death of Bach. At the outset of the baroque era the influence of Palestrina on many composers was so great that it led to the existence of two practices of writing—one emulating the Renaissance master Palestrina, and the other stressing the "spontaneous expression" of the composer himself.

It must be remembered that the Renaissance composer was as interested in the esthetic theories of the Greeks as the Renaissance painter and poet. In the music of the Renaissance composer there are a number of ideas pertaining to music that the Greeks embraced, but these ideas are expressed in a subtle and mild way. In the baroque era the composer used the same classical ideas that the Renaissance composer had used, but he employed them with exaggerated force. The Renaissance composer all but ignored the doctrine of affections, which was originally a Greek esthetic practice; the baroque composer used it with exaggeration. The composers of both eras were interested in the text—as their idols the Greeks were. The Renaissance composer frequently employed subtle word-painting (expressing through a musical idea the basic thought of a word or phrase). Nevertheless, he would not sacrifice his music for a text. The baroque composer, on the other hand, emphasized the sense of the text at the expense of the music when it served his purpose to do so.

The devices which the late baroque composers used to heighten the emotional intensity of certain words or passages in the libretto were familiar to almost everyone in the opera house. One motif, for example, suggested pathos, and another fear. This was the underlying principle of the doctrine of affections. The motifs that were used to portray the different emotions in the doctrine of affections were standardized, but, to a considerable degree, the types of expression were the same in all baroque forms of art. Composers matched wits and compared skills with each other in the way that they used these stylistic techniques. It was not an age in which composers dedicated their lives to being different from each other, but rather one in which they tried to improve stylistically on their contemporaries in expressing specific emotions. The feat of musically treating a specific emotion more ingeniously than other composers, had a ring of creativity about it to baroque listeners. In the world of painting the practice was quite the same. Painters portrayed similar scenes, the scene itself was never wholly demolished, as it so often is at present, but was retained and enhanced, in a peculiarly individualistic fashion. This was the painter's way of improving on his fellow artists.

The music of the Renaissance composer was written in such fashion that it could be performed either instrumentally or vocally. The baroque composer wrote his music around the specific characteristics of an instrument or voice and, therefore, his music could not be either sung or played at the discretion of the performer. Later on, the practice developed of transferring the musical techniques that were used to emphasize the peculiar characteristics of one specific instrument to another instrument, or to the voice. This practice even extended to transferring the musical characteristics that were associated with one musical form to that of another musical form.

In baroque music the *basso continuo* is the musical foundation on which the chords rest; the upper voice is free to carry the melody and produce individual expression. In Renaissance music all voices were equally balanced and dissonance was achieved through restrictive rhythmic techniques. Baroque music had a strong sense of tonality, chordal direction, and possessed a harmonic sense of polarity between the bass and soprano. Renaissance music was modal and, to use a metaphor, had a linear quality in contrast to the perpendicular quality of baroque harmonic tones. Finally, however restricted Renaissance rhythms were, they flowed with evenness and serenity while the baroque rhythms were often agitated and extreme.

Musical traditions are not found only in the changing styles of composition and alterations in public taste. Quite often personal sacrifices that composers make are very important. Of the three overpowering figures of the classical era, fate was kinder to Haydn than to Mozart or Beethoven. Haydn's genius shone through every musical form that he touched except one—the opera; this form he thought would bring him immortality, but not one of his operas is well remembered. The music that he wrote to be played during his patron's dinner parties we now listen to as though it were of sacred origin. Mozart, precocious child, master composer, defender of the under-privileged, died at the age of thirty-five and was laid to rest in an unmarked grave. His operas are satires on archaic customs, but they flow like wine and intoxicate us with laughter now that his world of inequities is gone. Contemporaries called his music "heart rending"; it sounds pleasant to us now. Beethoven broke rules of composition at random. He also changed the social status of the composer in the Western world. With music as his weapon, he showed his scorn for Napoleon in the same way that Mozart fought religious and political tyranny up to the day that he died.

The musical styles of the classical and romantic periods are neatly marked out in Nietzsche's distinction between the character of Apol-lonian and Dionysian art. One is calm and peaceful, the other is frenzied and bombastic. In classical musical styles, form and order are prominent; feeling and impulse do not run rampant but are expressed somewhat in the way a disciplined man tempers his desires and ar-ranges his life in an orderly fashion. The classical composer bears out Aristotle's theories on the creation and function of music. Aristotle pointed out that all men have a natural inclination to imitate nature and a very strong desire to impose order on nature. The classical musi-cian does not merely imitate the sounds of nature, but transforms them into sounds more imaginative and even more wonderful than they are. What the musician has actually accomplished by this feat is to supplement nature's world by making it more complete and better ordered than he originally found it.

Romantic musical styles are more expansive and less well-knit than classical ones. Feeling and emotion are freely expressed, quite often at the price of bringing disunity to a work. Romantic ecstasy knew no bounds in its degrees of expressiveness. Schopenhauer and Nietzsche, champions of the romantic cause, extolled the virtues of feeling over the power of reason. They warned composers to shun

Jack Levine (1915–   ), *String Quartette*. Tempera and oil on composition board, 47 1/2 by 67 1/2 in. The Metropolitan Museum of Art, Arthur H. Hearn Fund, 1942.

logic and reason and let mysticism guide them. Language and mathematics "can never adequately render the cosmic symbolism of music," wrote Nietzsche; music "symbolizes a sphere which is beyond and before all phenomena." [1]

Two composers who listened to the voice of mysticism went on to shatter the musical rules. Berlioz and Wagner, complained Schönberg, wrecked the diatonic system by letting their feelings run wild, and since this ancient system could not keep up with them, the system almost played itself out. Schönberg, therefore, took it upon himself to construct a new musical order that would be ruled by the strictest logic—atonality his disciples called it. Atonality was intended as a panacea for romantic decadence. Romantic composers had forced the diatonic system beyond its normal range. Esthetically they resorted to painting pictures and telling stories with melodic tones and rhythms. At first, atonality was like a muscle-bound athlete suffering from self-induced paralysis, incapable of flexing his muscles. Nevertheless, in recent decades atonality served a useful purpose by doing away with our obsession for tonally centered musical works. What seemed to be a restrictive system of mathematical inflexibility has turned out to be an important step in preparing us for imaginative nontonal music and electronic music.

Contemporary musicians and painters are guided by similar precepts in their work. They are concerned with creating an impersonal art, an art based on the merit of its structure alone and not on romantic associations. Much of the music of Stravinsky and Bartók has been written with a hymn-like directness and purity of style. Some of their music is marked by classical simplicity and the kind of integrity that one finds in the work of the elder Bach. Neoclassicism in music is similar to paintings which do away with sentimental references and pictorial illustrations. Paintings consist of colors, patterns, and contrasts; that is how they should be seen and judged. Music is made up of notes and sounds; the logic with which they are developed and the sincerity with which it is done are the things that count, not what we associate with them in our private lives.

The tape recorder and electronic music machines are important inventions of the twentieth century. A variety of music machines have existed for hundreds of years, but none with the potentialities of these two modern machines. Before this century is over, children who are yet to be born will be listening to music machines as part of their standard musical repertoire. Electronic machines will be employed extensively to teach harmony and sight reading. Machines which will function according to certain rhythms, pitch, and intensity will be used as diagnostic aids in medicine. Physicians will use them to test our reflexes, the conditions of our bones, and to record the oscillating tempo of our brains to check on mental disturbances. Anesthetists will use music machines in preference to, or in conjunction with, present types of sedation.

DOGMATISM

Dogmatism is a form of belief. It brooks no compromise and is resolute in the conviction that only one belief is right and all the others are wrong.

⌐

A full-fledged dogmatist is like an octopus whose tentacles reach out in all directions to grasp at everything within reach. Moralists and political fanatics who believe in one truth and one way of life are prone to seek control over every facet of our lives, including the kind of music we should have. They spread their gospel, and sometimes their venom, with ardent zeal. They try to control our lives by stifling our thoughts and having us act and think as they do. We are told what is good and what to avoid, both in actual life and in the arts. The penalty for not following this advice may be religious condemnation and political ostracism.

Tolstoy maintained that it would be better not to have any music than to have the wrong kind.[2] In his estimation, only music that fits the requirements needed to establish a brotherhood of man based on the original doctrines of Christ has any right to exist. His views are not very different from those we have seen in Plato and the three Western faiths. They are similar to those of the Soviet Union, as they would be to those of any authoritarian and totalitarian state.

Musical dogmatists would ban certain types of music when they have power in their hands and they will, on occasions, remove the works of certain composers from the repertoire and sometimes even change their names. The Nazis did not perform the works of composers who challenged their ideology, and they changed the names of Jewish composers to "Anonymous." Children were taught, on the basis of a pseudoracial theory, that Aryans were superior to Semites and Slavs. Since the Nazis could not deny that Mendelssohn's music sang as clearly as the nightingale and Heine's poetry was superbly articulate, they used the name "Anonymous" where the names of Mendelssohn and Heine should have been.

Dogmatism exists in milder forms too. During the first half of our century a group of well-intentioned "scientists" turned into a fraternity of fanatics over the merits of musical tests. These men, experimental psychologists by vocation, devised tests which they insisted could determine the innate musical potentialities of every child and late adolescent, from kindergarten age to college level. These tests were like a black plague in the musical world. Music administrators and supervisors became infected with the "scientific" bug. With these tests they separated the "sheep from the goats," the musical from the unmusical on the elementary school level. They used these tests as "scientific tools" in the entrance examinations required of candidates wishing to take a degree in music. The creators of the tests were quite smug and complacent about the validity of their findings. They were certain about one thing and with this "truth" they would not compromise: a child with a low score on a musical aptitude test could not improve his rhythmic and tonal perceptivity to any great extent.

Dogmatic positions can have elements of truth to them, but they are rarely the whole story; and, so it was with this unfortunate attempt to use "scientific" criteria to separate the musical from the unmusical child. Pitch and rhythm can be improved with training, a child's musical abilities are developed like any of the other faculties that he is born with. It is even possible to develop a capacity for passing aptitude tests, such as these zealous men conceived, that presumably test our native abilities.

These tests did not determine the staying power of a student. They were not capable of ascertaining how great or how little the intensity of his desire to learn was. How could such tests predict what contribution a student would make? If they were not equipped to do all this, how valid were they actually? The most tragic feature about them was that they excluded the sensitive child from their considerations. A child who froze emotionally before this type of artificial testing had a low place in this musical hierarchy. One wonders how Schubert and Chopin would have fared under such circumstances.

There has never been a period in history when some form of dogmatism did not exist. There have been very few periods in our history, and those relatively brief, when humanism prevailed. In the modern world purists contribute a good deal to the cause of dogmatism. They have no place in their temples for those of us who wear our hearts on our sleeves. One of their most able representatives, Clive Bell, stated: "I do appreciate music as pure musical form, as sounds combined according to the laws of a mysterious necessity, as pure art with a tremendous significance of its own and no relation whatever to the significance of life." [3]

Composers themselves are disposed to be dogmatic about a number of things, although they complain about the inflexible mentalities of critics. This dogmatism is expressed in forms of favoritism. Composers write for those instruments that best display their talents, such as the violin and piano, and ignore practically all the other instruments in the orchestra. They foster class distinctions between groups of musicians by favoring one group over another. They will not compose for new instruments except on rare occasions. Therefore, orchestral organizations have very little opportunity to perform music with new musical instruments, even if they want to. Several new instruments have been introduced into the orchestra in the last hundred years. These have been percussion instruments, a developed tuba, and the saxophone. The saxophone has been the most colorful of these instrumental additions. Debussy wrote a solo score with an orchestral accompaniment for it. With its variety of possibilities the saxophone still has the status of a prima donna in the world of jazz and the distinction of being a second-rate citizen in the symphonic orchestra.

Class distinctions between orchestral groups, and within the groups themselves, is modeled after society, with leaders and followers and a privileged aristocracy that is supported by the labors of others. Instruments that have been favored for solo work hold the highest social rank in the orchestral society; those that only support the efforts of these instruments are relegated to a secondary place. The social structure of the modern orchestra is a parody on society except that there is no democracy in an orchestra; it is purely an authoritarian structure with an iron-willed sovereign at the helm.

The Russian Five called Bach a petrified pedagogue who composed like a machine. They would have nothing to do with his work because it might get in the way of their ideas for a nationalistic school of music. We have composers of our own who will not listen or study the scores of the masters in order to insulate themselves from absorbing or being influenced by traditional ideas.

A composer must be imbued with a deep sense of spirituality, but many of our contemporary ones confuse it with sentimentality and associate it with an age of romantic chivalry which no longer has a place in a world explained purely in *mechanistic* terminology. Many contemporary composers will not toil and become proficient in their craft. They would rather be vague and subjective, and cloak themselves in esthetic purism so that there is no way to communicate with them musically. They simply follow their impulses, which is very good as therapy for them personally; but, unfortunately, they do not go beyond that point and the result is often chaos, not a well-ordered musical work. Many of our younger composers have lost the quality of humility, a most important element for serving the Muse. Without humility there is no love or charity, and dogmatism usually follows.

In former days students were strongly encouraged to imitate their elders, express musical ideas with the techniques of their mentors, but to do it better than they did. Students followed in the paths of their teachers; this is how it was in all the arts. Now composers "walk alone." Their individuality must not be blemished with the taint of anyone else's contribution even seeming to appear in their work. They make a fetish of originality, a form of dogmatism in itself. There is no such thing as originality in a pure sense. Every human creation is not without its debts to the accomplishments of others in the past.

However, such composers must not be discouraged; they are our best insurance against those who write altogether in a traditional vein. But the danger is that if we shun our tradition, become disrespectful of our heritage, a type of dogmatism emerges which holds that everything new is good, just because it is modern. Nothing could be further from the truth. It is a mental affliction which seems to be more rampant in our time than in any other in history.

Intolerance will produce dogmatism among music listeners in a variety of ways. Listeners who refuse to hear music composed by men of a religious faith or political concept different from their own simply carry their moral and social dogmatism into the esthetic realm. They willfully accept one dominating principle, laid down by church or state, to determine every thought they have and action that they make, whether it be listening to a certain composer or a particular kind of music that the "authorities" disapprove of.

It is easy to enjoy classical and popular music, but partisans of jazz and serious works are often so carried away by their views that they become dogmatists of sorts. Jazz devotees refer to classical works as skeletons of the past whose rattling bones have no attraction for them. Listeners of serious music sometimes sound as despairing as Arnold Toynbee does in this oblique reference to the significance of jazz in the modern world:

> The prevailing tendency to abandon our artistic traditions . . . is the deliberate abandonment of a style which is losing its appeal to a rising generation because this generation is ceasing to cultivate its aesthetic sensibilities on the traditional Western lines. We have wilfully cast out of our souls the great masters who have been the familiar spirits of our forefathers; and, while we have been wrapped in self-complacent admiration of the spiritual vacuum that we have created, a Tropical African spirit in music and dancing and statuary has made an unholy alliance with a pseudo-Byzantine spirit in painting and bas-relief, and has entered in to dwell in a house which is found swept and garnished. The decline is not technical in origin but spiritual.[4]

Music educators play the role of dogmatists when they refuse to expand the curriculum to comply with the growing application of music to industry and medicine. A minority (but a well-entrenched group of music educators) insist that courses in music therapy should be given in a medical school and not as part of the curriculum of a fine arts education; the effects which music has upon industry belong in classes of psychology and labor management. Sociological and political problems pertaining to music are not discussed in their classrooms; courses on the esthetics of music should be relegated to the philosophy department.

These educators are of the view that their task is to train and produce musicians, but they fail to teach them what their obligations are to society or what their art can do to enrich our expanding scientific world in forms other than a fine art. Music, like any other luxury, may become superfluous if it ceases to have any direct bearing on practical life. If we should ever reach a state of existence in which man is completely self-sufficient, thanks primarily to science, there will not be a need for music to ease the burden of living and working. But since this is still very far away, if indeed it will ever come, educators are not justified in keeping the curriculum narrowed down to courses in theory, analysis, appreciation, and technical performance only. A music department should have on its staff a specialist in esthetics, as it has in the different areas of theory and instrumental music. Music appreciation courses fall far short of covering a course in the esthetics of music. Instructors in music appreciation are not philosophically equipped and they simply do not possess the background to enable students to formulate value judgments and distinguish between superior and inferior types of criteria.

Dogmatism often grows out of insecurity and fear. This is as true of our musical prejudices as it is of so many other warped views that we hold. We defend pronounced likes and dislikes with vehemence without any insight into the motives that make us do so. We make a fetish out of our fears by eschewing all contemporary music and musical machines because we are afraid of the inroads they may make on our lives. Even though our natural bent is to search for new sounds, in order to satisfy our curiosity, most of us exhibit fear that something new will be found that will upset our equilibrium.

Now that the music machine has broken through the barriers of sounds that we are accustomed to and has produced new sounds that tingle the nerves and startle the imagination, many of us have become frightened. We agree that machines in general take the drudgery out of our daily chores. Machines can even be used to teach the fundamentals of music as they can of reading, writing, and arithmetic in general education. But a wailing voice laments that music machines will engulf us with sounds that are impersonal and have no direct relationship with life experience. These people have no compunction about the use of machines to automate the industrial world or to cure the sick; but when machines invade their private lives, as music machines do, they are fearful of losing their souls to them. The fact that much of our traditional music has reached its end, in many respects, does not bother them. They would rather live with archaic and monotonous musical forms and sounds than be challenged and frightened by new musical affects.

HUMANISM

Humanism is a philosophy of values based on precepts of tolerance. It favors a policy of equality among men and freedom to entertain their personal ideas but only to the point that they do not impinge on the welfare of others. Humanism creates the conditions which permit dogmatism to exist. It would even defend dogmatism against those who would attack it for its ideas. But dogmatism, if it had its way, would crush any humanistic tendency that might prevail. It would destroy the very values which made humanism's existence possible. This is the danger that besets humanism.

〜

Humanism is a relatively new concept in the world; it is synonymous with a democratic ideal. There is a strong trace of it in Pericles' funeral oration, as Thucydides later related it, for the soldiers of democratic Athens who died fighting oligarchic Sparta. The Periclean spirit unfortunately did not prevail; loquacious champions of

Sparta's way of life, of whom Plato was the most important, finally won the day. Rome was taken over and governed by iron monarchs; the Middle Ages came under the domination of an infallible spiritual leader.

During the Renaissance, Giordano Bruno, burned at the stake for his *pantheistic* heresy, tried to remove the yoke that the religious authorities had placed around the neck of the musician. He noted that there are as many sorts of rules as there are musicians in the world; there is no one rule that governs creativity except in the mind of some self-styled authority.[5] Humanism is the motive that spurred Milton to fight for a free press and Locke to give men equality under the law of the land. Humanism permeated the writings of Thomas Paine. It was the guiding principle by which Thomas Jefferson formulated our Declaration of Independence. John Stuart Mill summed up the humanistic cause in his essay on *Liberty:* "If all mankind minus one, were of one opinion, and only one person were of the contrary opinion, mankind would be no more justified in silencing that one person, than he, if he had the power, would be justified in silencing mankind." [6]

What benefits does the musician receive from the humanistic cause? He can create with freedom from the dictates of church, state, aristocratic benefactors, and big business. Such freedom has its dangers and forms of excess, but this is the price that humanism is ready to pay. The philosophy of art for art's sake grew out of the freedom that humanism in the guise of democratic forms of government produced. The irony of it is that many of our modern artists, like the ancient Greeks,[7] do not admit that they have an obligation to society as a whole.[8] They pose as men of ideas who have loyalty only to their art. Schönberg and Stravinsky have the privilege of declaring, in this kind of environment, that they create only for the few; they have no responsibility as artists to the masses. If Cézanne and Wilde had lived in the Middle Ages when the decrees of the Council of Laodicea were strictly enforced Cézanne could not have said that he paints only for a restricted group, and Wilde, that he never considers the public's welfare in his writings. Where humanism does not exist in our own time, outstanding composers of the land are brought up on charges before a political committee and publically humiliated because they presumably deviated from Marxist ideology. The measure of our strength as humanists in a democracy is that we can allow creators to have their eccentric ways and do not bear down on them because they refuse to create as we would like.

If we should begin to stifle the creator, our own freedom would very soon be curbed. By protecting his freedom, we help to assure the existence of our own. They are our first line of defense against men with rigid ideas, even though creative men may fit into this classification somewhat themselves. Should we insist that they create only in a certain way, their work would become commonplace and we would be the losers more than they. It is better to give them free reign than to make the mistake that Ruskin did in attacking Whistler for not following esthetic ideals compatible with socialism.

A composer is not necessarily a humanist by conviction because he deliberately appeals to mass taste. A composer is not lacking in humanism because he writes with an eye on posterity and his music is too advanced for the average person. Humanistic environments do not produce music in any one specific form or style. They differ from dogmatic environments in this very important respect. In one climate music of all kinds is encouraged for the needs of the many and the few. In the other the composer is restricted to certain types of form and style because he is expected to create for a chosen audience.

The precarious balance between humanism and dogmatism must rest on making our intelligence play the role of a fulcrum to keep the disparity between them from becoming extreme. Creativity is not always in the best interests of mankind, either in science or in art. But this is part of the challenge that comes with living in a democratic world. Although this may sound specious in our atomic age, the rewards are far greater than the risks we take. Compromise and reconciliation are required to achieve democratic ideals in all the different facets of our lives.

We are no more temperamentally suited to listen to one kind of music than we are mentally equipped to read the same books. Freedom of selection, however, does not mean that there are no standards of excellence and important esthetic criteria that must be considered. While we strive to better ourselves we must not be scornful of others whose tastes differ from ours. In the musical world there is a place for each of us.

MYTHS

Christians once believed that members of heretical sects surreptitiously injected their false doctrines into the souls of the faithful with songs that came from the theater, taverns, and ships. Myths such as these inspired great fears among religious leaders, of whom St. Augustine was one, so that they contemplated the banishment of music from the religious service altogether as a moral safeguard against heretical influences. In the modern world fears emanating from unfounded musical myths are political and cultural, as well as religious. The Soviets "guard" their citizens and youth from the musical influence of "decadent bourgeoise" and "corrupt" Western societies. Moralists in our own country ascribe to every musical innovation in popular music and dance forms a symptom of cultural decay that can only lead to a bad end.

Myths about music are as old as the stylized dances of the Magic Circle. In the mind of primitive man there existed a connection between music, and fertility and death. A chant which brought rain to replenish the earth and cured the sick was used until its magic charms gave out. It was then replaced with another chant by the head priest of the tribe. As primitive men edged upward toward civilized existence, their institutions became more stable; ceremonies and rituals were patterned and longer lasting than they had been previously. Traditions replaced the magic of the moment.

A primitive man beating on hollow logs, singing a chant for rain would directly associate a darkening sky, the eventual falling of rain, with the magic of his song. He did not know that music alone cannot bring rain, for this myth was his source of strength. It was his impression that with music he could converse with nature and be answered by the spirits of thunder and lightning. With music he could hold off unseen demons that spears could not pierce or stone and wood touch and thus ward off death. What music actually did was to diminish his fear by allowing him to think that he had a hand in shaping life and death.

Greek poets created the myth that the earliest musicians were the gods themselves. According to Greek mythology Athena created the flute. Hermes invented the lyre and gave it to Apollo. Hermes also made the shepherd pipe, but that instrument he kept for himself. Pan created the pipe of reeds which imitates the nightingale. The Muse of song did not invent an instrument, since she had such a glorious voice. She would rather imbue mortal musicians with powers of creation than be creative herself. If any mortal could approach the gods in inventiveness, it was Orpheus the sweet singer, himself a son of the Muse who gave him the gift of song.

Greek physicians and priests perpetuated myths about music that they inherited from cultures older than their own. These myths were that music could ward off plagues, cure the mentally deranged, heal bodily ills, and change the motion of the human soul.

Greek philosophers created myths about music, of which the most colorful was that of the harmony of the spheres. They also developed a theory that the world was constructed according to a mathematical formula and is governed by laws that are based on numbers. On the basis of this theory, they propounded the myth that harmony and dissonance in music rest on the same laws that rule the physical world. These two myths originated with the Pythagoreans and became the basis of Plato's philosophy of music.

Myths about the harmony of the spheres rose to a crescendo during the sixteenth and seventeenth centuries. At times these myths were used as metaphors and at other times with the utmost seriousness. Kepler believed that a Supreme Being had so arranged the planets that they would produce celestial music, inaudible though it might be to mortals. God ordained mathematics and created the world according to a definite plan. We need only "plot an average angular velocity" for each planet and then determine the ratios of these to each other to understand why heavenly bodies produce music. The mathematical ratios are the same for the relationship of one planet to another as that of a musical interval in a polyphonic score. What is more, each of the heavenly bodies produces melodic fragments, not isolated or disconnected sounds. God spaced the planets to produce a harmony of the spheres.

Accordingly the movements of the heavens are nothing except a certain everlasting polyphony (intelligible, not audible) with dissonant tunings, like certain syncopations or cadences (wherewith men imitate these natural dissonances), which tends towards fixed and prescribed clauses—the single clauses having six terms (like voices)—and which marks out and distinguishes the immensity of time with those notes. Hence it is no longer a surprise that man, the ape of his Creator, should finally have discovered the art of singing polyphonically (per concentum), which was unknown to the ancients, namely in order that he might play the everlastingness of all created time in some short part of an hour by means of an artistic concord of many voices and that he might to some extent taste the satisfaction of God the Workman with His own works, in that very sweet sense of delight elicited from this music which imitates God.[9]

Sir Thomas Browne, physician and essayist, discerned a clear relationship between astronomy and music with moral attitudes and the physical health of human beings. Wherever there is harmony there is music, whether it be in the celestial realm or the soul of man. Since there is harmony in the spheres, there is divine music; and if a man has harmony in his being he is well-disposed to music.[10]

The Christians created the myth that the seven tones of the scale had ethical significance because there were seven planets in the heavens, seven requests in the Pater Noster, seven capital sins, and seven virtues. Musical thirds were forbidden to be sung or played because the number three was associated with the Holy Trinity.

Father Mersenne tried to reconcile Greek myths with Christian theology in the same way that St. Thomas had reconciled faith and science. He intuitively surmised that musical tones exist in the heavens. These will always be inaudible to us, he held, in the same way that knowledge of the Holy Trinity will forever surpass our understanding. The twelve musical modes are comparable to the twelve pearly gates of the Celestial City. He found an analogy between the four singing voices of human beings and the tonal qualities of the planets: Saturn and Jupiter may be compared to a bass; Mars, to a tenor; Earth and Venus, to an alto; Mercury, to a soprano.[11]

Theorists were not alone in perpetuating musical myths. Poussin wrote about analogies that exist between the Greek theory of musical affections and styles in painting. Greek musical modes, he noted, were restricted to specific subjects and each mode expressed the mood of that subject. Painting should be governed by the same considerations. Each subject of a painting has a particular mood and should be illustrated in a style that suits the temperament of the work. A painter ought to portray moods with the same familiarity and definiteness of style as a composer does when he uses a musical motif in the doctrine of affections to pinpoint a specific emotion.

Poets originated musical myths and poets perpetuated them more than any other creative artists. Sir John Davies gathered these myths together in an Elizabethan poem, *Orchestra*.[12] Each musical myth is illustrated as a dance in poetic form. One is a version of the harmony of the spheres:

> *Like this he fram'd the gods' eternal bower,*
> *And of a shapeless and confused mass*
> *By his through-piercing and digesting power*
> *The turning vault of heaven formed was,*
> *Whose starry wheels he hath so made to pass*
> *As that their movings do a music frame*
> *And they themselves still dance unto the same.*

Another is that music can cure the sick in mind and heart:

> *And thou, sweet music, dancing's only life,*
> *The ear's sole happiness, the air's best speech,*
> *Lodestone of fellowship, charming rod of strife,*
> *The soft mind's paradise, the sick mind's leech,*
> *With thine own tongue thou trees and stones canst teach,*
> *That when the air doth dance her finest measure,*
> *Then art thou born, the gods' and men's sweet pleasure.*

In "A Song for St. Cecilia's Day" John Dryden unlocked the heavens and called upon the stars to sing loud and clear. Their songs are the myths that contain our primitive fears and civilized hopes, not quite as Pythagoras heard them sing. There is no poem that exists in which our musical myths are told more beautifully than this:

> From harmony, from heavenly harmony,
>   This universal frame began:
> When nature underneath a heap
>   Of jarring atoms lay,
>   And could not heave her head,
> The tuneful voice was heard from high,
>   'Arise, ye more than dead!'
> Then cold, and hot, and moist, and dry,
>   In order to their stations leap,
>   And Music's power obey.
> From harmony, from heavenly harmony,
>   This universal frame began:
>   From harmony to harmony
> Through all the compass of the notes it ran,
> The diapason closing full in Man.

GRAND CHORUS

> As from the power of sacred lays
>   The spheres began to move,
> And sung the great Creator's praise
>   To all the Blest above;
> So when the last and dreadful hour
> This crumbling pageant shall devour,
> The trumpet shall be heard on high,
> The dead shall live, the living die,
> And Music shall untune the sky![13]

Philosophers have remained loyal to the image of Plato. Three musical myths which he created have been faithfully repeated throughout the ages by philosophers in writings of their own. During the Middle Ages, theology and philosophy were inseparable; and since the Christians adopted Plato for their mentor in musical matters, it is quite understandable that the Scholastics would preserve his views.

But even as late as the Age of Enlightenment, Rousseau seriously believed that music composed in accordance with "natural laws" could mold the character of a child in the formative years of his life. Music had a very high place in education for purposes of character building in his estimation.

Plato's belief, that arts which are closer to reason are of a higher order than those which appeal to feeling primarily, has also been preserved and embellished by modern philosophers. Kant arranged his hierarchy of the arts in keeping with Platonic theory. He gave poetry the highest place in his system because it appeals to reason and is based on experience; next come sculpture and painting; music is the lowest of the arts in importance and merit because it appeals essentially to feeling. Hegel did somewhat better. He placed music between painting and poetry; music is lower than the former and higher than the latter.

Schopenhauer was so anxious to prove that feeling rather than reason brings us closer to unraveling the mysteries of music that he resorted to using illustrations that outdid his predecessors in phantasy. He described music as the pulse of life, the expression of the will to survive. He enhanced a myth that began with Father Mersenne, but he brought it into harmony with the tenor of his time by giving it a Darwinian character. The lowest harmonic voice, the bass, is likened to crude unorganized nature upon which all rested and from which everything that exists originated and developed. Gradations of "the objectification of the will" lie between the bass and voice carrying the melody; the leading voice carrying the melody represents "the highest grade of the objectification of the will, the intellectual life and effort of man."

The musical myths of the twentieth century are not very different from those of former times which dealt with the influence of music on human behavior. Even the issues with which these myths are associated have not changed greatly. When it was said of Arius, in the early years of Christianity, that his agents secretly inserted the heresies of their sect into the souls of the faithful through music, it was not only believed but feared and guarded against by the Christian hierarchy. A myth as incredulous as this is still in vogue today and is responsible for the restrictions that theologians and statesmen use to protect their flock from immorality and alien political influences.

The myth that the machine will destroy us is still prevalent in our day. It has its origin in the ancient myth that the gods will destroy us with our own inventions (if we do not do so ourselves) should we try to fly like birds and learn the secrets of the universe. The outcry against the electronic music machine by so many people is a modified version of this myth. Electronic machines are likened to a scourge that has come over the musical world; and, in the estimation of these antagonists of electronic music, something will shortly have to be done to stop the mechanization of music or it will soon be dead and forgotten.

MYSTICISM

What mysticism is cannot be completely taught or explained. It can be sought and found only by searching within ourselves. Once it is discovered, a feeling of overwhelming delight takes hold of us. It is an experience which illuminates and defines; the mysteries of life are made clear, not with logic and reason, but with feeling alone. Space disappears, time ceases to exist, and the infinite beckons unto us.

Mysticism has its origin in fear and wonder. Out of these two elements ancient religion was born; without them, music would never have emerged. Music without mysticism is comparable to religion without mysteries. Our responses to musical tones are very much like those to holy images. We endow rhythms and tones with our psychic lives, we endow our sacred rituals and ceremonies with the mysticism that prevailed in the Magic Circle. Music without mystical qualities would be the equivalent of listening to scales and arpeggios that are executed with skill but leave the heart cold indeed.

In religious worship we take refuge in a mighty fortress that God has wrought for us. In loving someone else we feel secure that we are loved in return or will be loved in time. But in music we are alone; there is no dependence on Heaven or man, but only on ourselves. Music cannot give us the factual knowledge about ourselves that science presumably can. Music does not give us what religion feigns to with dogmas and decrees. Music helps us measure our needs, weigh our hurts and joyous states, and, in this process of bare-faced confession, often saves us from spiritual destruction. In the mystical experience of becoming one with music, not detached from it as purists insist, life is unraveled, re-examined, and then put together again.

To ask whether music has a mystical quality for all men is like asking if all men dream. Some of us dream more than others; some claim they rarely, if ever, dream. Wherever music is associated with religion, toil, and hope, music is a mysterious power that man looks to in order to carry him into another world, a better one than he knows. Many great mysteries are revealed to us in music. We may discover ourselves becoming one with the universe, experiencing things from a different perspective, and then returning from whence we started.

The mystical experience which music gives us we cannot relate to others. Its very ineffability makes it impossible to tell someone, by word or deed, how we felt at that moment in our lives when music allowed us to brush aside the veil that hides reality from us, as Bergson [14] said, or to be carried out of ourselves and become one with the universe, as Plotinus [15] so beautifully expressed it.

Mysticism is frowned upon in the Western world; its home is in the East. We pride ourselves on our scientific accomplishments and practical way of life. But pragmatic values do not sufficiently fortify us; something is lacking in our lives. The missing element is mysticism; no human life is complete without it. Some of us search and find it in prayer, others listen and experience its presence in music. In the throes of a mystical experience the conflicting impulses in us are reconciled. Peace and serenity reign within us until we return to the practical world in which mysticism is not allowed.

The mystical qualities in music are greater than in any other art. Its nature evades definition, its affects overwhelm us and take charge of our mind and body. Music keeps its mysterious powers to herself; she will even twist and tie our tongues should we attempt to tell others how well we fathom her. Even when as gifted a poet as Coleridge touches on the mysteries of music, his words are pale and thin when compared to the musical experience itself.

Music is the most entirely human of the fine arts, and has the fewest *analoga* in nature. Its first delightfulness is simple accordance with the ear; but it is an associated thing, and recalls the deep emotions of the past with an intellectual sense of proportion. Every human feeling is greater and larger than the exciting cause,—a proof, I think, that man is designed for a higher state of existence; and this is deeply implied in music, in which there is always something more and beyond the immediate expression.[16]

Music possesses a quality that defies understanding, concluded Coleridge. No amount of logic can account for the impact that it makes upon our emotions. Analysis will not unfold its esthetic character completely. Poe claimed that he created "The Raven" according to a mathematical formula. Then he went on to discover that in every great work of art, even his own, "a suggestive indefiniteness of vague and therefore spiritual effect" exists. John Dewey noted that there is an implicit factor in art that the intellect cannot grasp.[17] He called music the most "mechanical" of the arts and also the most "ethereal."

Music without mystical qualities can never reach great heights or seriously influence our lives. Such qualities are not present in popular music of the day or in college drinking songs. This type of music is all too clear and pointed. There is little about it that is inexplicable that sentimentality alone cannot account for. In serious music we experience a spiritual uplifting, not an invitation to a ballroom dance or a call to march with a school band.

Music demonstrates its mystical qualities when it extends the areas of our consciousness and broadens our life experiences. A spiritual quality exists in music when as a result of having listened to it we experience life more keenly than we had ever been capable of previously. The mysterious element, of course, is in us. The song is within our own beings, not in the printed page. We have not progressed emotionally beyond our primitive ancestors who worshipped totem poles.

Thus we psychically endow our arts with certain attributes, as they did their divinities, except that we do it somewhat differently.

A composer whose life is without wonder and awe cannot produce music with mystical qualities. Whatever he writes will be cold and explicit. It is possible, nevertheless, for someone who does have wonder and awe in his life to convert this type of composer's utterances into mystical journeys of his own. The chances are, however, that an average listener is more apt to miss the deep mysteries imbedded in a musical work than to read into it what has been omitted. A conductor who cannot intuitively grasp the mysterious elements in a score may execute the work in a performance with exemplary craftsmanship, but his interpretation will not be satisfactory. A listener who does not gaze at the stars and marvel how waves break on a beach may recognize a structured fugue and associate a rondo with a past dance form, but this is as much as the music will draw from him. Without curiosity there cannot be any spiritual awakening in a human life—no mysteries to be found in music.

PROPHECY

Music in the next thousand years will have more importance in the life of man that it has at present. The more mechanized the world becomes the greater will be its need for music. It will be used as a shield against social and scientific forces that would depersonalize the human race. Should men's thoughts become regimented and their speech be controlled, music will remain unfettered; there will be no way to bind it. Instruments will join the march of the machine but the singing voice will remain what it always has been, a song of self-assertion: I am man.

There was very little change for several thousand years in the manner in which sounds were produced on musical instruments. Strings were plucked, struck, and scraped, and performers blew their breath into perforated and curved tubes to produce a variety of tones.

Not until the last century was there a modest change. Electronic instruments were invented but fared rather badly in a postromantic age. In the second half of the twentieth century electronic music entered a second stage; soon it will be well entrenched. What will it be like in the next thousand years?

Will music have as important a place in the life of man in the next one thousand years as it now has if social scientists succeed in creating an ideal state, and if physical scientists achieve a breakthrough in space that will carry us far beyond the earth? Will there be any need for music in this most ideal of worlds, and, if there is no need for it, will it cease to exist as a cultural phenomenon because of its superfluous status? It is very safe to predict that music will not disappear but will prosper in a number of remarkable ways to fulfill the emotional and cultural needs of man in the twenty-first century. Music will be as necessary for us who are moored to this planet as for those people who emigrate to other planets, should our science-fiction dreams be realized.

Of what use will music be to space travelers for whom night and day have turned into patterns of light and shade as they look back upon a world that they left, outward bound for another planet? There will be no dawn or dusk in the space that these people traverse or up and down as these people were accustomed to experience on earth. In order to sustain themselves they will have to follow routines of earthly life while in flight, and diminish anxiety in traditional ways; music will be one of these.

For those who remain on earth, music will have just as important a place in their lives as it does in the twentieth century. It is not possible to construct a civilized society that will be so completely perfected that it will extinguish anxiety altogether. Even if the social irritants which plague our present existence were to disappear, there would not be too much change in our lives. Conflict and tension are necessary for life to continue; without it man would decay and soon rot away. Different types of social orders have their individual effects on musical creation, but until a social scientist can divine an ideal society in which each man is wholly self-sufficient, music will have a reason for being.

Electronic music will be produced for mass consumption as radio and victrola records now are. These machines will be factory made with built in "brain controls" able to convert ordinary sounds into musical patterns of tones. Music machine manufacturers will vie with each other to make a product with the greatest fidelity and selectivity of tone. They will strive to outdo each other in producing a "brain control" that is responsive to gradations of sounds as a sensitive barometer is to the slightest change in the weather. These machines will receive sounds and transform them in a number of ways. Their mechanism will be somewhat like modern air conditioners. They will be equipped to absorb selective sounds from the surrounding atmosphere, and as waves of sounds pass through their complex mechanism they will be filtered, diffused, and then emitted in matters of seconds.

Some machines will be constructed to produce electronic music with formal characteristics that are reminiscent of traditional musical forms. Other machines will simply produce "interesting" and "exciting" sounds in sequences that cannot be altogether determined beforehand. The element of novelty, anticipation, and surprise will be one of the prominent features used as a selling point for these machines. Members of the musical avant-garde will construct their own "control brain" to receive and blend sounds so that the results will be more sophisticated than those produced for the general public. Many people will do without these machines and simply purchase a superelectronic radio which they will use to tune into a central station that will broadcast as our radio stations do, offering a balanced musical diet to their listeners.

Sound engineers will travel deep into the sea and far out into the earth's atmosphere to record sounds for musical purposes. Recordings based on the newest sounds will be sold commercially. These sounds will be taped and split and juxtaposed in an endless variety of ways. Some tones, which in their ordinary context are uninteresting, will be made extremely beautiful when electronically treated, as a glob of filthy oil is transformed into an esthetic masterpiece when magnified one hundred fold under a high powered microscope and photographed in color.

The music machine will make composers of all of us in a lesser sense, but the professional composer will be better schooled and discerning in his musical activities. He will create music in a past vein, and music suitable for an electronic age. His works will be performed in public places and sent out over the air ways not very differently from the way in which it is done in our day. His preparation to become a composer will consist of a course of study that will contain a musical system that somewhat approaches the Schillinger one, advanced studies in the science of acoustics and esthetic theory. He will compose with a set of tonal combinations already worked out by the musical engineers.

While the scientific world forges ahead in the next thousand years, there will remain very serious problems that will vex the human race because they cannot be solved even in such an enlightened mechanical age. Space men will be conveying cargoes of human beings to distant destinations, navigating by the stars as ancient mariners did, but war and emotional disease will still exist. In order to relieve fatigue, music machines will be strategically placed on moving roadways which travel at various speeds carrying pedestrians and gasless automobiles; but alongside these giant strides of mechanical advancement man himself will advance little beyond his present emotional state. These roads will go from one major town to another straight across the breadth of our land, and north and south as far as solid ground is found; but all along the way the countryside will be blotted with malignant symptoms showing that greed has not been erased.

Complaints will be numerous from indignant citizens that the public thoroughfares are clogged with music boxes that detract and annoy, as billboards marred landscapes in the twentieth century. Engineers will not be able to protect individuals from other peoples' musical programs, either in public places or in their homes. The inventive genius of the engineers will be unable to overcome this social problem of values and tolerance. Every device that they will construct to protect the individual from his neighbor's music, some perverse human will manage to nullify with a device of his own.

The greater the mechanization becomes in the next thousand years the greater will be the need for music in the life of man in order to break the chain of routine in his behavior which might well make a machine of him too. Although music will be strongly mechanized, man will use machines to offset the ills produced by them, almost in the same way that the Greeks used homeopathic remedies. The basic urge to survive will compel man to create another machine to protect himself whenever a machine is created that poses a threat to him.

People in the next thousand years will have concerts of ancient music performed with old instruments and in ancient dress. On less festive occasions such as regular weekly concerts, which only fortunate subscribers will attend since there will be so many people in the world that concert halls will be overcrowded, the masters of past centuries will be played. People with classical tastes will prefer this music to the modern kind of their day. Program annotators will note that Stravinsky's *Sacred Rites of Spring,* being played that night, has a classical serenity and poetic calmness in its allusion to the emergence of life. They will remind their readers that on its first performance, in a Parisian concert hall, the audience divided into two groups and fought each other, until the police arrived and separated them, because they found the score too frightening and turbulent.

In the twenty-first century, concerts of sacred music will be given by religious groups, and glee clubs will sing for the alumni of their colleges. Parents will attend their children's yearly recitals of instrumental and vocal music, and youth concerts will be a regular phase of liberal art studies. A school of eclectic esthetes may emerge; these esthetes will attempt to combine the best of the fine arts into one unified philosophy of art. Their motto will be one world and one art, but they are bound to fail from the start.

Although the political structure of the world in the next one thousand years will be more closely knit than it is at present, ethnic groups will firmly hold on to their traditions. They will retain their folk music and dances by performing them at every opportunity. It will be one of their strongest ways of preserving their identity. Contests will flourish and prizes will be awarded to the dismay of a progressive element who will complain that as long as these ethnic differences are allowed to be flouted and rewarded, assimilation of the entire human race is that much further away.

Of all the changes that will come over the musical scene, the one aspect of it that will change the least will be that of music for the human voice. The range and texture of the four main types of voices will remain the same and men will sing of love and hate, life and death, in the same way as they do now. Vitamins and tranquilizers, mechanics, and the science of geriatrics will have little effect on singers. The four main types of voices, the human instruments, preceded man-made instruments. The singing voice is in a sense the inner voice of man that will not be stilled by external forces so long as there is life in him.

The music form that will be the most vital and important in the future will be the operatic one. It will come about for two different reasons of which the second will be the more important. The technical character of the opera will profit from new inventions. Composers will use electronic singers along with human casts in increasing numbers. They will try to use an all electronic cast but will find that it will sound too much like a symphonic concert. That project will not get far. They will therefore enlarge the range of the operatic orchestra by adding electronic instruments to it, but they will in the main retain a live orchestra in the pit. Stage settings and choreography will make the most of new inventions so that the scenes will be spectacular beyond our comprehension. These operas will be televised far and wide with complete fidelity of picture and sound, and interference from the weather or other sources will be down to a bare minimum of what we are accustomed to expect.

Since there is no reason to assume that the human singing voice will change very much in the next thousand years, whatever biological mutations may take place in this atomic age, traditional forms of singing will prevail. It will not be possible to extend the range of the respective voices much beyond their present ones. Singers who try to execute rhythms that electronic instruments are capable of may ruin the *timbre* of their tones. They will sound like our singers do when they are trained for the classics and try their hand at jazz. Composers will therefore have no alternative but to write differently for the voice than for electronic instruments.

The human voice will yet be our salvation. It will remain the one personal element in a mechanized operatic world. It will symbolize the role of man in a changing universe. Speech and song are the two distinguishing features that separate man from all other forms of life—two weapons to speak and cry out, which the machine cannot drown out.

SUMMARY

The education of the composer has not always been what it is now. Centuries ago a young boy who displayed musical ability was apprenticed to a practical musician, as another boy, who showed skill in drawing, would be sent to live and work in the studio of a well-known painter. Composition was not taught in a formal way, as it is taught in our music schools; a musical apprentice was required to become proficient in every branch of music. Of all his studies, singing was considered the most important so that he would always know how to write for the noblest musical instrument, the voice, and make every other instrument sing like it. Singing in a church choir taught him the art of ensemble, harmony, and counterpoint. His musical education was not one-sided, mainly theory, as it so often is now.

In past centuries it was taken for granted that a composer could write and perform on all the instruments. He may have been more adept in writing and performing for one instrument than the others, but specialization, as it exists today, was unknown in earlier times. The musician was a well-rounded artisan, thoroughly versed in every facet of his craft. He wrote for the voice on the strength of having sung himself and not, as today, when many composers who have never sung themselves expect singers to perform their unsingable works.

In our time, the soloist is like the Queen of the May around whom all the other figures dance and prance; but this too was not so in former times. Solo performing was a phase of training for ensemble work, not for a grandiose career. The ensemble was more important than the solo performer, as the community overshadowed the individual.

The difference between dogmatism and prudence is a difficult thing to decide. We make laws to insure our survival and punish those who are a threat to our security. We insist that certain mores and customs must not be compromised lest our moral structure in a democracy should crumble; but we also guard eccentrics, who simply go their own way without any threat to us, from abuse. Full-fledged dogmatists do not have the problem of deciding, on a pragmatic basis, whether someone's thoughts or behavior are a threat to their own. In an authoritarian religion and a totalitarian state there is only one way to think and act, every other way is forbidden. This philosophy is carried over into every facet of public and private living, including the arts. Certain types of music have been condemned as "immoral" by churchmen and as characteristic of "bourgeoise decadence" by the communist ideologists because such music did not conform with the principles for planned living according to one "truth."

Humanists place the welfare of man above all other considerations in human relationships but they also acknowledge that we have our intimate moments of "truth" which remain locked within ourselves. These are moments of being alone, secure and exalted, in a private world with experiences from which we can never part or share with others. Mystics center their entire lives upon these private experiences and agree with humanists that these rare moments of insight cannot be expressed in language or taught. They can, at best, only be felt. But the mystic, unlike the humanist, dogmatically insists that only one "truth" exists—the one that he experienced. A humanist never insists that only his "truth" is right and that all others are wrong because they are unlike his.

There never was a time when the superstitions and fears of the period were not reflected in its musical myths. Platonic myths about music mirrored the average Greek's desire for order and certainty. If there was no peace and order in living, it could at least be acquired through musical phantasy. The Middle Ages were not a Christian paradise, and the fact that St. Thomas insists that musical works contain the three elements of integrity, proportion, and clarity implies that these ideals can at least be achieved in art, if not in actual life. In our electronic age mechanical devices regulate our lives and do much of our work for us. But machines have not yet brought us a social utopia or demonstrated that they are capable of satisfying our emotional needs. Until that time comes, however inconceivable it may be, we shall require music that offers us escape and phantasy to compensate for the mechanization and regulatory agencies that control us.

Mysticism is an invisible ingredient in music. It can only be alluded to, never detected and pointed out. Scriabin invented a chord consisting of a series of six fourths that he used as the harmonic basis of some of his work to give it a mystical quality which he thought would express in music his esoteric religious beliefs. But mysticism cannot be achieved in music through any obvious technique. Chords used in odd fashions will only give a musical work unique coloring, as it did to Scriabin's compositions. An arrangement of musical tones alone will not produce mysticism, any more than the words of a prayer will make us reverent if there is no religion in our lives.

During the next thousand years musicians will perform on instruments powered by electric batteries that are so small that they will be worn like boutonnières in a lapel. Listening to music at home will be a feast of sounds which will come out of every part of the room instead of one as it is now. Electronic machines will canvass the universe for new sounds. The human voice, however, will not progress very much. Its range and quality will take more than a thousand years to alter. Its repertoire will consist mainly of those things that machines cannot give us, such as love and devotion for example. Song, in the sense in which it has been used in this book from the outset, is a gift that man alone enjoys and even when he teaches a machine to sing, the voice is his.

NOTES

[1] *The Philosophy of Nietzsche, The Birth of Tragedy,* trans. Clifton P. Fadiman (New York: The Modern Library, Inc., 1937), p. 202.

[2] Leo Tolstoy, *What is Art?,* trans. Aylmer Maude (New York: Thomas Y. Crowell Company, 1899), p. 162. "Would it be preferable for our Christian world to be deprived of *all* that it now esteemed to be art, and, together with

the false, to lose *all* that is good in it? I think that every reasonable and moral man would again decide the question as Plato decided it for his 'Republic,' and as all the Church Christian and Mohammedan teachers of mankind decided it, i.e. would say, 'Rather let there be no art at all than continue the depraving art, or simulation of art, which now exists.' "

[3] Clive Bell, *Art* (New York: Frederick A. Stokes Company, 1914), p. 31.

[4] Arnold J. Toynbee, *A Study of History,* abridgement by D. C. Somervell (New York: Oxford University Press, 1947), p. 259.

[5] Giordano Bruno, "A Discourse on Poets," *Library of the World's Best Literature,* V. (1897), p. 2617. "Then they are wrong, those stupid pedants of our days, who exclude from the number of poets those who do not use words and metaphors conformable to, or whose principles are not in union with, those of Homer and Virgil; or because they do not observe the custom of invocation, or because they weave one history or tale with another, or because they finish the song with an epilogue on what has been said and a prelude on what is to be said, and many other kinds of criticism and censure; from whence it seems they would imply that they themselves, if the fancy took them, could be the true poets: and yet in fact they are no other than worms, that know not how to do anything well, but are born only to knaw and befoul the studies and labors of others; and not being able to attain celebrity by their own virtue and ingenuity, seek to put themselves in the front, by hook or by crook, through the defects and errors of others."

[6] John Stuart Mill, *Liberty,* II, line 28.

[7] Athenaeus, *The Deipnosophists,* VI, trans. Charles Burton Gulick (Cambridge, Mass.: Harvard University Press, 1937), Bk. XIV, 631-32. "In early times popularity with the masses was a sign of bad art; hence, when a certain flute [aulos]-player once received loud applause, Asopodorus of Phlius... said 'What's this? Something awful must have happened!' " The player evidently could not have won approval with the crowd otherwise.

[8] The Spanish philosopher José Ortega y Gasset, in *Dehumanization of Art,* trans. Helene Weyl (Gloucester, Mass.: Peter Smith, 1951), pp. 7, 12, looks upon modern art as a harbinger of the future. "A time must come in which society, from politics to art, reorganizes itself into two orders or ranks: the illustrious and the vulgar.... Even though pure art may be impossible there doubtless can prevail a tendency toward a purification of art. Such a tendency would effect a progressive elimination of the human, all too human, elements predominant in romantic and naturalistic production. And in this process a point can be reached in which the human content has grown so thin that it is negligible. We then have an art which can be comprehended only by people possessed of the peculiar gift of artistic sensibility—an art for artists and not for the masses, for 'quality' and not for hoi polloi. That is why modern art divides the public into two classes, those who understand it and those who do not understand it—that is to say those who are artists and those who are not. The new art is an artistic art."

[9] Johannes Kepler, *The Harmonies of the World,* trans. Charles Glenn Wallis in *Great Books of the Western World* (Chicago: University of Chicago Press,

1955), p. 1048. *See* John Hollander, *The Untuning of the Sky* (Princeton: Princeton University Press, 1961), pp. 38-40.

[10] Sir Thomas Browne, *The Religio Medici* (London: J. M. Dent & Sons, Ltd., 1931), pp. 79-80.

[11] Kepler, *op. cit.,* p. 1049. This analogy had already been made by Kepler: "For those same properties which ... custom ascribed to the bass and nature gave legal grounds for so doing are somehow possessed by Saturn and Jupiter in the heavens; and we find those of the tenor in Mars, those of the alto are present in the Earth and Venus, and those of the soprano are possessed by Mercury, if not with equality of intervals, at least proportionately."

[12] Sir John Davies, *Orchestra* (London: Chatto & Windus, Ltd., 1947), pp. 19, 46.

[13] *The Oxford Book of English Verse, 1250-1900* (Oxford: Clarendon Press, 1915).

[14] Henri Bergson, *Laughter,* trans. Cloudesley Brereton and Fred Rothwell (New York: The Macmillan Company, 1937), pp. 156-157. Composers "grasp something that has nothing in common with language, certain rhythms of life and breath that are closer to man than his inmost feelings, being the living law—varying with each individual—of his enthusiasm and despair, his hopes and regrets. By setting free and emphasising this music, they force it upon our attention; they compel us, willy-nilly, to fall in with it, like passers-by who join in a dance. And thus they impel us to set in motion, in the depths of our being, some secret chord which was only waiting to thrill. So art, whether it be painting or sculpture, poetry or music, has no other object than to brush aside the utilitarian symbols, the conventional and socially accepted generalities, in short, everything that veils reality from us, in order to bring us face to face with reality itself."

[15] Plotinus, *Enneads,* trans. Stephen MacKenna (London: The Medici Society Limited, 1926), IV, 4, 41. Music and prayer are very much alike as forms of mysticism according to Plotinus. "The prayer is answered by the mere fact that part and other part are wrought to one tone like a musical string which, plucked at one end, vibrates at the other also. Often, too, the sounding of one string awakens what might pass for a perception in another, the result of their being in harmony and tuned to one musical scale; now, if the vibration in a lyre affects another by virtue of the sympathy existing between them, then certainly in the All—even though it is constituted in contraries—there must be one melodic system; for it contains its unison as well, and its entire content, even to those contraries, is a kinship."

[16] Samuel T. Coleridge, *Biographia Literaria,* II, ed. J. Shawcross (London: Oxford University Press, 1954), *On Poesy or Art,* p. 261.

[17] John Dewey, *Art As Experience* (New York: G. P. Putnam's Sons, 1958), p. 194.

GLOSSARY OF NAMES

AELIAN, (d. A.D. 222), a Roman author and teacher of rhetoric described in his stories how the ancients used music to hunt and fish. This collection of writings was often used to convey moral lessons.

APOLLO was a Greek god, one of whose divine duties was to look after the sick. Songs and dances were rendered in his honor to heal various ills of body and mind.

ARCHYTAS of Tarentum, (first half of fourth century B.C.), a friend of Plato, was distinguished as a statesman and Pythagorean scholar. He contributed to the science of acoustics with theories on sound, pitch, and the numerical structure of musical intervals.

ARISTOPHANES, (444?–380? B.C.), a Greek poet and dramatist, crusaded against the musical innovations of his time.

ARISTOTLE, (384–322 B.C.), a student of Plato, tutor to Alexander the Great, founder of the Peripatetic school of philosophy, performed experiments in acoustics and perpetuated, in a moderately altered form, Plato's moralistic theories about music.

ARISTOXENUS of Tarentum, (latter half of fourth century B.C.), was a Peripatetic philosopher and a musician whose writings on the esthetics and structure of Greek music have survived in part. *The Harmonics of Aristoxenus* is one of our most important sources of Greek musical theories.

ATHENAEUS of Naucratis in Egypt, (earlier half of A.D. third century), has left us a collection of quotations and anecdotes on numerous topics. His comments on music cannot aways be regarded as reliable.

BACH, JOHANN SEBASTIAN, (1685–1750), introduced flowing melodies from Italian operas into the staid religious music of the Protestants as a part of his great contribution to the esthetics of music.

BACON, ROGER, (c. 1214–1294), a Franciscan monk with strong philosophical and scientific talents, stressed the importance of music as a mental discipline in education.

BEETHOVEN, LUDWIG VAN, (1770–1827), wrote music which, with few exceptions, was instrumental. His esthetic views became the gospel of romanticism.

BELL, CLIVE, (1881–   ), insists that the significance of music is unrelated to the significance of life. To him, esthetic emotions are different from emotions in ordinary life.

BERG, ALBAN, (1885–1935), perhaps even more than his teacher Schönberg, illustrated how it was possible to replace esthetically the diatonic system, in which the emphasis is on the tonic and dominant, with a system in which each note is as important as any other.

BERGSON, HENRI, (1859–1941), considered musical works as records of intuitions; every verbal effort to describe the creation and appreciation of a musical composition can be only an intellectual activity, a form of knowledge lower and less reliable than intuition.

BLAKE, WILLIAM, (1757–1827), a poet, believed that he was guided in his creations by a Divine Being. Yet he could be thoroughly realistic and point out that without strife and opposites there would be no progress or art.

BOETHIUS, (480–524), a Roman statesman and philosopher, made a serious effort to resolve the musical philosophies of Plato and Aristotle. His writings influenced the course of music in the Western world for a thousand years after his death.

BRAHMS, JOHANNES, (1833–1897), used traditional musical forms which kept him closer to the esthetics of the classicists than to that of the romanticists. But, in the manner of the romantic composers, he used folk material over and over again.

BROWNE, SIR THOMAS, (1605–1682), a physician and essayist, believed that wherever harmony existed music was also present. He applied this theory to the harmony of the spheres, and to explain why some of us are disposed to like music and others are not.

BROWNING, ROBERT, (1812–1889), wrote in *Abt Vogler* that the finger of God singled out the musician from all the other creators of art. The musician, like God Himself, transcends natural law in the creation of a masterpiece.

BRUNO, GIORDANO, (1548–1600), was burned at the stake for heresy. He championed a doctrine of pantheism which identifies the universe with God. This doctrine was contrary to orthodox Christian theology which holds that God is transcendent as well as immanent.

CALVIN, JOHN, (1509–1564), believed that music can ennoble and degrade character; music used for worship should be simple and modest so that it will not mar religious texts or draw men's minds away from prayer.

CASSIODORUS, (485–580), was a contemporary of Boethius, who, with Boethius, helped make the musical philosophies of the Greeks known to medieval scholars. He considered music to be a mathematical discipline, and attributed ethical qualities to musical modes.

CHOPIN, FREDERIC, (1810–1849), was the supreme master of the romantic instrument—the piano. His tonal combinations and intricate rhythms allied him with the neoromantic composers rather than with those of the first half of the nineteenth century.

CICERO, (106–43 B.C.), a Roman statesman and Stoic philosopher, was critical of Roman music because it only offered childish pleasure and did not contribute toward lasting happiness.

COLERIDGE, SAMUEL T., (1772–1834), a poet and philosopher, referred to music as the most human of the fine arts. He ascribed significance to music that transcended empirical understanding.

CROCE, BENEDETTO, (1866–1952), an Italian philosopher, maintained that music lives in the imagination only. There is no essential difference between the creation of a musical composition and the appreciation of one. They both have their life in imagination.

DARWIN, CHARLES, (1809–1882), set forth the view that, in the most primitive societies of men, music had its origin as a factor in attracting and selecting a mate. Music preceded the existence of articulate speech.

DAVIES, SIR JOHN, (1569–1626), in his poem, *Orchestra*, described the origin and functions of music in dance metaphors.

DEBUSSY, CLAUDE A., (1862–1918), a composer, on the one hand imitated the impressionistic painters in his music and on the other hand emulated Gluck's esthetic theories of the opera by advocating the greater importance of the text over that of the music.

DEMOCRITUS, (b. *c.* 460 B.C.), described music as the youngest of the arts which arose not from "necessity but from superfluity."

DESCARTES, RENE, (1596–1650), maintained that music is essentially mathematical and should be used as a discipline in preparation for philosophical studies. He also attributed moral values to rhythms because they could directly affect the soul.

DEWEY, JOHN, (1859–1952), whose instrumentalism denied eternal truths, held that beliefs about beauty and goodness can be grounded only in experience. Musical ideals, like scientific hypotheses, must forever be tested by individual experience.

DRYDEN, JOHN, (1631–1700), poet laureate of England and collaborator with Henry Purcell, wrote in his Preface to *Albion and Albanius* that: "An opera is a Poetical Tale, or Fiction, represented by Vocal and Instrumental Musick, adorn'd with Scenes, Machines and Dancing. The Suppos'd Persons of this Musical Drama are generally Supernatural, as Gods, and Goddesses, and Heroes."

ELIOT, T. S., (1888–   ), does not make a distinction between the intellectual and the emotional in poetry; both are fused in the esthetic experience, as they are in the act of creation. "...a 'musical poem' is a poem that has a musical pattern of sound and a musical pattern of secondary meanings of the words which compose it, and these two patterns are indissoluble and one."

ERIGENA, JOHN SCOTUS, (800–877), a medieval philosopher, has left us a highly mystical passage on polyphony in which he compares music to the harmonious character of the physical world.

EUCLID, (323–285 B.C.), a mathematician and Pythagorean, wrote a treatise on harmony.

EURIPIDES, (480–406 B.C.), a Greek tragic poet and dramatist, introduced new musical styles into his plays, and defended the musical innovations of others.

FICINO, MARSILIO, (1433–1499), a philosopher, believed that "poetry is superior to music, since through the words it speaks not only to the ear but also directly to the mind. Therefore its origin is not in the harmony of the spheres, but rather in the music of the divine mind itself, and through its effect it can lead the listener directly to God Himself."

FREUD, SIGMUND, (1856–1939), the founder of psychoanalysis, believed that the creation of a musical composition has its origin in the unconscious, and that sublimation is the process whereby a composer converts his repressions and unfulfilled wishes into tonal phantasies expressive of his desires.

GAUGUIN, PAUL, (1848–1903), was one of the original group of post-impressionist painters. His paintings of the Tahitian scenes and people with their "flat-patterning, linear harmonies, and brilliant color" are of rare beauty but are unfortunately fading prematurely.

GIDE, ANDRE, (1869–1951), was a French author whose writings were concerned with mass morality, and the conduct of the individual. His comments on music are mainly in his *Journals.*

GLUCK, CHRISTOPH W. VON, (1714–1787), fought against the loose structure of Italian opera. He succeeded in creating a new operatic style with emphasis on dramatic expression.

GOETHE, JOHANN W., (1749–1832), wrote poems and plays that were an endless source of inspiration to romantic composers. He held the view that music itself cannot be political any more than science can.

GOGH, VINCENT VAN, (1853–1890), used extraordinary brush strokes and sun-drenched colors which give his paintings a texture and clarity that are sometimes compared to the music of Berlioz.

HANDEL, GEORGE FREDERIC, (1685–1759), wrote oratorios that are a musical representation of episodes from biblical history. His musical themes in these oratorios are often set to Italian arias.

HANSLICK, EDUARD, (1825–1904), opposed the Wagnerian fusion of the arts and the romantic notion of uniting music and poetry. He maintained that music is an autonomous art and can express musical ideas only.

HAYDN, FRANZ JOSEPH, (1732–1809), brought the string quartet to esthetic fulfillment. Although he was a most gifted composer, his contemporary Schiller, the philosopher and humanist, considered him an uninspired and mediocre musician.

HEGEL, G. W. F., (1770–1831), characterized instrumental music as a romantic art. He preferred music with words to music without a text. Instrumental music merely produces "a subjective play of forms." Vocal music gives definiteness to the vague feelings of pure musical tones.

HELMHOLTZ, H. L. F., (1821–1894), held a theory that consonant intervals consist of tones whose fundamentals or overtones are free from "roughness"; "smoothness" is what makes a tone consonant.

HESIOD, (eighth century B.C.), a Greek epic poet, believed that musicians are divinely inspired and that they are representatives of the gods.

HINDEMITH, PAUL, (1895–   ), was one of the leading figures, in an early stage of his career, in a German movement known as Gebrauchsmusik, or "utility music." This music was characterized by forms of moderate length, a simplicity and clarity of style, small ensembles, and avoidance of technical difficulties so that it would be suitable for use by groups without professional training. The movement was both a social and esthetic reaction against romanticism.

HOBBES, THOMAS, (1588–1679), was a philosopher of the school of materialism.

HOMER, (*c.* ninth century B.C.), a Greek epic poet, characterized musicians as the favorite mortals of the gods. The Muse endowed them with the gift of song to gladden the hearts of men.

HORACE, (65–8 B.C.), a Roman poet, has left us a vivid description of the low level to which music degenerated in his time.

HUME, DAVID, (1711–1776), maintained that creativity in music can only come from one source—experience.

HUXLEY, ALDOUS, (1894–   ), tried to arrange the activities of characters in one of his novels in the manner in which counterpoint is constructed in a musical composition.

JOYCE, JAMES, (1882–1941), has one section of his book *Ulysses* in which there is a suggestion of prose writing in the manner of a fugue. His contribution to music is found in his comments about it, which are exceedingly discerning.

JUNG, CARL G., (1875–1961), concurred with Freud that the creation of music has its origin in the unconscious. To him music symbolizes the collective unconscious of the human race.

KANDINSKY, WASSILY, (1866–1944), painter of the abstract school, has written a good deal about the similarities between his paintings and musical works.

KANT, IMMANUEL, (1724–1804), placed music at the bottom of his category of the arts because it more strongly appealed to feeling and less to reason than any of the other arts.

KEPLER, JOHANN, (1571–1630), correlated musical tones and intervals with the movements of the planets.

LEIBNIZ, GOTTFRIED W., (1646–1716), described music as a manifestation of the universal rhythm whose essence consists of number and relation.

LESSING, GOTTHOLD E., (1729–1781), opposed a union of the arts. One art, such as music, should not be used to illustrate what is "natural" to another art.

LIPPS, THEODOR, (1851–1910), held the theory that consonant intervals are made up of simple ratios, and dissonant intervals of more complex ratios.

LISZT, FRANZ, (1811–1886), devoted much of his musical life to developing an intimate union between music and poetry. His musical works, however, are primarily instrumental.

LUCRETIUS, (95–52 B.C.), a Roman poet, wrote that man first learned to sing by imitating birds, and to invent instruments by observing how nature produces varied sounds.

LUTHER, MARTIN, (1483–1546), appropriated and simplified music used by the Catholic Church for the Protestant service. He changed the words that accompanied the music from Latin into the vernacular.

MAELZEL, JOHANN N., (1772–1838), was a musician and inventor whose fame is preserved by the metronome which he invented.

MANN, THOMAS, (1875–1955), wrote that music was an influence in shaping the structure and style of his novels.

MARITAIN, JACQUES, (1882–   ), is a philosopher whose esthetics of music is based on the writings of St. Thomas Aquinas.

MARX, KARL, (1818–1883), claimed that he was doing for the political economy what Darwin had so successfully done for the science of biology. The musical views of modern communism have their origin in his philosophy.

MENDELSSOHN, FELIX, (1809–1847), the musician of romanticism, wrote that music does not become more intelligible when accompanied by words, but less clear and meaningful.

MERSENNE, FATHER MARIN, (1588–1648), followed Kepler in correlating the structure of music with the movements of the planets.

MILL, JOHN STUART, (1806–1873), wrote "I was seriously tormented by the thought of the exhaustibility of musical combinations. The octave consists of only five tones and two semitones, which can be put together in only a limited number of ways of which but a small proportion are beautiful: most of these, it seemed to me, must have been already discovered, and there could not be room for a long succession of Mozarts and Webers to strike out, as these have done, entirely new surpassing rich veins of musical beauty."

MONDRIAN, PIET, (1872–1944), was an abstract painter whose work "Broadway Boogie Woogie" is an effort to capture the rhythm of musical jazz in geometric patterns of different sizes and colors.

MOZART, WOLFGANG A., (1756–1791), included, in his own operas, the operatic reforms which Gluck had made, but he held that poetry ought to be the obedient child of music rather than the other way around.

MUSE is a goddess presiding over music; the "mother" of inspiration.

NICHOLAS OF CUSA, (1401–1464), believed that human beings are able to profit from music, but animals cannot; that animals do not have the faculty of reason and, therefore, cannot learn music although they perceive sounds.

NIETZSCHE, FRIEDRICH, (1844–1900), believed that music can help man revalue his values, transform this "crude" world into a more imaginative and better place to live, and that it is within the power of a composer to redeem a "corrupt" society.

ORTEGA Y GASSET, JOSE, (1883–1955), stated that society will eventually organize itself into two orders or ranks both politically and musically—that of superior and that of ordinary men.

PICASSO, PABLO, (1881–   ), has been to painting what Stravinsky has been to music. Their contributions and styles have striking resemblances.

PLATO, (427–347 B.C.), is the most notable of all the Western philosophers who held that music should be used to achieve sound morality.

PLOTINUS, (204–269), a neo-Platonic philosopher with a strong mystical strain, compared music to "divine" rhythm.

PLUTARCH, (A.D. first to second centuries), was a Greek moralist and biographer whose writings are a storehouse of references to Greek music. Although his comments are often hearsay, the essence of what he has written, it would seem, is reasonably accurate.

POE, E. A., (1809–1849), attempted to imitate music in his verse and wrote about the relationship of music to verse.

PYTHAGORAS, (c. sixth century B.C.), holds the enviable position of being the father of Greek musical science, and the founder of an esoteric school of philosophy. We do not possess any of his writings.

QUINTILIAN, (b. A.D. 35), wrote that Roman music was corrupted by the degeneration of the Roman theater. The "effeminate stage has to no small extent destroyed such manly vigour as we still possessed."

RAMEAU, JEAN P., (1683–1764), was one of the important founders of our system of modern harmony. He described music as a science.

ROUSSEAU, JEAN J., (1712–1778), a French philosopher and composer, nurtured the belief that the French language was unsuitable for musical declamation. After writing extensively on this point, he changed his mind.

SANTAYANA, GEORGE, (1863–1952), was a philosopher whose writings on music are summed up in *Reason in Art*, one of the five books of *The Life of Reason*.

SCHILLER, FRIEDRICH, (1759–1805), believed that the play impulse is responsible for musical creativity. He pointed out that an esthetic education is necessary for a civilized existence.

SCHILLINGER, JOSEPH, (1895–1943), a musical theorist, believed that we can teach the average school child to create music by the use of mathematical formulas. His writings are essentially an effort to make music a mathematical science.

SCHONBERG, ARNOLD, (1874–1951), evolved a twelve tone system in which each of the twelve tones has equal standing. This system has been called atonality by his disciples.

SCHOPENHAUER, ARTHUR, (1788–1860), believed that music of all the arts is the most capable of helping man to escape from the irrational will which dominates his life. He thought that, although music does not express concepts and can only allude to human experience, we understand its significance and meanings more clearly than those of any other art.

SCHUBERT, FRANZ, (1797–1828), was the creator of the German *Lied*.

SCHUMANN, ROBERT, (1810–1856), was the successor to Schubert in the creation of German *Lieder*. In addition to his musical prowess he was a critic of unusual ability. Hanslick, however, attacked him for taking the position that the esthetic principles of one art are the same for all the arts.

SENECA, (4 B.C.–A.D. 65), a Stoic philosopher, noted that orchestras and choruses grew to such immense proportions in Rome that there were more performers in the theater than there were spectators.

SHAKESPEARE, WILLIAM, (1564–1616), wrote plays which contain references to the harmony of the spheres and music's powers as a therapy. Operatic composers, of whom Verdi is one, have found his plays a source of inspiration for their own masterpieces.

SPENCER, HERBERT, (1820–1903), ranked music as the highest of the fine arts on the thesis that it is "the one which, more than any other, ministers to human welfare.".

STRAVINSKY, IGOR, (1882–   ), has had a great and far-reaching effect on the musicians of two generations. Bartók and Stravinsky may rank in future generations as two of the most outstanding composers of the twentieth century.

ST. THOMAS AQUINAS, (*c.* 1225–1274), was separated from St. Augustine by eight centuries. These centuries marked approximately the beginning and end of medieval philosophy. There is very little about music in the voluminous writings of St. Thomas. The references to music that do appear in his works are as mystical and moralistic as those of the early Church Fathers.

ST. AUGUSTINE, (354–430), held puritanical views concerning the moral effects of music on behavior which are similar to those of Plato. The esthetic beliefs which St. Augustine fostered exerted a strong influence on the musical philosophy of the Catholic Church.

ST. BASIL, (330–379), wrote that the psalms were one of God's ways of teaching Scripture. In the psalms, melody and doctrine are blended "in order that through the pleasantness and softness of the sound" the young, the indifferent, and the illiterate "might unawares receive what was useful in the words."

ST. JOHN CHRYSOSTOM, (345–407), maintained, as St. Basil did, that God established the psalms to foster the Christian cause. St. Chrysostom wrote that it was the duty of the clergy to guard their flock against the influences of "immoral" music.

ST. JEROME, (c. 340–420), made a Latin translation of the Scriptures which came to be known as the Vulgate. He regarded music as a means to propogate the Christian faith.

THEOPHRASTUS, (fourth century B.C.), was a pupil of Aristotle whom he succeeded as head of the Peripatetic school at Athens. However, he disagreed with the view expressed by Aristotle that the Greek modes reflect ethical qualities.

TOLSTOY, LEO, (1828–1910), was a Russian novelist and moralist whose esthetic views rest on a social and religious condemnation of society and its art. Many of his views on music were incorporated into the musical philosophy of the Soviet Union.

TSCHAIKOVSKY, PETER ILICH, (1840–1893), did not share the views of or belong to the Russian Five, but he was as fervent a patriot as they were and sang of his native land as forcefully as any other nationalistic Russian composer. The descriptions which he has left us of his creative process are painstaking and detailed.

VERDI, GIUSEPPE, (1813–1901), the esthetic level of whose operas belied the Wagnerian thesis that Italian opera was not good theater, had very few composers equal him in melodic ability.

WAGNER, RICHARD, (1813–1883), attempted to gather and fuse the arts under one roof by creating the music drama. Whereas the vocal line was of primary importance to the Italian composers, Wagner sought to make the orchestra as important as the singers.

WHITMAN, WALT, (1819–1892), wrote poetry showing evidence of formal musical influences. There is even a suggestion of polyphonic writing in verse in "When Lilacs Last in the Dooryard Bloom'd."

WORDSWORTH, WILLIAM, (1770–1850), considered poetry the most philosophical of all writing: ". . . its object is truth. . . . Poetry is the image of man and nature." In his estimation the knowledge that we derive from poetry is superior to that which we gain from science.

YEATS, WILLIAM B., (1865–1939), whose musical sentiments are expressed in his essay, *Ideas of Good and Evil*, was one of the pioneers in the "Irish Renaissance."

GLOSSARY OF TERMS

ABSTRACTION is a term used with reference to painting and sculpture when the emphasis is on form and color and not on subject matter in the traditional representational sense. Abstract painting is often compared to neoclassicism in music.

A CAPPELLA is vocal music without instrumental accompaniment.

ACCIDENTALS are used to alter the musical pitch. The accidental signs are sharps, flats, double sharps, double flats, and naturals. A sharp raises and a flat lowers the pitch by a half-tone, a natural cancels these and restores the original pitch, double sharps and double flats raise and lower the pitch by two half-tones.

AFFECT, as the psychologists use it, refers to feeling. Musical affects are associated with mental and emotional states. The term "effect" is the result of a cause. There is a causal nexus between striking a group of piano keys and producing a series of musical sounds. These musical sounds may have an affect upon us.

ANXIETY, though closely related to fear, must be distinguished from it. Fear is a reaction to a danger actually present, whereas anxiety is a state that can occur in the absence of danger. Anxiety can be produced in a music listener through rhythmic and melodic suggestions of suspense, surprise, and uncertainty.

APOLLONIAN AND DIONYSIAN, terms used by Nietzsche in *The Birth of Tragedy from the Spirit of Music*, express the distinction between classical order and frenzied revelry. Nietzsche held that the basis of human values are will and desire. Not until will masters its environment and exerts itself can a full life be achieved. Since the world is ugly and men are crude, values must be transformed by imagination. The two ways of doing this, according to Nietzsche, are by the crea- to the formal order found primarily in dreams, and the other is ecstatic tion of the Apollonian and the Dionysian types of art; one is similar and intoxicating. Through the arts, particularly music, we realize the infinite imaginative possibilities of life and affirm our existence.

ATONALITY is a twelve-tone musical system which establishes and maintains a set of relationships (tone row) in which all of the twelve tones have equal value, instead of the primacy of the tonic and dominant which exists in the diatonic system.

BAROQUE MUSIC began about 1600 and lasted until about 1750.

BASSO CONTINUO, or thorough bass, is a musical type of shorthand. The bass line, originally uninterrupted from beginning to end, is numbered to indicate the chordal accompaniment, which is improvised. This term is sometimes used synonymously with figured bass.

CACOPHONY consists of discordant and harsh tones that produce an unpleasant affect.

CAMERATA is the name for a group of literary people, musicians, and painters who met, shortly before 1600, at the palace of Count Bardi in Florence. They met to discuss the problems which polyphony had created in the music of their time, and the need to develop new musical styles that would imitate the esthetic ideals of the Greek drama.

CANTATA is a vocal composition, usually with instrumental accompaniment. It may be made up of solo singing, choral singing, and occasional recitatives. Its text may be either sacred or secular.

CATHARSIS, according to Aristotle, is the purging effect of certain emotions that a tragedy, which engenders pity and fear, has upon the spectator. The implication is that certain esthetic experiences act in the same way that homeopathic medicine does. The arts can enable us to work off our fears and hostility in phantasy and thus help us to retain a proper emotional equilibrium. The arts can also help us to remain moral by diffusing our animal needs through a world of "make-believe."

CHORALE is a hymn tune and is associated with German Protestantism.

CHORDS consist of three or more notes played simultaneously.

CHROMATIC notes are "color" tones. A chromatic scale proceeds in semitones and includes the twelve tones of the octave.

CLASSICAL, in music, is generally considered the period of Haydn, Mozart, and Beethoven. The period of the Viennese classics was approximately from 1770 to 1830.

CONCERTO is a musical work for solo instrument with orchestral accompaniment.

CONSONANCE signifies musical tones which we find personally agreeable and which give us a sense of repose.

COUNTERPOINT is an independent melody set against another melody.

DIALECTICS, as the term is used by Hegel and Marx, signifies the mode of historical progression. History advances by the resolution of conflicts, which resolution in turn produces more conflicts which are resolved, the process terminating eventually in the Absolute in Hegel and a classless society in Marx.

DISSONANCE consists of musical tones which mentally disturb and produce an element of anxiety in us.

DOCTRINE OF AFFECTIONS is a term associated with the baroque era but is actually of Greek origin. The Greeks used specific modes to evoke definite moods. Baroque composers used stereotyped musical motifs to evoke definite emotional responses from their audience.

DOGMATISM is a type of self-styled authority concerning esthetic values. Musical dogmatism can be personal and can also stem from religious and political sources and groups in the community with vested interests.

ELECTRONIC MUSIC is produced by various electronic devices.

EMPATHY is the process by which we project into music our own values and experiences.

EMPIRICISM is the position that the only valid source of knowledge is experience.

ENTERTAINMENT is distinguished from amusement throughout this book in that it must appeal to the intellect while amusement need appeal only to the senses.

ESTHETICS, as a field of philosophy, is concerned with the study of artistic values, just as ethics is concerned with moral values, metaphysics with the nature of being, epistemology with theories of knowledge, and logic with the principles of reasoning.

FORM is common to all art. In music the term can be used in different ways, the form in which a work is written according to traditional principles and also the structural form of the composition.

FUGUE is a composition in contrapuntal texture, usually identified by a stark opening subject. The fugue was developed during the seventeenth century and brought to a musical culmination in the compositions of Johann Sebastian Bach.

GOTHIC is used with reference to the history of music of approximately the thirteenth up to the middle of the fifteenth century. The term is usually employed, with reference to music, as a comparison to the other arts of the period. Gothic is also used as a metaphor for spirituality in describing the religiosity of Bach's scores. Neo-Gothic is used in a similar metaphorical way when modern music is described as possessing the characteristics of this late medieval school of art.

HARMONY is a term which does not mean the same thing when applied to different arts. The term harmony, in music, is often identified with chord. Musical harmony, however, does not stop with the construction of chords, but includes in its province the succession of chords and the esthetic relationships between them.

HARMONY OF THE SPHERES is a Greek myth that the stars produced celestial music as they spun about in their orbits.

HEDONISM is a doctrine which states that the ultimate good is pleasure.

HOMEOPATHIC therapy is a form of medical treatment which is founded on the principle that "like cures like." Greek physicians were known to treat frenzied patients with "wild" types of music to which they danced until they were exhausted, after which they would fall to the ground, and when they revived they would be cured of their frenzy.

HUMANISM is a philosophy of values focusing on human welfare, particularly in terms of the world of everyday experience and not of a theological hereafter. Humanism differs from dogmatism by emphasizing tolerance and democratic ideals. Dogmatism is based on precepts of intolerance and authority.

IDEALISM, in metaphysics, is the view that reality is ultimately mental or spiritual. In ethics it is the view that one's behavior ought to be guided by absolute moral principles.

IMMANENCE, in theology, is the doctrine that God is part of, or within, the universe. It is opposed to the doctrine of transcendence which holds that God is outside the universe.

INSTRUMENTALISM is the philosophic position associated primarily with John Dewey. Ideas are tools or instruments employed by humans in adjusting to the environment.

INTERVALS are differences or relations in pitch between two tones produced simultaneously or in succession. Intervals are perfect, major, minor, augmented, or diminished.

INTUITION is a mode of obtaining knowledge. Intuitive knowledge is nonmeditated and nondiscursive. Intuitionists claim that we are endowed with a faculty to apprehend "truth" and that this faculty is independent of reason and experience. Certain philosophers and theologians believe that we are born with an intuitive ability to make moral and esthetic judgments.

KEY is a group of musical tones held together by their relationship to a tonic. A key derives its name from the tonic.

LEITMOTIV is a representative theme which is used to announce a particular character or situation in a musical composition. This term is usually associated with Wagnerian operas. Thomas Mann uses the term *leitmotiv* in his account of the influence of music on his literary creativity.

LIED is a German art song. It was brought into existence by the union of romantic poetry and music in the eighteenth century. The *Lied* is probably the most sophisticated art song that we possess.

LITURGICAL DRAMA is a religious play that grew out of the art of troping, a form of medieval music.

MATERIALISM is the view that reality is ultimately material, that matter is the basic stuff of the universe.

MECHANISM is a form of materialism. Mechanism is the position that all human behavior is explicable in mechanical terms and that biology is an extension of physics and chemistry. Love and hate, and the functions of the mind are processes that can be explained in terms of physics and chemistry.

MELODY consists of a series of successive musical tones which are arranged with logic and a sense of order for the purpose of evoking certain emotional responses from listeners.

METAPHYSICS is one of the traditional fields of philosophy and is concerned with the study of the nature of being. Philosophical arguments based on suppositions that transcend the physical universe are traditionally characterized as metaphysics.

METER is the arrangement of note values and accents in a musical work. Musical rhythm is as dependent on meter as a human body is on its skeletal structure.

MODES consist of a selection of tones arranged in the manner of a scale upon which the composition rests. Our major and minor modes are an outgrowth of the Greek modes.

MODULATION is the act of moving from one musical key to another. There are twelve major and twelve minor keys in our system of classical harmony.

MONOPHONIC music consists of a single melodic line. Primitive music was essentially monophonic; folk music has retained this characteristic to a large extent. Greek music was monophonic and so was a great deal of early Church music, such as the chants.

MOTETS were considered the most important form of early polyphonic music during the Middle Ages and the Renaissance. They were composed for both sacred and secular occasions.

NATIONALISM in music rests on the belief that a composer should draw upon the folk music and dance rhythms of his country for musical inspiration. The music should be expressive of cultural traits and a form of glorification of the history of the nation.

NATURALISM, as distinguished from realism, has taken on political significance in the modern musical world. The Soviets contend that naturalism in music is found in the imitation of the cuckoo in Beethoven's *Pastoral Symphony* and the bleatings of the lambs in Strauss's *Don Quixote*. This type of naturalism has been carried to extremes by composers who imitate the roar of locomotives and the clatter of industrial machinery. Realism in music, wrote Shostakovich, means to "generalize upon the great experience of living, and at the same time to single out that which is most important in the process of living." Music must "become once again a great social force serving humanity in its struggle for progress and the triumph of Reason."

Naturalism, in philosophy, is the view that the physical universe is self-sufficient and can be adequately interpreted by science. It denies that the world had a supernatural cause and that a Divine Being guides the course of nature or human events. Values are a product of experience and require no supernatural justification.

NEOCLASSICISM is a term associated with a movement of "back to Bach," a reaction against the romantic movement. The underlying esthetic principle on which this movement was based was that the composer's function is not to express emotion or indulge in extra musical devices for theatrical effects, but as Stravinsky stated: "I move towards a greater abstraction." Neoclassicism is thus only a new era of classicism, with Stravinsky as its ablest champion. Law and order are his guideposts. Music "is given to us with the sole purpose of establishing an order among things," summed up his musical philosophy. "Once the construction is made and the order achieved, everything is said."

NEUROSIS is a form of mental or emotional disturbance. Freud maintains that the creative artist is close to being a neurotic personality. Through the process of sublimation he is able to convert his anxiety, guilt, and repressions into works of artistic achievement. These artistic expressions are forms of wish-fulfillment.

OPERA is a term ordinarily used for a play in which the dialogue is sung throughout and is accompanied by an orchestra, although some operas contain spoken dialogue.

ORGANUM strictly speaking is the oldest type of polyphonic music in the Western world.

PANTHEISM is the doctrine that God and nature are identical. Orthodox theologians have regarded pantheism as heresy. Giordano Bruno was burned at the stake by the Catholic hierarchy for holding to this belief, and Benedict Spinoza was excommunicated by the elders of his synagogue because of his pantheistic views.

PHANTASY is a form of mental imagery. Musical phantasies are very often projections of our psychological needs.

PLAIN SONG and plain chant are terms which are used as synonyms for Gregorian chants. Plain song also refers to other chants associated with the Catholic Church and with ancient forms of monophonic music that prevailed in the liturgies of other religious services.

POLYPHONY is music in which two or more melodies are sung or played simultaneously. During the late Middle Ages religious authorities complained that this type of music obscured the words in sacred music and gave more importance to melody than to the Holy Text.

POLYRHYTHM is the simultaneous use of contrasting rhythms in a musical composition.

POLYTONALITY is the presence of several simultaneous keys in the fabric of a musical work.

POSITIVISM is a philosophic work restricting inquiry to problems that lend themselves to scientific methods.

PRAGMATISM is a school of philosophy opposed to any form of absolutism or dogmatic reasoning. Its two chief doctrines concern meaning and truth. The meaning of a statement lies in its consequences for experience. The truth of a statement is its practical efficacy.

PSALMS are of Hebraic origin and psalm singing is the oldest form of Christian music.

PSYCHOANALYSIS is a school of depth psychology which emerged out of the research of Sigmund Freud into the nature of mental disorders. The primary tenet of this psychology is that our conscious actions are governed by unconscious forces.

PSYCHOSIS is a severe form of mental or emotional disturbance. The difference between a psychotic and a neurotic individual is that the latter does not experience hallucinations and is capable of distinguishing between reality and phantasy in a psychological sense.

PURISTS are concerned with structure and form and not with our emotional response to a musical work. An example of musical purism is Hanslick's statement that the function of music is to express musical ideas only and Stravinsky's remark, "I evoke neither human joy nor human sadness [in my music]."

RATIONALISM, in philosophy, is the theory that reason or intellect is the "true" source of knowledge rather than the senses.

RECITATIVE is a style of singing which emphasizes the inflection of the words in a prose passage. It was introduced into the first operas by the Camerata "to imitate the delivery of an orator."

RENAISSANCE (c. 1450–1600) was a period of profound scholarship and great wealth in the Western world. Musicians, their fellow artists, and scholars became so enamoured with the intellectual and esthetic theories of the Greeks that they tried to model their thought on Greek philosophy and their art on Greek styles. It was during this period that the opera was born in an effort to imitate Greek tragedy.

RHYTHM is the source of life to a musical work. It is to a musical composition what the flow of blood is to a living human body.

ROMANTIC musicians, poets, and painters thought of beauty as a lofty goddess. They hoped that by the sheer beauty of their art it would be possible to spark the imagination of nineteenth century man and free him from the dogmas of religion and the greed of a materialistic society.

SCALES are arrangements of a series of tones in the order of their pitch. Different musical systems arrange their scales in different ways. Every musical system in the world is in some way based on the structure of its scales. Scales are to music what an alphabet is to language.

SINGSPIEL in Germany, opera buffa in Italy, opera comique in France, ballad opera in England are nationalistic types of operas with spoken dialogue.

SONATA is an instrumental composition which usually consists of three or four independent movements. It is written for a particular instrument or group of instruments.

STYLE of a musical composition may mean the manner in which the composer expressed himself or the historical period in which it was created. A musical work may possess characteristics that are associated with the style of certain countries and schools.

SYMPHONY is a large scale work for orchestra, usually arranged in several movements which contrast in character and in mood.

SYNCOPATION is the inclusion of a rhythmic accent where an accent would not normally appear. It is a deliberate effort on the part of the composer to disrupt the even character of his rhythm.

SUBLIMATION, according to Freud, is the process in which the hostility and repressions of a creative person are converted into works of art. Noncreative persons convert their guilt and anxiety into dreams and phantasies which remain private and cannot be esthetically shared with others.

TELEOLOGY is the view that all events occur for a purpose or an end, even though the purpose or end may not be apparent.

TEMPO is the rate of speed at which a musical work is sung or played. A musical composition marked "allegro," for example, moves at a lively speed, and one marked "adagio" at a slow speed.

TIMBRE is the quality or color of a musical tone. The same tone produced on different instruments or rendered vocally will have different qualities.

TONE POEM, OR SYMPHONIC POEM is a type of orchestral music which is based on extramusical ideas of a poetic or descriptive character.

TRANSCENDENT, in theology, refers to God as existing apart from the world. In philosophy, it refers to that which is outside the pale of empirical investigation.

UNCONSCIOUS, in Freudian usage, is the welter of thoughts, feelings, and emotions not available to ordinary consciousness. Freudians maintain that the unconscious is the storehouse of our repressed emotions, and, according to Jung, is the source of all human creativity.

UTILITARIANISM is the doctrine that all actions are to be judged in terms of their utility in promoting the greatest good for the greatest number of people. Good is defined as pleasure or happiness.

VOLUNTARISM is the view that will, not reason, is the basic force in human conduct.

WISH-FULFILLMENT is the realization of repressed emotion in works of art. Freudians hold that all art, to a lesser or greater degree, is a form of wish-fulfillment. Artists create for the same reason that children play games—to work out their inhibitions in phantasy.

BIBLIOGRAPHY

ALLEN, Warren Dwight. *Philosophies of Music History*. New York: American Book Company, 1939.

APEL, Willi. *Harvard Dictionary of Music*. Cambridge: Harvard University Press, 1945.

ARNHEIM, Rudolf. *Art and Visual Perception*. Berkeley: University of California Press, 1954.

ARISTOTLE. *The Basic Works of Aristotle*. ed. Richard McKeon. New York: Random House, Inc., 1941.

———. *On the Art of Poetry*, With a Supplement *Aristotle on Music*. trans. S. H. Butcher; ed. Milton C. Nahm. New York: The Liberal Arts Press, 1948.

AUBRY, Pierre. *Trouvères and Troubadours*. trans. Claude Aveling. New York: G. Schirmer, Inc., 1914.

BACH, J. S. *The Bach Reader*. ed. Hans T. David and Arthur Mendel. New York: W. W. Norton & Company, Inc., 1945.

BELL, Clive. *Art*. New York: Frederick A. Stokes Company, 1914.

BERGSON, Henri. *Laughter*. trans. Cloudesley Brereton and Fred Rothwell. New York: The Macmillan Company, 1937.

BLOM, Eric. *Mozart*. New York: Farrar, Straus and Cudahy, Inc., 1949.

BOSANQUET, Bernard. *Three Lectures on Aesthetic*. New York: The Macmillan Company, 1915.

BROWN, Calvin S. *Music and Literature*. Athens: The University of Georgia Press, 1948.

BUKOFZER, Manfred F. *Music in the Baroque Era*. New York: W. W. Norton & Company, Inc., 1947.

CARPENTER, Nann Cooke. *Music in the Medieval and Renaissance Universities*. Norman: University of Oklahoma Press, 1958.

COLERIDGE, Samuel T. *Biographia Literaria*. ed. J. Shawcross. London: Oxford University Press, 1954.

COLLINGWOOD, R. G. *The Principles of Art*. New York: Oxford University Press, 1958.

CONFUCIUS. *The Wisdom of Confucius*. trans. Lin Yutang. New York: The Modern Library, Inc., 1938.

COOKE, Deryck. *The Language of Music*. London: Oxford University Press, 1960.

CROCE, Benedetto. *Aesthetic.* trans. Douglas Ainslie. London: Macmillan & Co., Ltd., 1929.

DEWEY, John. *Art as Experience.* New York: G. P. Putnam's Sons, 1958.

EINSTEIN, Alfred. *Mozart, His Character, His Work.* trans. Arthur Mendel and Nathan Broder. New York: Oxford University Press, 1945.

———. *Music in the Romantic Era.* New York: W. W. Norton & Company, Inc., 1947.

FARMER, Henry George. *Historical Facts for the Arabian Musical Influence.* London: William Reeves, 1930.

FARNSWORTH, Paul R. *The Social Psychology of Music.* New York: Holt, Rinehart and Winston, Inc., 1958.

FLEMING, William. *Arts and Ideas.* New York: Holt, Rinehart and Winston, Inc., 1955.

FLEMING, W., and A. Veinus. *Understanding Music.* New York: Holt, Rinehart and Winston, Inc., 1958.

FERGUSON, Donald N. *Music as Metaphor.* Minneapolis: University of Minnesota Press, 1960.

FORTE, Allen. *Tonal Harmony in Concept and Practice.* New York: Holt, Rinehart and Winston, Inc., 1962.

FREEMAN, Kathleen. *The Pre-Socratic Philosophers.* Oxford: Basil Blackwell & Mott, Ltd., 1949.

FREUD, Sigmund. *Introductory Lectures on Psychoanalysis.* trans. Joan Riviere. New York: Liveright Publishing Corporation, 1935.

GILBERT, K. E., and H. Kuhn. *A History of Esthetics.* New York: The Macmillan Company, 1939.

GRADENWITZ, Peter. *The Music of Israel.* New York: W. W. Norton & Company, Inc., 1949.

Grove's Dictionary of Music and Musicians. New York: The Macmillan Company, 1946.

HANSLICK, Eduard. *The Beautiful in Music.* trans. Gustav Cohen. Novello and Co., 1891.

HEGEL, G. W. F. *The Introduction to Hegel's Philosophy of Fine Art.* trans. Bernard Bosanquet. London: Kegan Paul, Trench, Trübner and Co., 1905.

HILLER, L. A., and L. M. Isaacson. *Experimental Music.* New York: McGraw-Hill Book Company, Inc., 1959.

HINDEMITH, Paul. *The Craft of Musical Composition.* trans. Arthur Mendel. New York: Associated Music Publishers, Inc., 1942.

———. *A Composer's World.* Cambridge: Harvard University Press, 1952.

HOLLANDER, John. *The Untuning of the Sky.* Princeton: Princeton University Press, 1961.

HORACE. *Ars Poetica.* Albert S. Cook edition. New York: Stechert-Hafner, Inc., 1926.

HOSPERS, John. *Meaning and Truth in the Arts.* Chapel Hill: The University of North Carolina Press, 1946.

HUXLEY, Aldous. *Point Counter Point.* New York: Harper & Row, Publishers, 1928.

IDELSOHN, A. Z. *Jewish Music.* New York: Tudor Publishing Co., 1944.

JUNG, Carl G. *Modern Man in Search of a Soul,* New York: Harcourt, Brace & World, Inc., 1934.

KANDINSKY, Wassily. *Wassily Kandinsky Memorial,* ed. Hilla Rebay. New York: Museum of Non-Objective Paintings, Guggenheim Foundation., 1945.

KANT, Immanuel. *Critique of Judgement.* trans. J. H. Bernard. London: Macmillan & Co., Ltd., 1914.

LANG, Paul H. *Music in Western Civilization.* New York: W. W. Norton & Company, Inc., 1941.

LANGER, Susanne K. *Philosophy in a New Key.* New York: Mentor Books, 1942.

———. *Feeling and Form.* New York: Charles Scribner's Sons, 1953.

LEIBNIZ. *Philosophical Writings.* trans. Mary Morris. London: J. M. Dent & Sons Ltd., 1934.

LEICHTENTRITT, Hugo. *Music, History, and Ideas.* Cambridge: Harvard University Press, 1946.

LEVARIE, Siegmund. *Mozart's Le Nozze di Figaro.* Chicago: University of Chicago Press, 1952.

———. *Guillaume de Machaut.* New York: Sheed & Ward, Inc., 1954.

MACRAN, Henry S. *The Harmonics of Aristoxenus.* Oxford: Clarendon Press, 1902.

MANN, Thomas. *Stories of Three Decades.* trans. H. T. Lowe-Porter. New York: Alfred A. Knopf, Inc., 1946.

MEYER, Leonard B. *Emotion and Meaning in Music.* Chicago: University of Chicago Press, 1956.

MUNRO, Thomas. *The Arts and Their Interrelations*. New York: The Liberal Arts Press, 1949.

MURSELL, James L. *The Psychology of Music*. New York: W. W. Norton & Company, Inc., 1937.

NAHM, Milton C. *The Artist as Creator*. Baltimore: The Johns Hopkins Press, 1956.

NETTL, Paul. *Luther and Music*. trans. Frida Best and Ralph Wood. Philadelphia: Muhlenberg Press, 1948.

NEWMAN, Ernest. *The Life of Richard Wagner*. New York: Alfred A. Knopf, Inc., 1933-1946.

NIETZSCHE, Friedrich. *The Philosophy of Nietzsche*. New York: The Modern Library, Inc., 1937.

OATES, Whitney J. *The Stoic and Epicurean Philosophers*. New York: Random House, Inc., 1940.

ORTEGA Y GASSET, José. *Dehumanization of Art*. trans. Helene Weyl. Gloucester, Mass.: Peter Smith, 1951.

Oxford History of Music. London: Oxford University Press, 1938.

PANASSIE, Hugues. *The Real Jazz*. trans. Anne Sorelle Williams. New York: A. S. Barnes and Company, 1960.

PARKER, DeWitt H. *The Principles of Aesthetics*. New York: Appleton-Century-Crofts, 1946.

PATER, Walter. *The Renaissance*. London: Jonathan Cape, 1873.

PLATO. *The Dialogues of Plato*. trans. Benjamin Jowett. New York: Random House, Inc., 1937.

PLUTARCH. *Plutarch's Miscellanies and Essays*. Boston: Little, Brown & Company, 1898.

PORTNOY, Julius. *A Psychology of Art Creation*. Kenan Fellow Study, Chapel Hill: The University of North Carolina Press, 1942.

———. *The Philosopher and Music*. New York: The Humanities Press, Inc., 1954.

PRALL, D. W. *Aesthetic Judgment*. New York: The Thomas Y. Crowell Company, 1929.

PRATT, Carroll C. *The Meaning of Music*. New York: McGraw-Hill Book Company, Inc., 1931.

RADER, Melvin. *A Modern Book of Esthetics*. New York: Holt, Rinehart and Winston, Inc., 1960.

REESE, Gustave. *Music in the Middle Ages*. New York: W. W. Norton & Company, Inc., 1940.

———. *Music in the Renaissance.* New York: W. W. Norton & Company, Inc., 1954.

SACHS, Curt. *The Commonwealth of Art.* New York: W. W. Norton & Company, Inc., 1946.

———. *The Rise of Music in the Ancient World, East and West.* New York: W. W. Norton & Company, Inc., 1943.

ST. AUGUSTINE. *The Fathers of the Church,* II. New York: Cima Publishing Co., Inc., 1947.

SALAZAR, Adolfo. *Music in Our Time.* trans. Isabel Pope. New York: W. W. Norton & Company, Inc., 1946.

SANTAYANA, George. *Reason in Art.* New York: Charles Scribner's Sons, 1931.

SCHILLINGER, Joseph. *The Mathematical Basis of the Arts.* New York: Philosophical Library, Inc., 1948.

———. *The Schillinger System of Musical Notation.* New York: Philosophical Library, Inc., 1946.

SCHOPENHAUER, Arthur. *The World as Will and Idea.* trans. R. B. Haldane and J. Kemp. London: Routledge and Kegan Paul, Ltd., 1909, 1948.

SCHWEITZER, Albert. *J. S. Bach.* trans. Ernest Newman. London: A. & C. Black, Ltd., 1935.

SLONIMSKY, Nicolas. *Music Since 1900.* New York: Coleman-Ross Co., Inc., 1949.

STOLNITZ, Jerome. *Aesthetics and Philosophy of Art Criticism.* Boston: Houghton Mifflin Company, 1960.

STRAVINSKY, Igor. *An Autobiography.* New York: Simon and Schuster, Inc., 1936.

———. *Poetics of Music.* trans. Arthur Knodel and Ingolf Dahl. Cambridge: Harvard University Press, 1947.

STRUNK, Oliver. *Source Readings in Music History.* New York: W. W. Norton & Company, Inc., 1950.

TOLSTOY, Leo. *What Is Art?* trans. Aylmer Maude. London: Oxford University Press, 1946.

TOVEY, Donald F. *Beethoven.* London: Oxford University Press, 1945.

WAGNER, Peter. *Introduction to the Gregorian Melodies.* trans. Agner Orme and E. G. P. Wyatt. London: The Plainsong and Mediaeval Music Society, 1901.

White List of the Society of St. Gregory of America, Papal Documents on *Sacred Music, From the 14th to the 20th Century*. New York: The Society of St. Gregory of America, 1951.

ZUCKERKANDL, Victor. *The Sense of Music*. Princeton: Princeton University Press, 1959.

———. *Sound and Symbol*. trans. Willard R. Trask. New York: Pantheon Books, Inc., 1956.

INDEX*

Acoustics, 6, 57, 68, 73, 166, 177, 180, 252
Adam de la Halle, 114n7
Adler, Alfred, 21
Aelian, 195–196
Aeschylus, 220n4
Aiken, Conrad, 130
Alcaeus, 2
Alexander, 94, 207–208
Anesthesia, 191–192, 231
Anthem, 113, 121
Antisthenes, 94
Apollo, 2, 6, 188, 202, 203, 241
Apollonian, 13, 32, 122, 228
Architecture, 31, 76, 113, 119–121, 126, 129, 130, 132, 137, 145–148, 151, 152n26, 159, 160, 183
Archytas of Tarentum, 165
Aristophanes, 93, 149, 224
Aristotle, 5, 6, 8, 9, 32, 42, 50n9, 79n6, 80n6, 83, 94–95, 96, 113, 126, 148, 149, 151n1, 156, 157, 158, 161, 165–166, 168, 186n11, 189, 190, 201–202, 203, 207–208, 220n6, 221n16, 222n26, 228
Aristoxenus, 68, 73, 95, 166, 168, 182, 186n14
Arius, 240, 245
Arnheim, Rudolf, 153n27
Artist, general, 16, 18–19, 22–23, 26, 31–33, 46–49, 101–102, 120–123, 126–128, 163, 168, 190, 198, 200, 238, 239, 243
Astronomy, 154, 164, 166–167, 186n8, 203, 242
Athenaeus, 219n2, 258n7
Atonal music, 66–67, 72, 73, 183, 230
Bach, C. P. E., 101
Bach, Johann Sebastian, 41, 42, 62, 101, 109, 128, 140, 159, 169, 182, 226, 230, 234
Bacon, Francis, 160
Bacon, Roger, 167–168, 190, 203–204, 217
Baroque, 66, 69, 71–72, 78, 120, 128, 140, 182, 184, 226–227
Bartók, Béla, 230
Beethoven, Ludwig van, 43, 44, 49, 97, 101, 120, 174, 228
Beliefs and myths about music, dogmatism, 231–237
    humanism, 237–240
    mysticism, 246–249
    myth, 240–246
    prophecy, 249–255
    summary, 255–257
    traditions, 223–231
Bell, Clive, 233
Berg, Alban, 133, 142
Bergson, Henri, 13, 247, 259n14
Berlioz, Hector, 169, 179, 230
Bible, 2, 3, 4, 78, 81, 82, 83, 159, 188, 225

* The notation 50n9, for example, refers the reader to the note number (9) on the page given (50).